YALE PUBLICATIONS IN RELIGION, 9

DAVID HORNE, EDITOR

———◆———

Published under the direction of the Divinity School

NIHIL OBSTAT: Walter H. Peters, S.T.L., Ph.D.,
Censor Librorum

IMPRIMATUR: ✠ Leo Binz,
Archbishop of St. Paul

April 29, 1963

THOMAS STAPLETON

AND THE COUNTER REFORMATION

by Marvin R. O'Connell

New Haven and London, Yale University Press, 1964

For PHILIP HUGHES

Wer so viel Huld vergessen kann,
Den seh' man mit Verachtung an.

PREFACE

The ecumenical dialogue which we enjoy on all sides today would have bewildered the subject of this book. Thomas Stapleton's life and career were fashioned by that violent reaction to Protestantism which we call, perhaps incorrectly, the Counter Reformation. Because he was articulate and intelligent and admirably placed in the university life of his time, Stapleton played a great part in the intellectual debates which dominated the thinking of Europeans in the latter half of the sixteenth century. Up to now that part has gone virtually unexamined. As might be said of most of his contemporaries, on both sides of the quarrel, the value of his work must be found beneath his understandable prejudices. I have let him speak for himself, insofar as that was possible, in the hope that he, a witness of the events and a student of the issues, can help us understand what really divided our Christian ancestors four centuries ago.

The book is divided roughly into three parts. The first three chapters include an essay on the Counter Reformation itself, a summary of Stapleton's life, and an analysis of his literary work. Chapters four through six treat of Stapleton's views on justification, the issue which he considered the primary cause of the Reformation controversies. The last four chapters examine his criticism of various Protestant notions of Church government, with special emphasis on the Elizabethan Settlement of 1559. In quoting from Stapleton's works, I have modernized his English spelling without spoiling, I hope, the sixteenth-century flavor of his prose. All translations from the Latin are my own.

Much of the research for this book was done while I was Lingard Fellow in the University of Notre Dame. To the President of the University, to the history faculty, and particularly to the

Reverend Thomas T. McAvoy, C.S.C., formerly Head of the History Department and now University Archivist, I am very grateful. To the President of the College of St. Thomas, Monsignor James P. Shannon, who during these past four years has never ceased to encourage me, I can only say that I consider it rare good fortune to be a member of his faculty. I have never hesitated to seek the advice of my friend and mentor of former years, the Reverend Patrick H. Ahern of the St. Paul Seminary. The Reverend Terrence J. Murphy, Executive Vice President of St. Thomas, and Professor Robert Fogerty of the College history faculty have helped me in various ways, and I thank them for their kindness. I am grateful as well to Mrs. Kathleen Boyd who typed the manuscript. Were it not for the interest of Mr. David Horne and his colleagues at the Yale University Press, Thomas Stapleton would not have emerged even this far out of the shadows, and for this both he and I thank them.

Finally, in the place of honor, I thank the man to whom this book is dedicated, because what is good in it is very largely his.

M. R. O'C.

St. Paul
April 1963

CONTENTS

ABBREVIATIONS

WORKS BY STAPLETON

Antidota apostolica	*Antidota apostolica,* in *Opera, 3* (Paris, 1620), 347–993
Antidota evangelica	*Antidota evangelica,* in *Opera, 3,* 1–344
Counterblast	*A Counterblast to M. Hornes Vayne Blaste against M. Feckenham* . . . , Louvain, 1567
Fortresse	*A Fortresse of the Faith First Planted among Us Englishmen* . . . , St. Omer, 1625
Justificationis	*De universa justificationis doctrina hodie controversa libri duodecim,* in *Opera, 2,* 1–377
Principiorum	*Principiorum fidei doctrinalium demonstratio methodica,* in *Opera, 1,* 1–503
Relectio	*Relectio scholastica et compendiaria principiorum fidei doctrinalium per controversias, quaestiones et articulos tradita,* in *Opera, 1,* 507–838
Returne	*A Returne of Untruthes upon M. Jewelles Replie* . . . , Antwerp, 1566
Speculum	*Speculum pravitatis haereticae per orationes ad oculum demonstratae,* in *Opera, 2,* 379–475
Tres Thomae	*Tres Thomae, seu res gestae S. Thomae Apostoli, S. Thomae Archiepiscopi cantuariensis et martyris, Thomae Mori Angliae quondam cancellarii,* in *Opera, 4,* 932–1065

OTHER WORKS

DB	Henricus Denziger and Clemens Bannwart, *Enchiridion symbolorum, definitionum, et declarationum de rebus fidei et morum,* ed. Carolo Rahner, Fribourg, 1952
DD	*The First and Second Diaries of the English College, Douay,* ed. Fathers of the Congregation of the London Oratory, London, 1878

DNB   *Dictionary of National Biography*, Oxford, 1917

DTC   *Dictionnaire de théologie catholique*, Paris, 1902–50

GH   Henry Gee and W. J. Hardy, *Documents Illustrative of English Church History*, London, 1896

Chapter 1

THE COUNTER REFORMATION

The historian cannot help feeling a twinge of envy and self-pity as he approaches his material. The tools available to his colleagues of other disciplines are for the most part lacking to him. He cannot isolate his data; he cannot control his experiment. When he divides his subject, as he must to get any intelligibility out of it, he has to make so many reservations and qualifications that the division often tends to obscure rather than to illuminate the facts. If he constructs a theory which, after painful research and analysis, will explain a series of events, he knows there is always a chance that someone will advance an opposite theory based not necessarily upon further and deeper observation but simply upon the lacunae in his own. The historian lives in mortal fear of the crushing remark, usually delivered in a crowded room, "But haven't you read Schwartz on this subject?" Schwartz is an invisible enemy, immortal and omnipresent, and an encounter with him is possible round the next corner. Plagued by unknowns, the historian spends his scholarly life dealing with that most inconstant of constants, the activities of dead human beings. He may explain in the greatest detail the causes which contributed to the assassination of Julius Caesar, and all the time a little voice back somewhere in a corner of his mind keeps saying, "But perhaps on that mid-March morning Brutus' breakfast eggs were overcooked, and perhaps Brutus couldn't abide overcooked eggs."

Take, as an instance of the problem, the history of Europe between the publication of Luther's Ninety-five Theses and the conversion of Henry of Navarre. Normally, this period is divided into the eras of Reformation and Counter Reformation, the break coming sometime about mid-century. That this is a useful division no one can deny, for as certainly as the Protestant movement dominated men and events during the first half of the sixteenth century, so reaction to it dominated the second half. But, as one attempts to become more precise, the validity of the division shows signs of strain. Does the Reformation period close with the death of Luther (1546) when Calvin lived almost two decades longer (d. 1564)? Does the Counter Reformation begin with the opening sessions of the Council of Trent (1545) or with the closing sessions (1563), with the peace treaty of Cateau-Cambrésis (1559) or perhaps with the excommunication of Elizabeth I (1570)? These are questions without answers, because the strands which compose the fabric of human events cannot be so nicely separated.

Thus, in the very years which saw the Jesuits score remarkable triumphs for Catholicism in the Rhineland, Calvinist preachers were crisscrossing Holland and France with a similarly dedicated and successful mission of their own. There is no question that significant internal reform did not affect the college of cardinals before the time of Pius IV (1559–65), and yet, as early as the 1520s, the papal princes had had the virtue to elect an Adrian of Utrecht, sandwiching him incongruously between two Medici. If Luther and Calvin and their followers revealed vast new theological vistas during the first half of the century, Cajetan, a generation before their activity, had given a powerful new impetus to the old theology, and Erasmus had provided the critical method that each side would employ in the ensuing verbal conflict. The Counter Reformation, we are correctly told, was a time of Catholic resurgence, and yet, in the midst of it, England and the Netherlands were lost definitively to the ancient Church, and a sizable part of France's most productive classes was alienated. One of the most eminent of the Catholic reformers, Cardinal Contarini, died before the opening of the Council of Trent, and one of the most successful Protestant reformers, Theodore Beza, flourished at Geneva into the first years of the seventeenth century. And if the Catholics, in the days of their darkest confusion, could produce a theologian of the stature of St. John Fisher, the Protestants, when their own theology was allegedly on the wane, could boast of Richard Hooker, serene and unruffled after four decades of attack on the foundations of his intellectual position.

Difficulties abound, therefore, in the traditional division. The river of human events stubbornly refuses to be dammed up, and, the moment one attempts to divert it into this or that reservoir, a thousand leaks gush out. The events of the latter half of the sixteenth century seem particularly uneasy jammed into their Counter Reformation compartment. Nevertheless, the division is useful, and, if the constant need for qualification is borne in mind, it can elucidate many a man and many a movement, because, despite the qualifications, Philip II's era did differ radically from Charles V's.

It was largely a difference in the spirit which animated two generations of Catholics. Charles Hapsburg, born the year (1500) of Pope Alexander VI's gaudy jubilee when Europeans still took for granted a Christendom which was Catholic, united, and rural, became, through a series of bizarre dynastic accidents, Holy Roman Emperor, Count of Flanders, Archduke of Austria, Most Catholic King of Aragon, Castile, Sicily, and all the Indies—possessor, in short, of so many titles that no man could number them. He promptly found himself, along with his contemporaries, caught between dedication to the hallowed slogans of an earlier, simpler time and the hard realities of a life dictated by powerful new forces. Already those two lusty young giants, capitalism and nationalism, were flexing the muscles that were ultimately to build the modern world. Already feudal barons and estates general had given way to entrepreneurs and nationalist monarchs, even if words and symbols and habits of mind had not yet adjusted to the fact. Charles' generation found it impossible to believe that it was committed to an ideal as outmoded as the bow and arrow, impossible to abandon the old vision of Christian Europe peopled by noble lords, happy peasants, and an occasional industrious burgher. The infamous circumstances of the imperial election of 1519 provide a case in point. The ideal of the presidency of Christendom embodied in the office of the Holy Roman Empire was ancient and attractive, and, in centuries past, it had been politically useful. But the facts of sixteenth-century life made it necessary for Charles to pay cash for the empire, to haggle for it as though it were a sausage or a cheese. In order to become the anointed successor of Charlemagne, he had to call upon the bourgeois bankers, who alone could supply him with enough money, at ruinous rates of interest, with which to outbribe his rival candidate.

But if Christendom was bankrupt as a political and economic idea, there still remained the prop of religious faith. States and social systems had gone the way of all flesh, but the Holy, Catholic, Apostolic, Roman Church had gone on as though even the gates of hell could not prevail against her. In Charles V's boyhood the Church appeared possessed of her traditional serenity, blessed anew, so to speak, by the gorgeous creations of Renaissance art. Except for a handful of eccentrics, everyone agreed that Christ was in the Church, that, indeed, the Church was herself the extension of Christ. In her doctrine, moral code, and ritual, therefore, were buried the deepest roots of Christendom, because in them was contained the basic reason for the unity of Western man. Of course, nobody was so naïve as to believe that all was well with the Church, or, for that matter, had ever been. Had not St. Bernard, centuries before, given it as his opinion that hell was paved with clerics' tonsured pates? The sour-sweet smell of ecclesiastical corruption was strong in sixteenth-century nostrils, and priests and laymen railed at one another about the colossal financial chicanery, clerical ignorance, and widespread popular superstition. Though it was hard for a priest, especially a priest in high places, to win the argument, it was even harder to fix precisely the responsibility for the perpetuation of a dishonest system from which so many different people profited. In any case, the Church had suffered from grievous internal complaints in the past and had always managed to survive them. But between 1516 and 1519, while Charles V was accumulating his various thrones, a Saxon friar named Martin Luther, in pamphlets brilliant in their indignation and rhetoric, if not always in their logic, hurled a challenge not at ecclesiastical abuses but at the traditional Christian notion of man's relationship to God. With the sound of Luther's trumpet, the walls of Christendom, already shattered, came tumbling down.

The Protestant movement's chances for survival must have appeared slender to Charles V's contemporaries in, say, 1520. No doubt Pope Leo X (d. 1521) spoke for most of his contemporaries when he dismissed Luther as "this troublesome friar." Four tumultuous decades later, the Reformed gospel could count its converts in the millions. The fantastic success of the Reformers left a generation of Catholics stunned and fearful and quite prepared to believe that their time would witness the end not only of Christendom but of the faith as they had known it. Defections from the Roman Church occurred on every level, from the kings of England and the heads of religious orders to ordinary people who found the poise and dedication of the Reformers a striking contrast to their parish priests' ignorance and greed. The new creed was not something to be muttered about in corners. On the contrary, it inspired its adherents with an intense zeal with which they ascended any available rooftop, there to proclaim, in tones both sweet and strident, God's revelation to sinful humanity. They displayed the same fiery persuasiveness as their heroes and rhetorical exemplars, the Old Testament prophets, and they called down the same kind of doom upon those who rejected their message. The Reformers were not, however, simply hot-eyed fanatics. They included in their ranks some of the most brilliant and best-educated men of their time, men skilled in the use of the latest scholarly devices. The ancient Church, crippled by internal woes, drifted leaderless under their sustained assault. She was betrayed by popes who were dilettantes and by bishops who were, at best, politicians. When she turned to the intellectuals, she learned to her dismay that they had ceased to be Christian or else had ceased to think, imprisoned within a theological structure the moorings of which had been nibbled away by two centuries of nominalism. What she had indulgently called her secular arm she now found too busy with secular matters to be much concerned over her plight. Even laymen of good will, convinced that through a cynical acceptance of abuses the priests had brought the catastrophe upon themselves, were anxious that the priests should learn a salutary lesson from it. The heretics will be attended to, the laymen reasoned, in due course. Then, one fine morning, they awoke to discover that it was too late.

For a man who held as many scepters as Charles V, abdication was a complicated matter not to be accomplished with a single ceremony or signature. The series of abdications began in Brussels on October 25, 1555, and the event almost shouted out its symbols. The Emperor rode slowly and painfully from the Louvain Gate to the Great Hall of the Dukes of Brabant. He wore simple black garb, the severity of which was relieved only by the jewel of the Order of the Golden Fleece, which hung upon his breast. Although he was only fifty-five, Charles had been an old man for a long time, and on this day he appeared particularly stooped and weary. He grimaced at every step taken by the horse beneath him. At the end of the short journey, as his retainers helped him to dismount, late arrivals might have seen that the man who for forty years had exercised more political authority and administered dominions more vast than any European since Constantine was physically a shambles, his eyes dull and the jutting line of the Hapsburg jaw somehow slack under the grizzled beard.

The abdication ceremony was brief and moving. In the Great Hall was assembled a glittering company, more than a thousand people altogether, including the Knights of the Golden Fleece, the foreign ambassadors, and the princes and deputies of the Netherlands. On the dais, flanking the Emperor, sat William, Prince of Orange, and Charles' son Philip. A hush fell on the crowd as Charles rose with difficulty, leaned for support on Orange's shoulder, and began to speak. It was a halting, barely audible address, delivered in Charles' lisping French and interrupted at least once by the speaker's tears. No one in the large and distinguished audience doubted the Emperor's sincerity when he explained that he wept not at the loss of sovereignty but at the loss of friendships and associations of forty years' duration. And though not a few openly wept with him, others with colder eyes appraised the young man who stood stiff and unblinking by his father's side. After all, it would not be many days before the old Emperor retired to a remote retreat in the Spanish mountains, there to rest his gouty limbs and ponder his imminent encounter with a king who could neither deceive nor be deceived. The future lay with Philip, for whom the moment had come to assume the Hapsburg burden and receive the inheritance of Charles' checkered career.

Historical opinion has always considered Philip II leader of the movement called the Counter Reformation, and, with the proper qualifications, this judgment is undoubtedly correct. But the qualifications are considerable, because the man is as difficult to categorize as the era in which he lived. That Philip himself never strayed from the path of religious orthodoxy, that he was, compared to his fellow monarchs, remarkably pious, that he remained all his life an adamant foe of Protestantism and was more than once a savage persecutor of it, that he consistently supported religious projects ranging from endowment of Catholic universities to holy war against the Turk—none of these points need be debated. There need not be much discussion, either, about the position of Spain as the natural base for the reaction against Protestantism. Touched hardly at all by heresy, she became, during Philip's long reign (1556–98), the arsenal of orthodoxy, providing Catholic Europe with the finest theological schools, a renewed and vital mystical tradition, and, most notably, the Society of Jesus. She guarded her own religious purity as a matter of national policy through the relentless activity of the government-operated Inquisition. If a situation called for force, and the sixteenth-century man never hesitated to use force in behalf of religion, Spain's military might made her the ideal Catholic champion and gave lively expression to the whole bellicose approach of the Counter Reformation.

But if Philip could rightly claim leadership of the resurgent Catholics, the part he played was too ambiguous to admit of easy explanation. He suffered no illusions, as his father had, about the

glories of Christendom. Philip was a Spaniard to the marrow of
his bones, then a Hapsburg, then a Catholic. Although he was
a kind of senior partner within the family coalition, he never
wore the imperial crown or aspired to a mythical presidency of
Christian Europe. Instead, he substituted an illusion of his own:
what is good for Spain, he might have said, is good for the family
and good for the Church, and anything else is bad for all three.
For Philip the interests of all three merged, and this parody of
the Trinity dominated his entire policy. It had begun to do so
even before his father's abdication. As had been predicted, his
marriage to the unhappy Mary Tudor proved a major disaster for
English Catholicism, but, since it had seemed at the time (1554)
consistent with Spanish interests, Philip had overridden all opposition.[1] The same notion dictated his attitude toward France,
whose strength was sapped throughout the Counter Reformation
period by a series of religious civil wars. Philip gave aid and
comfort to the Catholic side, enough to keep it fighting but not
enough to give it victory. The Most Catholic King of Spain assumed that a weak and distracted France would please God more
than a peaceful and united France, even if Catholic. When it became apparent that Henry of Navarre intended to submit to the
Roman Church and thus bring an end to the dreary bloodletting,
Philip did all in his power to prevent Henry's rapprochement
with the pope—a curious line of action for the Catholic champion.[2] But Philip was a curious man, riddled with inconsistencies
and burdened by contradictions whose true nature he never understood. Without him the English mission would never have existed,
and some of the most glorious pages in the Counter Reformation's
history would never have been written. And yet, had he given it
his ungrudging and unsuspicious support or had his mind been
supple enough to distinguish its true objectives from those of
Spanish foreign policy, perhaps the mission would not have ended
in futile heroics and wretched quarrels.

1. For details of the match see Philip Hughes, *The Reformation in England,* 2 (New York, 1954), 203 ff.
2. See L. Pastor, *The History of the Popes,* 23 (St. Louis, 1933), 59 ff.

There is a final irony to note. Few great men have been as humorless and stuffy as Philip II. He was an executive who gloried much more in meticulous attention to detail than in dramatic action, and it would not be hard to imagine him every morning in an office somewhere in the bowels of the Escorial, his vast palace-monastery, carefully counting paper clips. Somehow the grim-visaged Philip appears a distorted symbol of the Counter Reformation, the predominating spirit of which was a renewal of Catholic optimism and buoyancy. The abdication of Charles V and Philip's assumption of power must not, therefore, be strained into explaining more than they can. What was really significant about these isolated events was that they represented the coming of age of a generation which had not directly felt the stunning blows of the old Reformers, successful, it seemed, everywhere. Catholics of an age with Philip were not at all attuned to defeat as their fathers, by 1555, had become. These young adherents to the old faith possessed a new confidence and composure in which they asked themselves why territories and populations so quickly lost might not be just as quickly regained. Only a few months before Charles' abdication had come the election of Pope Paul IV, first in a series of remarkable popes who were to provide them with the zealous and resolute leadership woefully lacking to their fathers. The long delayed Council of Trent, in recess in 1555, was a far cry from the drab Council of the Lateran held when Charles V was an adolescent. At Trent the complex doctrinal points raised by the Reformers elicited from the Fathers of the Council a clear restatement of ancient Christian Catholic belief, while the ecclesiastical corruption, which had so facilitated the reception of the Reformers' evangel, was finally given the attention it deserved. In the decrees and canons of Trent the new generation's Catholic intellectuals could find, they thought, principles from which they hoped to derive a brave new ecclesiastical world.

The Catholics could take heart, too, from the fact that by 1555 the Protestant movement was in deep trouble, in danger, perhaps, of utter fragmentation. Even in the Reformation's first rush of fervor there had appeared that fatal flaw in the doctrine of abso-

lute biblical freedom. Luther had hardly returned to Wittenberg
from the Wartburg (1522) and the prodigious literary labors of
the ten months spent there when he had to face the vexing divi-
sions already created within the tiny reformed camp by Carlstadt,
Münzer, and other extremists. In German Switzerland, meantime,
the reform movement, under the leadership of the brilliant humanist Ulrich Zwingli (d. 1531), followed a direction repugnant to
Luther who, after his famous encounter with Zwingli in 1529,
wrote to a friend: "At the end [of the conference, Zwingli et al.]
asked that we at least recognize them as brothers. . . . It was impossible for us to do so."[3] But it was after the towering figure of
Martin Luther had departed the scene (d. 1546) that the quarrels
among the Protestants assumed really grave proportions. What
had formerly been controversial positions now became sects.
Lutheran unity crumbled into a confusion of squabbling factions.
The mantle of Zwingli fell upon the frail shoulders of that dour
genius, John Calvin, who combined intellectual and moral gifts
of the highest order with a terrible ferocity toward any deviation
from his own views, whether held by Lutheran, Anabaptist, or
papist.[4] And in England political expediency seemed poised, by
the middle of the century, to swallow the Protestant movement
whole, with the man in the street baffled and irresolute and his
civil and ecclesiastical superiors ready to jump from Protestant
to Catholic or something in between at the whim of the monarch.
Writing in 1564, one of the new generation of optimistic Catholics described, tongue in cheek, the lengths to which the doctrinal
confusion had gone:

> Now, so ye be no papist, ye may be a Sacramentary, an
> Anabaptist, or a Lutheran; and then a Civil, a Zealous or a
> Disordered Lutheran, among all which ye may choose of

---

3. See *DTC*, *3*, cc. 1711–12.

4. "Le Philippisme aboutit à une défaite: ses dosages savants, ses multiples
efforts vers la concorde échouent à réconcilier la pure doctrine de Luther tant
avec la tradition chrétienne qu'avec la raison humaine. . . . Voici venir de
France le robuste et large génie qui sauve le Protestantisme." Albert Dufourcq,
Histoire moderne de l'Église, 8 (Paris, 1933), 50–51.

what sort in each branch ye list to be; whether ye allow two sacraments with the Zealous Lutherans, three with the Leipsians or four with the Wittenbergers; whether ye will be an Osiandrin, a half-Osiandrin or an Antiosiandrin; whether a close Anabaptist or an open Anabaptist, a new Pelagian or a new Manichee. Whether ye say the body is with the bread, or the bread without the body, or a pledge to assure the body, or the very value and effect of the body. All these, with a number of other doctrines professed and defended freely of Protestants, hath God now revealed for truths, faiths and gospels to recompense the darkness of nine hundred years.[5]

"What a perpetual shame it is to you," wrote the same young man to one of Elizabeth I's bishops, "and to all your holy brotherhood, that yet to this hour the tragedy of your horrible dissension lasteth, even in the first foundation of your ragged gospel."[6] "Perpetual shame" it may have been, but (and this is the point here) golden opportunity for the enemies of Protestantism it assuredly appeared to be.

The chief of these enemies was logically the Bishop of Rome, who claimed the august role of shepherd to all Christians, successor of St. Peter, Vicar of Christ. Much more important to the history of the Counter Reformation than the armies of Philip of Spain was the dramatic reversal in the character and activity of the papacy which took place after 1555. It is a commonplace that during the early years of the sixteenth century and for many, many years before that, the hands which guided the Church had grown palsied, had occupied themselves more with petty politics than with men's salvation, and had been soiled by theft and murder and crimes more flamboyant still. When the crisis of the Reformation arose, and when Luther excoriated the papacy as the Antichrist and the new whore of Babylon, the effete Leo X was incapable of grasping the issues raised, much less of dealing

5. *Fortresse*, p. 223.
6. *Counterblast*, fol. 432.

effectively with them. With the nerve center of the Church struck by a moral paralysis, the task of the Reformers was made immeasurably easier. It was not really until the election of Paul IV (in that symbolic year, 1555) that this situation changed drastically enough for the papacy to provide the supranational leadership necessary for a supranational movement against Protestantism.

It did not come overnight. Through six consecutive pontificates, over which presided at least three of the most remarkable men who ever wore the tiara, the weapons of leadership were forged. The obstacles were formidable because they lay at the heart of the Church's administration, in the Roman Curia itself. There could be no true reformation of the Church until reform came to the Curia. And as long as it was possible for a clever young man to find employment within the sprawling organization of Christendom's ecclesiastical center and to accumulate thereby a half dozen benefices, to look forward, if Providence smiled upon him, to a red hat and the bounteous favor of princes anxious to keep a friend in consistory and conclave, to aspire, no matter how mean or obscure his birth or unsavory his past, to the throne of St. Peter itself, then the cry for reform would go largely unheeded, as it had for generations. Rome, as one sixteenth-century observer put it, was no longer a city; it had become instead a place where foreigners came to make their fortunes.[7]

If the problem had been one of simple venality, a solution might have been quickly, if painfully, found. It was, however, much more complicated. There were structures no pope could compromise, even if they did provide occasion for corruption. Thus, the absolute power of Christ's Vicar could never be qualified, though it might be abused by a wicked or weak man. Thus, the independence of the Papal States had to be maintained in order to guarantee the popes' freedom of action in the spiritual realm, even if this policy opened the door to bureaucrats and adventurers. A pope, once elected, was accountable to no power on earth, but he achieved such heady eminence only through the votes of his

7. See Pastor, *Popes, 16,* 58 ff.

former colleagues, and he could not dismiss his debt lightly. In any case, he needed the cardinals' cooperation if his administration was to function smoothly. Then, too, the papacy, as an elective monarchy, rarely had an incumbent who ruled for more than a decade. The pope was normally an elderly and careful man who had long outlived any youthful penchant for revolutionary change. Often he had been elected chiefly because he had been an opponent of his predecessor, and, as a result, the papacy was not famous for consistent policy, surely a necessary ingredient in any reform program. The difficulties, therefore, that faced a pope of the Counter Reformation who would wield a new broom within his own administration were not all traceable to the neopagan viciousness which had infected Renaissance Rome. Some of them were endemic to a mysterious institution which, while it claimed to be the extension of Christ's Body, yet had to acknowledge that it was made up of sinful men and situated in an imperfect universe.

The imperfections in his own immediate area were enough for the first of the Counter Reformation popes, Paul IV (1555–59). A fiery Neapolitan whose great age (he was 79 in 1555) had neither slowed his step nor diminished the violence of his temper, Paul was a man opposed in every way to the kind of papacy personified by Leo X. For almost six decades he had been associated with movements within the Church to reform her "both in head and members" (to use the popular expression of the time). Once he had come to supreme power, he rushed headlong against the entrenched self-interest of clerical Rome. He attempted a purge of the college of cardinals, long a home for men who represented the worst in Renaissance civilization. He brandished every ecclesiastical weapon at his command to force upon bishops their fundamental (and often cynically neglected) duty of residence and to root up the simoniacal practices which flourished luxuriantly in the Curia and elsewhere. The Kingdom of Heaven, it is said, suffereth violence, but Paul IV's violence was a two-edged sword. He had no gift for diplomacy. His judgment of people was always rash and usually deplorable. He inspired fear rather than respect. But though he left many pieces for his less tempestuous successors

to gather up, Paul IV gave them a goal to strive for and an example
of honest, disinterested action.[8]

Paul IV's successor, judged by his experience and background,
gave little evidence at the time of his election of dedication to
reform. His personal life was not without its blemishes, and more
damaging to his reputation had been his long and active association with his brother, one of the era's more unscrupulous condot-
tieri. Aside from this unsavory connection, Pius IV (as he styled
himself) had been known primarily as a genial, talkative man,
clever at law and abounding in relatives. Among his nephews, as it
turned out, was the Pope's happy genius, the brilliant and saintly
Charles Borromeo. As temperamentally different from his predecessor as can be imagined, Pius IV brought tact and diplomatic
skill into the service of the Holy See at a time when those qualities
were sorely needed. Under his direction, and with his nephew acting as his right hand, the Council of Trent was reconvened and
brought to a successful conclusion despite enormous difficulties.

Pius IV (1559–65), whatever his past had been, carried the
Counter Reformation a giant stride forward. He had several things
working in his favor besides his own good will. The disciplinary
decrees of the Council of Trent struck at the heart of the system
which brought talented but unscrupulous or unreligious men into
the papal service by forbidding the accumulation of benefices and
by imposing the duty of residence upon benefice holders. A Roman
career, once it became clear that Pius meant to enforce the decrees
with rigor, no longer appealed to the merely ambitious or greedy.
The Pope began with his own household, dismissing four hundred
superfluous functionaries, and bishops were soon scurrying out of
Rome, packed off unceremoniously to the dioceses they had never
seen.[9] Moreover, the political importance of the States of the
Church had declined sharply since the early years of the century
when Borgia and Della Rovere popes dreamed dynastic and imperial dreams. Secular princes were no longer, by 1560, so con-

8. Ironically, much of Paul IV's reform activity was hampered by his ex-
cessive attachment to his nephews. See ibid., *14,* especially 206 ff.

9. Ibid., *16,* 81.

cerned about the outcome of papal elections or so willing to engage in the bribery necessary to secure the choice of a well-disposed
candidate. One seldom heard anymore of "French" or "Spanish"
cardinals, terms which had referred not to the nationality of individuals but to their status as lobbyists for the several European
governments.[10] This new indifference of the Catholic monarchs,
together with the loss of contacts in Protestant Germany and
England, proved a blessing to the college of cardinals and worked
a dramatic change in the character of its membership. Since from
this august body the popes themselves were invariably chosen, it
meant that the Church could look forward to a new kind of supreme pontiff. The day of the simoniacal pope, the militarist pope,
and the dilettante pope had ended.

There could scarcely have been more spectacular confirmation
of this than the papal election of 1566. Michele Ghislieri was a
Dominican friar, ten days short of his sixty-second birthday when
his unexpected elevation took place, and he was a saint.[11] Two
different modern legends have grown up about St. Pius V. On the
one hand, we are told that he typifies, in his famous personal
austerity, his forbidding appearance, frigid manner, and, above
all, his ideas of religious persecution (he had been Grand Inquisitor
during the preceding two pontificates), the stern and ruthless
fanaticism of the Counter Reformation. On the other hand, he is
sometimes described as a kindly old gentleman whose most characteristic activity was the fervent recitation of the Rosary during
the Battle of Lepanto. The truth, of course, lies somewhere in
between, because Pius V was as human and in his own way as
complicated as his more sophisticated predecessor. His contemporaries regarded him as that great rarity, the public figure who is
also a holy man, unselfish and unstinting, a ruler hard on others
but hardest of all on himself, "il papa santo." It had been almost
three hundred years since a saint had worn the tiara, and he,
Celestine V, had found the burden not only intolerable but also
inconsistent with the life of holiness to which he had dedicated

10. Ibid., p. 78.
11. For the career of St. Pius V see ibid., Vols. 17 and 18, passim.

himself.[12] Pius V, on the contrary, searched out his sanctification precisely in the tedious and often disedifying business of papal administration. In this spirit the projects of basic reform initiated by Pius IV were continued and intensified, and this spirit more than compensated for whatever human blunders Pius V's inflexibility and inexperience led him to make.[13]

The average man does not find life with a relentless ascetic particularly comfortable, and it was with some relief that the Catholic world heard of the election, on May 13, 1572, after a remarkably short conclave, of a man with a happy omen in his name, Ugo Boncompagni. The new pope, who assumed the name Gregory XIII, had been a compromise candidate, acceptable to all the factions because he was "good natured and a lover of peace."[14] Gregory proved in his thirteen-year pontificate (1572–85) to be a great deal more. An expert in civil and canon law, he had served in various academic and administrative posts, had come back from Trent with his reputation much enhanced, and had managed the considerable feat of getting on well with both Paul IV and Pius IV, who made him a cardinal in 1565. His relations with his immediate predecessor, however, had not been pleasant, for Boncompagni had never lived the rigorous kind of life which alone recommended a man to the severe affections of Pius V. There was nevertheless no pause in the march of the Counter Reformation. Indeed, this was one of the most remarkable features of the movement, that the popes who led it maintained a continuity despite their differences and mutual dislikes.

By 1572, Rome, with her own house reasonably in order after three successive reform pontificates, was ready finally to assert her rightful leadership in the greater Christian world. Because he possessed an "insatiable love of work, marked aptitude for govern-

12. Pope Celestine's "gran rifuto" earned him Dante's contempt and a place beneath the whirling banner at the gate of the Inferno: "After I had recognized some among them, I saw and knew the shade of him who made, through cowardice, the great refusal."

13. Perhaps the most mooted of Pius V's measures was the excommunication of Elizabeth I in 1570.

14. Pastor, *Popes*, *19*, 13.

ment, breadth of view, keen insight, firmness, . . . extraordinary power of organization and a clear grasp of the real forces of life,"[15] Gregory XIII was an ideal captain. Enforcement of basic Tridentine reforms like the duty of residence became the business of the Pope and his representatives all over Europe. The old temporary legations were replaced by dozens of permanent nunciatures, the tasks of which were religious and not financial or political, stimulation of reform at the grass roots level and not the collection of papal revenue or useless agitation for a crusade against the Turk. The Society of Jesus, by Gregory's time grown in number and stature sufficiently to constitute a powerful force, gave the Pope an evangelizing arm as its members marched across the world stating the case of the Roman Church with a zeal heretofore identified with the Calvinists. Missionaries made their hazardous way to the ancient empires of the Orient and preached the gospel to naked savages in the Americas. There even appeared, during Gregory's pontificate, a slim chance that both Russia and Sweden might seek reunion with Rome. This hope proved illusory, but victory for the reform movement in Poland, Germany, and the Low Countries was a measure of compensation. Disaster befell the Counter Reformation in England, and there was a frustrating stalemate in France, but even these failures did not conceal the new vitality of the old faith among large sections of the English and French populations. In Milan, Charles Borromeo set a vigorous example to the rest of the Catholic world by his energetic attack on the theological illiteracy of the clergy. In Spain that no-nonsense mystic, St. Teresa of Ávila, went about the reform of the Carmelites like a busy housewife at spring-cleaning time. And in Rome itself St. Philip Neri founded the Oratory and taught a generation of intellectuals that one's love for God might well be gauged by one's capacity for genuine gaiety. Over all this activity presided Gregory XIII. The years of his pontificate numbered more than those of his two predecessors put together, and he wasted hardly a moment of them. Nothing escaped the eye of the Pope; not the canon law or church music or even the Julian

15. Ibid., p. 3.

Calendar was safe from reform. When he learned, toward the end of 1583, that some of the cardinals were deep in intrigue with regard to the next conclave (the Pope was a hearty 81), he created nineteen new cardinals at once, which upset the calculations of the college's most astute pollsters. Alert and active to the end, he handled business as usual up to the very day of his death, April 10, 1585.[16] Time had been on the side of Gregory XIII. The unusual length of his pontificate made possible the accomplishment of long-range projects which might have languished with an unsympathetic successor.

The election of 1585 did indeed bring to St. Peter's throne a man whose dislike for Gregory was profound and whose brilliant and willful character made an appreciation of mere humans unthinkable. He had no quarrel with the aims and ideals of the Counter Reformation but what he considered his predecessors' use of wasteful and compromising means infuriated him.[17] Peretti, he might have said contemptuously, will not need half the time given to Boncompagni. In his five-year reign (1585–90), Felice Peretti, Sixtus V, very nearly proved his case. A stocky, extraordinarily ugly man, Sixtus possessed so colorful a personality that his contemporaries appear grey in comparison. He had grown up in the squalor of rural poverty, and to a degree he always remained the peasant—shrewd, grasping, wary. He combined boundless energy with a sublime confidence in his own powers which eliminated, he thought, any need for the advice of others. Few popes have ruled as tyrannically as Sixtus V, and few have ruled as well. He had first earned his reputation in the Church as theologian and preacher and thus attracted the notice of Pius V, who made use of his talents in various posts and gave him a red hat in 1570. Night descended on his career two years later, however, for Gregory XIII cared little for mendicants in general and Peretti in particular. (Peretti was a Franciscan, an astonishing tribute to

16. Gregory XIII surely stands as one of the most underestimated public men in the history of the West. For his career see Pastor, Vols. 19 and 20, passim.

17. Pastor, 21, 53, especially n. 2.

the flexibility of the Little Poor Man's Institute.) For the next thirteen years he occupied himself with his studies and waited. His colleagues who elected him in the conclave of 1585 surely had no premonition of the whirlwind they were loosing upon the Church and the world. A legend, too good to be true, points up this fact. During the conclave, we are told, Peretti gave every appearance of desperate illness, as he spoke only in a hoarse whisper and leaned heavily upon his stick. Once the electors had made their choice, however, the new pope threw back his shoulders, tossed aside his cane, and looked round triumphantly at the startled cardinals who realized now that they had chosen no mere caretaker.

Sixtus V plunged with a fury into the multitude of tasks that faced him. He introduced massive reforms into the financial and administrative machinery of the Papal States. He declared full-scale war on the brigands who had roamed the environs of Rome with impunity for years, preying upon commerce and travelers. Within a few months of Sixtus' election, one observer noted that bandits' heads exposed on the bridge of St. Angelo were as common a sight as melons in the market. His other legislation was similarly harsh: in 1586, included among criminals subject to capital punishment were verbal calumniators and parents who "allowed" their daughters to be seduced. He executed such legislation with rare impartiality; he only laughed when a cardinal protested at the public flogging of a member of an Imperial embassy who had been apprehended bearing weapons, contrary to the law. Many grumbled at the heavy, Draconian hand, but Rome and central Italy gained as a result of it a peace and prosperity they had seldom known. The city itself found the same hand lavish indeed, and she blossomed anew with monuments and projects, from a vast system of aqueducts to the mighty dome of St. Peter's, so that one visitor to Rome was moved to write a friend: "Here I am in Rome and yet I cannot find the Rome I know, so great are the changes . . . with which Sixtus has beautified this old and ruinous city."[18]

18. Ibid., 22, 305.

The new streets, fountains, and public buildings, the novel absence of violence in the hinterland, all of which made it difficult for a former resident to recognize the "old and ruinous city," had a kind of sacramental significance. For Rome, beneath its brightly scrubbed and bustling exterior, had become once again an Imperial city. There were no tramping legions, to be sure, and no monarch trembled any more at the thought of Canossa. Rather, the papacy's disillusionment with politics and art as substitutes for religious endeavor had been transformed by Sixtus V's time into the realization that Rome was again the ecclesiastical center of the West in a way in which Wittenberg or Geneva could never be. With this in mind, the imperious Sixtus did not hesitate to revamp the government of the universal Church so that it might meet its universal responsibilities. Two particularly important administrative reforms must be mentioned. Sixtus revived the practice by which every diocesan bishop, in person or by delegate, reported the religious condition of his diocese to the Holy See at regular intervals. This *ad limina* visitation, as it was called, had practically disappeared during the preceding two centuries. It would be hard to overestimate the importance of this prescription, which made "possible a more practical and well informed intervention in every religious development . . . caused the bishops to keep a closer watch over the spiritual welfare of their subjects and urged them to a keener sense of duty."[19] Secondly, Sixtus abandoned the consistory, that joint committee of all the curial cardinals chaired by the pope, as the normal instrument of ecclesiastical government. Waste, like thievery and adultery, was for Sixtus one of the bad things God meant him to destroy, and the consistory, he proclaimed, wasted too much time and too much money. Ignoring the sensibilities of the cardinals, he decreed that various congregations, nine in all, would hereafter handle the routine business of the Church. Each congregation would be staffed by several cardinals, with a prefect at its head, and each would concern itself with some particular facet of administration. It was a sensible and simple plan, for which Gregory XIII had laid

19. Ibid., *21*, 135.

the foundation (though Sixtus would never admit this). It was no more than the creation of a modern bureaucracy, which amounts to saying that it was as revolutionary, in its own way, as the invention of the wheel.

The establishment of the cardinalitial congregations made civil servants of men who had been princes, and it marks one of the climaxes of the Counter Reformation. The consistory continued to meet regularly every Wednesday, but it served mostly as an occasion for Sixtus to harangue the cardinals at numbing length about the poverty he had experienced as a boy or, perhaps, about the wealth the Holy See had accumulated during his pontificate. This latter was not an empty boast, as the work of physical restoration in Rome amply demonstrated. The ill-fated Spanish Armada, as expensive a political misadventure as a pope was ever involved in, was also financed partly by Sixtus V's treasury. More to the point, the financial solvency of the papacy was a sign of the vigor which had buoyed the Church since the days of Paul IV and which reached its culmination under the leadership of the vigorous Sixtus V. He died (August 27, 1590) in a predictable manner; fancying himself an expert in medicine, he refused to pay the slightest heed to his physicians.[20]

The fame of Sixtus V rests to a large degree upon the disproportion between the magnitude of his accomplishment and the shortness of time at his disposal. With a man so violently talented, it might be argued that he was fortunate in his death, that more years could have meant only decline into eccentricity or worse, that a comet is meant to light up the sky with its brilliance for a moment and then to sink silently and quickly from sight. However that may be, Sixtus' successor, Clement VIII (1592–1605), last of the Counter Reformation popes,[21] presents no such perplexing problem to later analysts. He reminded his contemporaries more of a fussy bank clerk (which he had been at one time) than of a shooting star. Ippolito Aldobrandini (b. February 24, 1536) ruled

20. Ibid., passim; 22, 1–311.
21. There were three short pontificates (one lasted only 13 days) between those of Sixtus and Clement.

the Church of Christ for thirteen years with competence rather than brilliance.[22] He consistently displayed caution, patience, and a hardheaded approach to the realities of life, qualities which served him well as pope and which led directly to the solution of the French problem with the conversion of Henry of Navarre, the high-water mark of the Counter Reformation. Clement VIII was by no means an extraordinary pope; extraordinary popes are rare, and by the end of the sixteenth century the ordinary pope, interested in God and God's people and unafraid of work, could guide the bark of Peter. The worst of the storm had passed.

It is always a temptation for one who looks back upon the times of his ancestors to assign a mystical significance to this event or to that individual. The historian must ever beware the "turning point," the easy association, or the coincidence which explains too much. "There are more things in heaven and earth, Horatio, than are dreamt of in your philosophy." And there are more events in human affairs caused by habit, temperament, and accident than the most astute observer can measure. Let 1555, then, stand as a momentous year, filled with portents of the future, but let it also be remembered that the Counter Reformation, like any historical era, is part of a seamless garment, "woven from the top throughout." If 1555 marks a convenient starting point for it (and there could well be others), this is true only because a 1554 and, indeed, a 1454 had gone before. With this in mind, it can be noted that a fortnight before the abdication of Charles V, a young man named Thomas Stapleton, Fellow of New College, Oxford, watched Nicholas Ridley and Hugh Latimer, sometime bishops in the Church of England, burned to death for heresy. The experience, he noted later, had moved him not at all. Though the punishment was, he granted, severe, the crime was, he felt, heinous enough to warrant it.[23]

---

22. For Clement VIII see Pastor, Vols. 23 and 24.

23. "If visions appearing to some and not to all that are present seem fabulous, let it be a fable (as indeed it is, being thereof an eyewitness myself) that [John Foxe in his *Acts and Monuments*] telleth of Latimer's heart blood, when he suffered in Oxford." *Fortresse*, p. 62.

Chapter 2

THE MAN

When Clement VIII sat down in lonely papal splendor to take his meals, he customarily had theological treatises read to him. Whether this practice served as an aid to the pontiff's digestion has not been recorded. At any rate, among the authors most frequently chosen for these occasions was Thomas Stapleton, an English refugee who, since 1590, had been Regius Professor of Scripture at the University of Louvain.[1] The choice was appropriate, because of all the intellectuals who had worn the livery of the Counter Reformation, few enjoyed Stapleton's high reputation. An Oxford chronicler, writing when the flames of religious controversy had burned down to a cold ash, described him as "the most learned Roman Catholic of all his time."[2]

This judgment might seem to reflect a narrow parochial pride, possible for a seventeenth-century Oxonian to feel even for a champion of popery as long as he had also been a Fellow of New College, and no doubt to some extent it does. After all, Stapleton's time saw the likes of Baius, Baronius, and Robert Bellarmine. Though later generations have forgotten him and not them, Stapleton's contemporaries did not hesitate to place him in their distinguished company. There is a significant point to be made here: Stapleton, whom nobody read for three hundred years, hardly outlived the tumult and shouting of the era which bred him. Baius, on the other hand, founded a sect whose gloomy votaries are with us still. Baronius paved the way for all the ecclesiastical

1. Pastor, *Popes*, *24, 437.*
2. Anthony Wood, *Athenae Oxonienses, 1* (London, 1820), 669.

historians who have followed him. Bellarmine constructed a lofty theological synthesis the ramifications of which have not even to this date been fully explored. One might conclude from this that Stapleton, in comparison with these others, had little to say to the ages. But one might also maintain, on the same evidence, that he had a great deal to say about and to the age he lived in. Perhaps the man who just misses the particular spark of genius which would set him above his time speaks more eloquently for his time than the man who possesses it. Only a certain amount of detachment can make a Bellarmine, and Stapleton was incapable of detachment. Precisely because he was an Englishman, he could not escape a personal and emotional involvement in the Counter Reformation unthinkable to an Italian. For him, as for many other English Catholics who refused to accept the Elizabethan Settlement, the movement was a holy war against very concrete foes, against those forces of evil which had seized his unhappy homeland. Stapleton's nationality makes all the difference in assigning him his proper place among the leaders of the Counter Reformation. When a man suffers the indignities of exile, when he is deprived of the respect of his countrymen, the sound of his native tongue, and the sight of the familiar things with which he grew up, detachment comes hard. A modern critic has chided Stapleton for the severity of his language in a controversy with an Anglican divine and has compared him unfavorably in this regard to Bellarmine, who took pains to treat the same adversary with great respect.[3] Such criticism misses the mark. An exiled Englishman

3. James Brodrick, *The Life and Work of . . . Cardinal Bellarmine*, I (New York, 1928), 176: "Döllinger held that in the matter of controversy Stapleton was a greater man than Bellarmine. He was alone in his opinion, and one cannot help feeling that something more than pure reason went to [sic] its making, but even supposing it correct, there are other laurels for a writer besides those of learning and Bellarmine assuredly has them all. A comparison of the works of the two men who, by the way, were friends, makes that conclusion plain. They had a common foe in [William] Whitaker and their attitude toward him may serve as a test for the quality of their minds. Stapleton, great man though he was, became ill-tempered in the debate, and belabored the doctor furiously. . . . All the way through he writes with a pen dipped in gall." If Father Brodrick will pardon me, I fail to see the point of

could not have reacted to the taunts of a Cambridge don with the imperturbability of one who had never seen the Thames and perhaps never heard of it. Would it be presumptuous to suggest that St. Robert's admiration for his opponent's argumentative skill might have been tempered had that opponent habitually taken his evening constitutional along the banks of the Arno?

If Stapleton's passionate concern for England set him off from the leading continental intellectuals and perhaps compromised the permanent value of his work, his talents nevertheless made him singular among the English exiles. He stood head and shoulders above all of them in erudition and literary skill. Not one of them could match the volume and variety of his work, to say nothing of its quality. On the other hand, Stapleton had no gift whatever for the activities which occupied his most eminent fellow exiles. William Allen and Robert Persons, for example, were first-rate controversialists, but they were men of action, too, organizers, popularizers, and politicians. They judged Stapleton for what he was, a bookish recluse, and though they rejoiced in his intellectual triumphs and were prepared to exploit them, they never allowed him into their inner counsels. Indeed, at certain moments of distress, they did not hesitate to remind him to keep his place. This does not indicate a difference in goal or an unusual amount of friction or personal animosity. Their cause bound the exiles together even when their talents and inclinations took them in various directions. Stapleton, without peer in the study and the lecture hall, simply could not have created the College at Douay

---

his comparison. One cannot help thinking that something more than pure reason went to its making; perhaps that "something" is made up of the fraternal bonds of that noble Society to which both Robert Bellarmine and Father Brodrick have belonged. The observation of the most recent researcher in this area might be pertinent: "On sait que le cardinal Duperrom et, plus tard, l'historien Döllinger estimaient plus l'œuvre polémique de l'Anglais que celle de l'Italien et qu'aux yeux de Paquot les études de Stapleton apparaît plus empirique, celle du saint Docteur plus rationnelle." Pontien Polman, *L'Elément historique dans la controverse religieuse du XVIe siècle* (Gembloux, 1932), p. 514. The two men, by the way, were not friends.

or the English Mission any more than Allen could have written Stapleton's tract on justification. As far as intrigue was concerned, Stapleton never overcame a childlike inability to engage in it. As it turned out, Allen, Persons, and the rest achieved little success in that same department, but it was not for lack of trial or ability. Stapleton, whom the other exiles nicknamed Cajetan,[4] was content with the unglamorous but congenial task of hurling verbal thunderbolts at the common enemy.

The bare outlines of his life should suffice to explain this difference. Stapleton was born at Henfield, Sussex, within days of the execution of Sir Thomas More, in July 1535.[5] His father, William, a man of some prominence in the neighborhood, was not sympathetic with the religious changes which had come lately upon the realm. Though he took care to keep his misgivings to himself, the Christian name he chose for his infant son may have been significant. In any case Thomas Stapleton toward the end of his life called it a "bonum communis nominis omen" which linked him to the great Chancellor. "I remember well," he wrote in 1588, "and numberless people can testify with me, that the fame of this man and the memory of his martyrdom acted as a stimulus to us young people who wanted to hold fast to the Catholic faith."[6] Stapleton the boy learned the rudiments of grammar

---

4. See Thomas Graves Law, *A Historical Sketch of the Conflicts between Jesuits and Seculars in the Reign of Queen Elizabeth* . . . (London, 1889), p. 113 n.

5. There is a curious metrical autobiography of Stapleton and a short memoir of him by a sometime student, both of which can be found at the beginning of the first volume of *Thomae Stapletoni angli, sacrae theologiae doctoris et professoris regii, Duaci primo, deinde Lovanii, opera quae extant omnia,* ed. Robert Fouet, Nicholas Buon, and Sebastian Cramoisy (4 vols. Paris, 1620). Neither the "Compendium breve et verum studiorum Thomae Stapletoni ab ipsomet . . . comprehensum" nor the "Vita admodum eximii viri Domini Thomae Stapletoni, sacrae theologiae doctoris et professoris celeberrimi," the latter written by Stapleton's fellow exile, Henry Holland, possesses pagination in this edition. The biographical sketches in *DTC,* in Hurter's *Nomenclator literarius recentioris theologiae catholicae* and in the *Catholic Encyclopedia* (1912 ed.) are so inaccurate as to be useless. Thompson Cooper's article in *DNB* is good but incomplete.

6. *Tres Thomae,* p. 935.

at Canterbury School and passed from there to the preparatory school at Winchester where, he said, he found the studies "more rewarding." At the age of 15 he went up to Oxford, and on January 18, 1553 he was elected Fellow of New College. He received his bachelor's degree in arts on December 2, 1556. Because of his association with the latter two institutions ("splendid colleges" he called them many years afterward), Stapleton could assume the proud title "Wiccamite," (i.e. Wykehamist) and he liked to boast that the alumni of William of Wykeham's schools had played a prominent role from the beginning in the resistance to the Elizabethan Settlement.

The need for such resistance, however, was not yet apparent to the young scholar when, early in 1558, he was ordained a priest and was collated to the prebend of Woodhouse in Chichester Cathedral. His piety and intelligence, wrote Henry Holland somewhat defensively, more than compensated for his youth. However that may be, Mary Tudor still ruled England, Cardinal Pole presided at Lambeth, and the heir to the throne, the Lady Elizabeth, piously attended Mass. The future seemed bright for a bookish young Catholic, pious and intelligent, already accepted in highly restricted academic circles and secure financially by reason of his benefice. The change, swift and dramatic, was not long in coming. On November 17, 1558, the unhappy Mary died and, by a curious coincidence, so did Reginald Pole. By Christmas it was clear that whatever her real religious sentiments, the new queen, Anne Boleyn's daughter, was not a Catholic. The Parliament which met the following January (1559) framed the government-sponsored legislation, the Acts of Supremacy and Uniformity, which re-established the state Church and the Protestant worship as they had developed in the days of the Queen's father and brother. The Englishman, therefore, had to shift his religious allegiance once again, a practice to which he was becoming wearily accustomed. But in striking contrast to the similar situation created by Henry VIII twenty-five years earlier, this time many eminent Catholics declined to jump. The bishops refused to a man the new Oath of Supremacy and were deprived and, by the early months of 1560, replaced. Others, not so highly placed, avoided the oath, hoped, and waited. Still others, in imitation of the Protestants at the beginning of Mary's reign, decided to do their waiting abroad.

Among these latter was Thomas Stapleton who, late in 1559, departed England for the Low Countries. The details of his going remain obscure, but evidently it was illegal in procedure. "Fearing the contagion of schism in my tender years," he explained vaguely, "I came a fugitive to the learned benches of Louvain."[7] "Misliking the proceedings of the realm," wrote William Barlow, the new Bishop of Chichester, "[he] conveyed himself over the seas without licence under the wings of Count Feria."[8] It is possible that Stapleton did leave England in the company of the Spanish ambassador who had married an English wife and had included several English clerics in his retinue.[9] Once in Belgium, however, Stapleton obtained the necessary royal license which permitted him to remain outside the kingdom for three years. The time was spent, characteristically, in study: theology at Louvain and linguistics at the University of Paris. Toward the end of the three-year leave, Stapleton made a pilgrimage to Rome. When he returned to Louvain, he found waiting for him several letters from his father calling him back to England. Whether domestic crisis, government pressure, or some other reason prompted William Stapleton's summons, we do not know. "I was scarcely home," his son wrote, "when I was called before the mock tribunal of the heretic jester to whom fair Chichester had become subject." He told Bishop Barlow that he was perfectly willing to swear part of the new Oath of Supremacy and that the Queen was indeed supreme governor in temporal matters, "at what time, upon refusal of the other part, he deprived me (as much as lay in him) of my prebend in (Chichester) Church." If Stapleton had hoped that during his

---

7. "Compendium," *Opera, 1,* no pagination.
8. Quoted in H. N. Birt, *The Elizabethan Religious Settlement* (London, 1907), pp. 424–25.
9. See the references in Robert Lechat, *Les Réfugiés anglais dans les Pays-Bas durant le règne d'Elizabeth* (Louvain, 1914), pp. 23, 139, 165.

sojourn on the continent the clouds of heresy over England would pass away, and with them the dangers to his own career, by early 1563 he knew better. Together with his father and the rest of his family ("all of them very good Catholics, pious and devout"), he emigrated to Louvain. He never saw England again.[10]

Stapleton spent the rest of his life in the Low Countries. Except for an occasional journey to France and one to Italy, he never left them. Indeed, to the very eve of his death, he was busy parrying the Pope's invitation to take up residence in Rome. He kept close contact therefore with his fellow refugees, the bulk of whom settled in one Belgian town or another and waited, in the pathetic tradition of political exiles, for the day when the rascals at home would be turned out. Their hopes were lively in the early years; any moment, they reassured one another, the heretics would fall from power. After all, the faith that the Tudor family had at first disavowed it had later restored, and perhaps it could be persuaded to restore it again. This optimism, so completely out of tune with political reality, inspired an avalanche of polemical prose in English, most of it emanating from presses located in the Netherlands. In this movement Stapleton made his controversial debut, or, as he put it, "At this time I began to write my first books against the heretics, but in the vernacular tongue only."[11] He joined a band of dedicated and talented men who poured forth a voluminous literature astonishingly high in quality of content and literary style.[12] But warriors, even verbal warriors, need more solid nourishment than dreams, and, by the time the 1560s had run their course, even the most sanguine among the exiles realized that their books had brought them not a whit closer to the common rooms they had left at Oxford and Cambridge. If anything, they had prematurely tipped their own hand and strengthened

10. Stapleton, "Compendium," and Holland's "Vita," *Opera, 1,* no pagination.

11. "Compendium," ibid.

12. A. D. Southern, *Elizabethan Recusant Prose* (London, 1950) has provided a most interesting and useful study of this literature.

the government's by contributing, in some measure at least, to the abortive Rising of the North in 1569.[13]

Another factor helped cut short this renaissance of English Catholic literature. Like Stapleton, most of the exiles did their writing in the Low Countries (as close to England as they could safely be) and depended for publication on Belgian printers. Toward the end of the decade the English discovered that the place in which they had chosen to await a fairer day for themselves had its own dreadful agony to pass through and that, as a result, their war of words must fade into the background. After 1566, the crucial military battles of the Counter Reformation were fought in the Netherlands. Here, for thirty years, wrestled giants like William of Orange and the Duke of Alba. Across this stage strode colorful characters like Don John of Austria, Alessandro Farnese, and the nameless Dutch Sea Beggars who drove the Spanish admiralty to distraction. The lush, wealthy Netherlands were the choicest of Philip II's provinces as well as the pivot round which swung his French and English policy, and he fought like a tiger to maintain their integrity. But he was faced by determined men who would discard the unnatural union with Spain at all costs and who would find in Calvinism a fierce benediction for their cause. The struggle in the Low Countries ended in a bloody draw and thus provided one more symbol for the Counter Reformation.

Thomas Stapleton, theologian and academician, had no direct part in the violent drama, but nobody could live in the Netherlands in those unhappy years and remain unaware of the riots, the purges, and the frenzied rush of armies. Stapleton, of course, took sides as everyone did. He described himself in 1597 as "a true and trusty servant to his Majesty of Spain," who alone, it seemed to him, stood between Christianity and the abyss.[14] With his preconception and his personal experiences, it was easy for

---

13. Stapleton was one of those divines who the Earl of Northumberland, in 1568, had hoped would teach Leicester and Cecil "to have discerned cheese from chalk" in matters of religion. See Hughes, *Reformation*, 3, 267–68.

14. Stapleton to Robert Persons, April 16, 1597 (*DD*, pp. 390–91).

him to see the Dutch resistance to Philip as simply an instance of what he called "the lewd, loose liberty of this wicked time,"[15] which aimed ultimately at the destruction of church and state. Stapleton, who had a genius for the dissection of abstract arguments, never grasped the complex issues involved in the revolt of the Netherlands. He could penetrate every shade of meaning in so difficult a doctrine as justification, and the maze of church-state relations, insofar as it presented a scientific problem, held no terrors for him. But he viewed the great political and military crisis of his time with utter simplicity: the blacks were Calvinists, the whites Catholics.

It would have been understandable enough if only for the fact that he had lived through the terrible night of August 19–20, 1566. The experience of those wild hours served as a confirmation sufficient for him for the rest of his life. "In the chief church of Antwerp town, the brethren . . . toward evening, at the anthem time, between five and six of the clock, began first by certain boys to play their pageant, mocking and striking by way of derision the image of Our Lady, then especially visited and honored for the . . . memorial of her glorious Assumption." The Prince of Orange, governor of Antwerp, had left that very day for Brussels and the Lady Regent's court. The chief officer in his absence was the town margrave, who, when informed of the disturbance, hastened to the church. "But the brethren by this time were become lords of the church and had shut the doors against the Margrave." The officer eventually found an open entrance and appealed to the Calvinists, in the King's name, to disperse. "Many words passing between the Margrave and them, their number being great and increasing still, the Margrave departed the church, nothing prevailing, neither by fair words nor foul."

The rejection of the royal officer's plea was only the beginning:

> The Margrave being thus rejected (as unable indeed to withstand the faction of the rebels, as it appeared well even that

15. This phrase was a kind of tag line with Stapleton, who used it often, e.g. in *Fortresse*, p. 285.

night) the holy brethren went to their drudgery. First they
sang Psalms, pretending that only to be the cause of their
meeting there at that time. At their psalmody, rushed in great
numbers of people, some to see and be gone again, some to
remain and accompany them. I was myself present at the beginning of the tragedy (coming by chance to town that afternoon), and I saw after the Margrave was gone out of the
church, and their psalmody begun, not past (I verily suppose)
three score persons assembled. There rushed in continually
great numbers of such as tarried still with them. All this was
before six of the clock. From that time forward, their melody
soon ended, they proceeded to sacrilege, to breaking of im-
ages, to throwing down of altars, of organs and of all kind of
tabernacles, as well in that church as in all other churches,
monasteries and chapels of Antwerp, to stealing of chalices,
to spoiling of copes, to breaking up of seats, to robbing of
the church wardens' boxes, as well as for the church as for
the poor. And herein, I will report that which I saw with my
eyes. In St. James' Church, the spoil there being not so outrageous . . . all the settles, benches and seats, made about the
church pillars and altars for folk to sit and kneel in, were
in manner left whole, one only excepted, placed at the west
end of the church, in the which there were diverse little
scobbes and boxes of gatherings for the poor. These scobbes
only were broken up and the contents visited, for to them
was their chief devotion; all the rest remained whole and
unspoiled. To be short, all that night (which to him that had
been present thereat, as I then was, might well seem Nox
Siciliana) the zealous brotherhood so followed the chase that
they left not one church in Antwerp, great or small, where
they hunted up not good game and carried away flesh good
store. Chalices, patens and cruets of gold and silver, copes
and vestments of silk and of velvet, fine linen and coarse,
none came amiss; they took all in good part and took no
more than they found. What shall I speak of the very
libraries spoiled and burned, namely, of the Grey Friars and

of the Abbey of St. Michael? To describe particularly the horrible and outrageous sacrileges of that night, an eternal document of the gospellike zeal of this sacred brotherhood, would require a full treatise of itself.[16]

There were other riots, other acts of pillage and desecration, and other nights reminiscent of the Sicilian Vespers, suffered and perpetrated by both sides during the course of that unreasoned confessional conflict. Because this was the case, one can search high and low without finding the calm and neutral observer. It should come as no surprise that Stapleton saw Antwerp ruffians who overturned tabernacles and rifled poor boxes as members of the same gang of desperadoes who had thrown down St. Thomas à Becket's image from London Bridge and who squatted impudently at that moment in the canons' stalls in Chichester Cathedral.

Until this violent summer of 1566, almost all the Catholic emigré books had been printed in Antwerp. Included among the prominent publishers of such materials was John Fowler, himself an exile and a Wykehamist, who printed several of his schoolfellow Stapleton's works. After the riots of August and September, however, the English printing operation moved en masse to Louvain, and two years later, when fresh and much graver troubles broke out, it ceased altogether. At roughly the same time as the literary effort of the English Catholics was stifled at its mechanical source, the market for its product was being sealed off by an increasingly repressive and watchful English government.[17] As far as Stapleton was concerned, this disadvantageous combination contributed to a profound change of direction in his career. After 1567, he never again published a book written in his native language, even when he dealt with specifically English topics. Latin became henceforward the exclusive vehicle of his thought. This was not so much due to a considered decision as to

16. *Counterblast*, fols. 18–21, 432–33. For the general accuracy of Stapleton's narrative see E. de Moreau, Pierre Jourda, and Pierre Janelle, *La Crise religieuse du XVIe siècle* (Paris, 1956), pp. 282 ff.

17. See J. H. Pollen, *The English Catholics in the Reign of Queen Elizabeth* (London, 1920), p. 109.

a chain of circumstances which included an ever widening range of interests and associations as well as the conviction that Calvinism was an international movement best combated in an international tongue. But also involved was the more mundane economic fact that a writer, whatever his subject, must have a public if he is to live to enjoy any satisfaction from his art. The literati of Europe did not buy books written in English.

This development still lay in the future. In 1568 what concerned Stapleton and all his fellow exiles was the opening, on Michaelmas Day of that year, of the new Collège des Prêtres Anglais. Located at Douay, a south Belgian town halfway between Lille and Cambrai, it consisted of two large houses with attached gardens and four students (three of them Oxford men) who shared a common life and took their courses in the new University of Douay. Their avowed purpose was to prepare themselves for the inevitable day when the Elizabethan regime would collapse and England would have an immediate need for trained priests. It was a modest beginning, based on a forlorn hope and supported by funds donated by a pair of sympathetic Benedictine abbots, and yet it proved to be the beginning of a great adventure. The English College gave birth to a generation of heroes and martyrs who have been the pride of English-speaking Catholics ever since. By 1574, with Elizabeth I still flourishing, the fateful decision was made to send the young graduates back to their homeland as missionaries. There were a hundred of them at work in England in 1580, and by the time Elizabeth died (1603), 450 Douay priests had served on the English mission, and 110 of them had suffered martyrdom.

At the head of this bold new venture stood William Allen (1532–94) who, with the opening of the College at Douay, assumed the leadership of the English Catholic resistance to the Elizabethan Settlement.[18] Allen would have left the imprint of his remarkable intelligence and organizational ability upon whatever environment he lived in. But given the particular circum-

18. See Hughes, *Reformation*, 3, 283 ff.

stances he actually faced, his endless tact served him perhaps better than any other gift. He led a party which might at any moment have disintegrated into a band of disgruntled expatriates. Instead, he inspired them with a confidence and cohesion that saw them through many a disaster and saved them for a generation from falling into desperation or eccentricity. When he described the regime he established for the students at Douay, Allen summed up his method of ruling men: "A little government there is and order but no bondage or straitness in the world. There is neither oath nor statute nor other bridle nor chastisement; but reason and every man's conscience toward other."[19] As long as Allen lived, this policy prevailed and guided the movement through good times and bad. It is a measure of his personal strength that at the final reckoning none among his followers, sensitive intellectuals for the most part, had anything but admiration for him. When he died, there was literally no one to take his place; without him the cause languished and the Catholics frittered away their energies in fruitless and unworthy quarrels.

The exiles rallied around Allen and his College. Before long, Douay was headquarters for the disaffected English Catholics. Owen Lewis was already on the scene in 1568, and Gregory Martin, destined for immortality as translator of the Bible, was among the first of the collegians to be ordained, in 1573. Eventually, if reluctantly, the Jesuits came too; though few in number, they included men of the highest caliber, like Robert Persons and Edmund Campion. Thomas Stapleton arrived at Douay in 1569 and promptly matriculated in the university. Whether or not he came at Allen's invitation remains unclear, though Stapleton took some pains not to give that impression: "Next I went to Douay and there I continued my studies, not without success," he wrote simply.[20] His association with Allen, in any case, was friendly but never close. Together they began to teach in the university's faculty of theology in 1569 and together they were promoted to the doctorate (July 10, 1571). As the historian of the university has

19. Ibid., p 288.
20. "Compendium," *Opera*, *1*, no pagination.

put it: "Aux premiers rangs des professeurs qui ont fondé l'enseignement de la théologie à Douay se placent deux des plus illustres docteurs de la nouvelle Université, que les persécutions d'Elizabeth avaient chassés d'Angleterre, Guillaume Allen et Thomas Stapleton."[21] In a book published many years afterward, Stapleton penned a dedicatory note to Allen which, in its balance of warmth and formality, may very well indicate the kind of relationship that existed between the two men:

> There are customarily two considerations, most distinguished Cardinal, which influence literary men in their selection of an esteemed person to whom they dedicate their labors: there is first the distinction, dignity, and greatness of the man they so choose, and, on their own side, there is affection and desire to please and joy in doing so. . . . Both these considerations have contributed to my dedication of this book to you, for you are the person by whose favor it can best be adorned and by whose patronage best defended, and my feelings toward you are such that I could wish it to be dedicated to no one else more happily or with greater pleasure in my heart. . . . And, indeed, to whom could I offer more happily this polemic in defense of the Catholic faith than to my old colleague and confrere in this kind of business, who is, besides, my well-beloved friend? For it was once our common fortune to be colleagues in the study and teaching of theology. Now in the splendor of your dignity as Cardinal of England you still deign to count me as a friend and to embrace me with fraternal benevolence. Surely this is a sign of your humanity and, I might say, of your humility. Receive then, distinguished Eminence, this defense which I have dedicated to you most heartily, as a testimony to my old friendship and to my present esteem.[22]

21. Georges Cardon, *La Fondation de l'Université de Douai* (Paris, 1892), p. 335.

22. Thomas Stapleton, *Autoritatis ecclesiasticae circa Scripturarum approbationem . . . defensio* (Antwerp, 1592), dedication in *Opera, 1,* 841–42.

Stapleton's retiring nature and bookish habits inclined him to work within the larger sphere of the university rather than within the single-minded atmosphere of the English College. This indicated no lack of sympathy for the cause or for the leader, but Stapleton never considered himself Allen's protégé. What he wrote in 1580, after Allen and the College had departed Douay for Reims, applied to his whole career: "I am convinced that I must devote myself to study and literary labor in which alone I can be of service to the Church of God."[23] Allen evidently appreciated this attitude and never attempted to draw Stapleton either into the routine work of practical formation carried on by the College or into the web of intrigue which, as the years passed, occupied more of his own attention. For example, in November 1576, on the eve of Stapleton's departure on a trip to Rome, Allen gave him a letter to deliver to Owen Lewis, at that time just beginning his brilliant work in the papal service. The letter, written partially in cipher, contained news about the progress of the "enterprise," that is, about the progress of plans to enlist foreign intervention to topple the Elizabethan regime by force. "Our master, Doctor Stapleton," wrote Allen, "is of himself quite eager to undertake the pilgrimage to Rome for the sake of devotion, but he knows nothing at all about the enterprise." If he did not allow Stapleton to share his secrets, however, Allen had no doubts about his colleague's loyalty, usefulness, or courage: "[Stapleton]," the letter continued, "will be a very fit person to send among the leaders with the fleet."[24]

Unaware that a fleet had even been thought of, and so spared

23. *Speculum*, p. 379.

24. See the references given by Martin Haile, *An Elizabethan Cardinal: William Allen* (St. Louis, 1914), p. 150. Lewis had an equally high regard for Stapleton, as his letter of introduction to his own patron, the learned Cardinal Sirleto, testifies (March 30, 1577): "Commendo cum favori vestro prolixe quia dignus est omni commendatione et favore, cum sit doctissimus et pientissimus et utile memorum sanctae matri ecclesiae, quam contra haereticos saepe et cum magno fructu defendit. Is est suae Sanctitati notus, eidem Sanctitati suae per me commendatus et credo per alios quoque." For the full text see *DD*, pp. 307–08.

the pangs reserved to the leaders of a hopeless project, Stapleton
had plunged into the full swim of the congenial academic life.
Shortly after his arrival in Douay, he formed a close attachment
to the chancellor of the university, Mathieu Galenus, to whom he
entrusted the direction of his studies leading to the doctorate. This
extraordinary scholar made a deep impression on Stapleton, who
described him as "theologoum decus, sacerdotum speculum . . .
scholae theologicae lumen."[25] The relationship between the two
men ripened into one of mutual regard, and Galenus, before he
died in 1573, provided Stapleton with a canonry in the local
church of Ste. Amoure. Through Galenus, Stapleton also met
François Richardot, Bishop of Arras, who had taken a prominent
part in the founding of the university's theology faculty and who,
until his death in the summer of 1574, exercised a kind of general
direction over it. Richardot had endeared himself particularly to
the English because, as Stapleton put it, he had "aided with his
constant alms so many penniless and despairing exiled students."[26]
Stapleton himself had financial problems which in the early years
of his sojourn in Douay were alleviated through the help of the
two Benedictine abbots who had acted as patrons to the English
College. Jean Lentailleur, abbot of Anchin, and Arnould Ganthois,
abbot of Marchiennes, had each endowed a university foundation
named after his own abbey. Although both the Collège d'Anchin
and the Collège de Marchiennes were staffed exclusively by Jesuits,
their founders made an exception for the young English secular
who in 1570 assumed the post of lecturer in Holy Scripture in
both institutions. This arrangement tided Stapleton over for two
years, until his university professorship and canonry afforded him
relatively permanent financial security. More than that, it gave
him the occasion for friendship with Lentailleur and especially

25. Thomas Stapleton, "Oratio funebris et panegyrica in laudem Matthaei
Galeni, Academiae Duacenae cancellarii," *Opera 2*, 486–92. For a short account
of Galenus' career see *DTC*, 6, Pt. 1, cc. 1054–56.

26. Thomas Stapleton, "Oratio funebris in laudem Fran. Richardoti," *Opera*,
2, 475–80.

Ganthois,[27] two of the most colorful figures in Counter Reformation Belgium, and also the opportunity to work closely with the Society of Jesus, an experience which was to affect his personal and professional life profoundly.

In the autumn of 1571 Stapleton was named university professor of catechetics, a position he filled until three years later when, as he explained flamboyantly in his metrical autobiography, "I was elevated to a still higher plane and henceforward had to expound in their full sweep the dogmatic controversies with the heretics."[28] During the winter term of 1574–75 he served in the honorific, though largely ceremonial, office of rector of the university.[29] But early in 1578 the pleasant round of academic routine was rudely interrupted. For almost two years the bloody war between the Spanish and the supporters of the Prince of Orange had been raging with particular fury. Though the Spaniards won a great victory at Gembloux in January 1578, peaceful settlement continued to elude them, and popular sentiment continued to grow against them. The March elections brought into power in Douay a slate of magistrates hostile to the Spanish and to the friends of Spain. The English Catholic refugees and their College were counted among the latter. On the morning of March 14 Stapleton was summoned by the university officials and instructed to inform the English community that it had two days to vacate the town. The only exceptions were university professors, the aged, and women and children. Next day came a mitigating decree and then a cancellation. For a week the matter hung in suspense, and then on March 22, the eve of Palm Sunday, the

27. Stapleton also preached the funeral orations over the remains of Lentailleur and Ganthois. See *Opera, 2,* 495 ff. Of the latter of these sermons Cardon, p. 471, says: "Cette oraison funèbre . . . nous fournit les principaux renseignements sur la vie de [Ganthois] l'abbé de Marchiennes."

28. "Compendium," *Opera, 1,* no pagination. For an interesting reaction to this promotion see Thomas Fuller, *The History of the Worthies of England, 2* (London, 1811), 398.

29. Cardon, p. 353.

expulsion order was renewed. The English College made its historic move to Reims.[30]

The blow was not totally unexpected. Since the autumn of 1576, Allen had been quietly preparing for such an eventuality. Indeed, for over a year he had been little more than a commuter in Douay. He had resided for the most part at Cambrai where he held a benefice, and he had made frequent journeys to France in hopes of locating a new home for the College if it were needed. The university town of Reims appeared to him the best choice. "I do not see in what place our men can be placed more apt for missions to England than this is," he wrote simply, "until Belgium recovers peace from these disturbances." By November the Calvinist faction in Douay had been turned out of office and the magistrates invited the English to return. Allen frostily refused,[31] and for fourteen years the English mission had its headquarters under the protection of the Most Christian King of France rather than that of the Most Catholic King of Spain. This difference in location was to contribute in time to the factionalism which brought ultimate doom to the mission.

The events of 1578 presented Thomas Stapleton with a cruel dilemma. As a university professor, the March decree excepted him from the expulsion. As an Englishman, his heart went with those exiles who, in Henry Holland's words, "were not even permitted exile."[32] However it wrenched his feelings, he chose to remain in Douay close to the familiar academic life and intellectual work in which he was convinced he could best serve the cause. Later the same year, a confirmation of this point of view appeared with the publication of his significant treatise on the constitution of the Church. Three years later, when he published his equally important tract on justification, it was clear that the departure of the College had not unsettled him to the point of incapacitating him for serious work. Nevertheless, the separation from old comrades underscored a weary dissatisfaction with his

30. Haile, pp. 137–38.
31. Pollen, *English Catholics,* pp. 269–70.
32. "Vita Stapletoni," *Opera, 1,* no pagination.

own efforts and encouraged a hankering to join another group of men for whom he had the greatest admiration. "Year followed year," he wrote, "and I grew tired of studies spoiled by contention, and longing for a kind of life in which the things of this world count for nothing I fled to the cool shadows and hid myself in the cloisters of those fathers whom we call by the blessed name of Jesus."[33]

In 1585 Stapleton resigned his professorship and canonry and presented himself to the Jesuits at Douay. They received their old friend—now, at fifty, a famous theologian—with kindness but probably with some reservations. For his part, Stapleton tried hard to adjust himself to the life of the Society. "For almost two years I put my powers to the test,"[34] but in the end he had to admit failure. Holland described the decision and some reaction to it:

> But finding after a long and careful probation that the pious Society suited neither his temperament nor his habits of a lifetime, he left with as open a mind and as good a conscience as he had entered it. . . . Many good men rejoiced over his return and they congratulated him warmly over his decision; for they judged that at his age to embrace the religious life was not really feasible, and besides that he could accomplish more good for the Church, through his writing, outside the religious state.[35]

The experience resulted in no bitterness and Stapleton remained what he had always been, one of the Jesuits' most steadfast friends and defenders.[36]

33. "Compendium," ibid., no pagination.
34. Ibid.
35. "Vita Stapletoni," ibid.
36. The Society has received few tributes more moving than the one Stapleton paid it in 1567 with these words which closed *Counterblast* (fol. 542): "Neither can I either too much think upon or too much praise the wonderful Providence of God. . . . Now, in the latter days, the Empire of Constantinople becoming Turkish, and, in our own days, a great part of our own Europe being (the more pity) carried away with errors and heresies, God

This loyalty, and the convictions which underlay it, cost Stapleton dear in the years immediately after his trial with the Jesuits. He still haunted the cloister's "cool shadows" when a sharp controversy, ultimately to affect him, broke out at Louvain. Leonard Lessius (1554–1623), a brilliant Jesuit whom Stapleton had known at Douay for fifteen years, was formally censured on September 9, 1586 by the theology faculty of the University of Louvain. The next year the Douay faculty followed suit and charged, as Louvain had, that Lessius' book, *Theses theologicae* (1586), contained semi-Pelagian doctrine. Behind the assault was wily old Michael Baius (1513–89), the revered Louvain professor of Scripture, who for a quarter of a century had been evading condemnations of his own views on grace and who judged, accurately, that Lessius' book had been primarily an attack upon him. This

---

hath of his wonderful mercy and goodness, in man's remembrance, opened and revealed to us as it were a new world, of which neither by writing nor otherwise we ever heard anything before. And which is a cause of deeper and more ample thanks, he hath by his Providence so ordained that the said countries of Asia and Africa have become of plain and open idolators, of Moors and saracens, very good Christians, and that chiefly by the great help and travail of those blessed and virtuous Jesuits, whom you [Robert Horne, Protestant Bishop of Winchester] so lewdly call Jebusites. By whom also God hath showed such wonders and miracles as the hearing or reading of them were to any good Christian heart of all things most comfortable. And surely, if a man would deeply and thoroughly weigh and consider the greatness of this benefit, he might well doubt whether after the creation of the world and the redemption of mankind by the passion of Christ, there be any one benefit or work of God more wonderful than this; or whether there be any one state or vocation in Christ's Church, after the apostles, more worthy laud . . . than these, that you so villainously call Jebusites. So filthily your blasphemous mouth can rail against God's truth. No, no, M. Horne, these be no Jebusites. The Jebusites be the cursed seed of Cham, cursed of Noah their father for dishonoring of him. Ye, ye are the Jebusites that the celestial Father, with his own mouth, hath cursed for making his spouse, your Mother (the Church), an idolatrous strumpet and harlot. Whom the blessed Jesuits, as good, gracious children, honor and reverence. Who worthily bear that name also, their works being correspondent to their name, which doth signify a savior. For they, by their preaching, have saved and brought from damnation many an hundred thousand of souls to the everlasting bliss of heaven, the which God of his goodness and mercy grant unto us."

is not the place to elaborate on this dispute which made up only one chapter in the long story of Jansenism and in the controversy (with us still) between Dominicans and Jesuits over God's foreknowledge and human free will. Suffice it to say that Stapleton went vigorously to Lessius' defense in 1587 and protested Douay's act of censure. The immediate result of his stand was ostracism from his beloved university, which had no intention of reversing itself. "It was not difficult to see," he wrote in May, 1588, "that I did not like the censure and that my love for the Society was not less than formerly. I do not know whether the Faculty [of theology at Douay] sensed this. At any rate I have had no contact with it since." Ultimately, Lessius appealed the verdict of the universities to Rome, and Sixtus V, without deciding the doctrinal issue, quashed the censures. Stapleton meanwhile, restored to a canonry at Ste. Amoure but unwelcome at the university, devoted himself to "private studies" and perhaps pondered the fact that the "chaos of controversy," so easily laid at the door of the Protestants, could confuse the Catholic ranks as well.[37]

As it turned out, the ill wind of the Lessius affair in time blew Stapleton good. When Michael Baius died in 1589, he left behind not only a host of friends who had with reason loved and admired him but also a party of disciples eager to build a religious system upon the master's questionable theories. The business of choosing his successor in the prestigious chair of Scripture at Louvain aroused, therefore, not a little interest. The appointment was reserved to the king of Spain, and Philip II, though he might battle popes over policy matters, still considered doubtful orthodoxy the worst charge that could be brought against one of his universities. Thomas Stapleton had many influential friends[38] who pointed out to the King that the Englishman possessed an un-

---

37. See *DTC*, 9, Pt. 1, cc. 453 f; Pastor, *Popes, 21,* 188–92; Cardon, *Université de Douai*, pp. 337–38.

38. Most notable among them perhaps were the brothers Pamele of Bruges. The elder of the two, Guillaume (1528–91), spent his whole life in public service and became, in 1575, President of the Council of Flanders. See *Biographie nationale . . . de Belgique, 16,* cc. 526–28. Jacques Pamele (1536–87), at the time of his death Archdeacon of St. Omer, was one of Stapleton's

disputed reputation for theological scholarship, was demonstrably loyal to Spain, and enjoyed the confidence of the highest circles in Rome. Philip proceeded in his wonted leisurely fashion, and, on July 13, 1590, he signed the letters patent which conferred on Stapleton the professorship and annexed to it a canonry in the Church of St. Peter, at Louvain. Stapleton returned to the place where he had first sought refuge thirty years before. The passage of time had not significantly modified his attitude, as he described it in 1594:

> When I was called here to Louvain four years ago and received the regius professorship of Sacred Scripture, there was nothing on my mind except a determination to do my work faithfully in this office for the glory of God and the benefit of my students. I judged that I should best accomplish this if I treated the genuine and literal sense of the Divine Word as well as its use best accommodated for these times. And indeed in my lectures I have always given the exact sense of the passage in question succinctly in the form of short glosses. Now it seemed to me that the use of Scripture study best accommodated to our times consisted in this, that I should treat principally those passages which either can score against the contemporary heretics or are commonly cited by them against the orthodox faith. Therefore, after touching with a light stroke those matters, whether dogmatic or moral, which have no relation to the present controversies, I took it upon myself to deal much more carefully with those passages which concern the novel or controverted dogmas of our time.[39]

This was the nature of the work, all of it directed "contra venenum Bezaeque Calvini," which occupied Stapleton during

---

closest friends. He was, says E. Amann (*DTC 11*, Pt. 2, c. 1839), "un des grands représentants de l'érudition patristique au XVIe siècle." See also E. de Moreau, *Histoire de l'Église en Belgique* (Brussels, 1952), Vol. 5, pp. 70, 142.

39. *Antidota evangelica*, p. 1.

the eight years he spent at Louvain. He also found time to take up again the practice of private tutoring which he had pursued successfully at Douay. Needless to say, even first-rate intellectual and literary work, usually routine and unspectacular, does not as a rule lead to high ecclesiastical preferment.[40] Even so, this last period of Stapleton's life was not without its honors, and it abounded in rumors. He had not been long at Louvain when Philip II gave him the deanery of Lilverenbeck in the diocese of Bois-le-Duc, a benefice which yielded a revenue of a thousand florins a year (and, noted Anthony Wood, "little enough, God wot, for such a rare and learned clerk as he was").[41] This handsome income, Holland reported, together with the fees he received for "sharing his board with certain noble students," made it possible for Stapleton to increase the financial aid he had habitually given to refugees and to impoverished Belgians as well.[42]

Soon, however, talk began to circulate about a higher honor for Stapleton than a deanery. William Allen, universally acknowledged leader of the English Catholics and a cardinal since 1587, died on October 16, 1594. His passing gave rise to a flurry of speculation that the Pope might soon choose a successor as "Cardinal of England." Gossip in the Roman salons quickly narrowed the field of candidates to two: the red hat would be given Stapleton or Owen Lewis.[43] The unpleasant reality with which the glib prognosticators did not reckon was seen clearly enough by the politic Clement VIII: Allen had been that rare man for whom

40. Fuller, in *Worthies of England*, 2, 398, found this truism well exemplified in the careers of Allen and Stapleton: "[Stapleton's] preferment (in mine eyes) was not proportionate to his merit, being no more than canon and master of a college in Louvain. Many more admired that Stapleton missed than that Allen got a cardinal's cap, equalling him in strictness of life, exceeding him in gentility of birth and painfulness of writing for the Romish cause. Such consider not that Stapleton's ability was drowned with Allen's activity; and one grain of the statesman is too heavy for a pound of the student, practical policy in all ages beating pen-pains out of distance in the race for preferment."

41. Wood, *Athenae Oxonienses*, 1, 670.

42. "Vita Stapletoni," *Opera*, 1, no pagination.

43. Pastor, *Popes*, 24, 11.

there was no successor. Both Stapleton and Lewis possessed fine gifts and eminent reputations, but neither of them had the stature of Allen. Indeed, they were sponsored by rival factions whose mutual animosities now, with Allen gone, came violently to the surface. The appointment of either of them to the college of cardinals would have meant a party victory and would have hastened the disintegration of the English Catholic effort. As events developed, that disintegration came quickly anyway.

Stapleton remained far from the conversation and the intrigue. Working furiously at Louvain on his Scripture commentaries, he knew little of what went on in Rome. This in itself gave emphasis to the factional problem at hand, for it was obvious that Stapleton would not dream of challenging Lewis, an administrator of long experience and proved ability, for Allen's mantle. The real opposition lay between Lewis and the seculars on the one hand and Robert Persons and the Jesuits on the other.[44] Persons, by the rule of his Order, could not actively aspire to the scarlet, but he could be expected to do all in his considerable power to secure the appointment of an Englishman friendly to the Society and to its point of view.[45] Stapleton would have been an ideal figurehead; he was a secular, the most eminent English theologian, a staunch ally of the Jesuits, and a child in the realm of practical affairs. An irony of the situation was the close friendship which had bound Lewis and Stapleton for forty years, beginning when they had been schoolfellows at Winchester.

> Our friendship [Stapleton wrote in a dedicatory note to Lewis early in 1594] is . . . so old, so agreeable, strengthened by so many mutual duties even from a tender age. . . . Brought up together in the school at Winchester, comrades in the

44. See Law, *Historical Sketch,* p. 113 n.

45. Shortly after Allen's death, Thomas Worthington, once a student of Stapleton, circulated a petition among the English exiles which begged the Holy See to promote Persons to the college. Enrico Caetani, Cardinal Protector of England, favored the Jesuits, but Lewis, by this time Bishop of Cassano, could balance this with the favor of the Aldobrandini family. See Lechat, *Réfugiés anglais,* p. 179, and the references cited there.

same College at Oxford, exiles together here at Louvain, colleagues as professors in the University of Douay, afterwards joined in close familiarity at Rome. Indeed, necessity has bound us together for more than four decades, and I should like to make clear to all the world, through this public testimony, how long-lasting and wonderful this friendship has been.[46]

Owen Lewis' death, almost a year to the day after Allen's, put an end to the unfortunate competition, but the speculation went on. In the spring of 1596 Stapleton received an invitation to Rome to join the household of the cardinal-nephew, Pietro Aldobrandini. Some months later a second proposal was made: Stapleton, if he liked, might take a chair in the Sapienza. Both these offers the Englishman respectfully refused on the grounds of age (he was 61), contentment with "the honest state" he had attained at Louvain, and the desire to complete certain literary projects.[47] Stapleton's attitude shocked and exasperated Robert Persons, who now began to have second thoughts about his candidate.[48] Meanwhile, in Rome, trouble had broken out between the students at the English College, who were seculars, and their Italian Jesuit faculty. In the midst of the crisis, Persons was appointed rector of the College and ultimately restored peace.[49] But before he did, he learned of a remark of Clement VIII, always a little distant in his relations with the Society, which gave further pause to his campaign for Stapleton. In the middle of September 1596 Richard Barret, the wholeheartedly pro-Jesuit rector of the English College now restored to Douay, had a stormy audience with Clement VIII. After Barret had finished an impassioned plea in behalf of

46. Thomas Stapleton, *Promptuarium quadragesimae*, in *Opera, 4,* 684.

47. Lechat, p. 179.

48. Persons had gone so far as to suggest, late in 1595, that, if the Pope found too much opposition to Stapleton's candidacy to the college, he should as an alternative formally appoint him to one of the principal English sees and create him apostolic legate.

49. Peter Guilday, *The English Catholic Refugees on the Continent, 1558–1795* (London, 1914), p. 97.

the Society, the Pope said: "Do you seriously think that the whole
world would perish if the Society were to relinquish its government of the English College here in Rome?" And then Clement
added: "Would not Stapleton come if I were to send for him?"
Barret answered heatedly that he believed in conscience that the
English Catholics might well perish if the status of the Society
were modified in behalf of a gang of unruly students. As far as
Stapleton was concerned, he boldly told the Pope, he was not
sure what that "old man totally taken up by literary pursuits"
might do, since he had every reason to be content at Louvain.[50]

The broad hint that Clement might summon Stapleton to Rome
to settle the wrangling in the English College was not lost on
Persons. He was further disquieted when rumors reached him
that Stapleton had been secretly in sympathy with the rebellious
students and had even lent them his encouragement. If these reports were true, the Society should oppose rather than support
such a man's entry into the college of cardinals. There was another consideration which weighed heavily with Persons. Many
influential Jesuits did not think Stapleton properly fervent in his
devotion to Philip II, and, by the end of 1596, Persons, who was
willing to gamble the whole English endeavor on the wheel of
Spanish policy, had just about come to agree with them.[51] At

50. Barret to Persons, Sept. 28 (or 26), 1596 (*DD*, pp. 384–86).
51. This suspicion of Stapleton arose despite the publication of his *Apologia
pro Rege Philippo II, Hispaniae Rege* (Coutance, 1592). This pamphlet was
provoked by Elizabeth's proclamation of Nov. 20, 1591, which, among other
things, attacked the seminary priests as "a multitude of dissolute young men
who have, partly for lack of living, partly for crimes committed, become fugi-
tives, rebels and traitors." Stapleton responded with stinging accusations against
the Queen as a persecutor, a woman of light morals and questionable ante-
cedents, and the responsible party in an alleged collapse of morality and
religion in England. For an analysis of this untypical (as will be seen below)
bit of Stapletoniana, see Joseph Bernard Code, *Queen Elizabeth and the English Catholic Historians* (Louvain, 1935), pp. 57–63, but beware the curiously
illogical conclusion. The pamphlet, however, had not satisfied the more extreme pro-Spanish Jesuits, among them Alphonsus Agazzari, who wrote to
Persons in Sept. 1596 (*DD*, p. 389): "Quel punto di Stapletono importa;
però V. R. ci pensi, procuri di remediare, facendo promover presto qual che
persona che sia fedele alla corona, della quale non si pessa dubitare."

about the same time, Stapleton received his third invitation to
Rome in ten months. "I received upon St. Thomas of Canterbury
his eve [December 28, 1596], at the hour that my friends invited came to dinner," a letter from Cardinal Aldobrandini in
which was contained "an offer of his Holiness to be a prothono-
tariat, one of the seven participants now vacant." This papal in-
sistence could not be ignored, and so "only for hope to be a man to
help my country and countrymen . . . in this new vocation, I did
accept the last offer."[52] To Robert Persons the timing of the invitation and the acceptance appeared ominous.

He had from the beginning misjudged his man. When Stapleton dispatched his affirmative answer to Aldobrandini in January
1597, he was blissfully unaware of the concern his Jesuit friends
in Rome and Madrid felt over his loyalties. Persons, who had
been willing enough to use Stapleton's indifference to ecclesiastical
politics for the interests of the Society (and, needless to say, of religion), should have realized that the man who would not, or
could not, intrigue for the red hat would hardly mix himself in
the shabby affair at the English College. By April, Stapleton had
heard the charges. "Not only I never liked," he wrote testily to
Persons, "but have always utterly misliked and condemned such
unquiet heads against their superiors and namely against the
Society . . . to which is conjoined the wealth and advancement
of the Catholic religion as well abroad as especially at home." To
his mind, he added, the dissension at the College in Rome had
been "an unhappy brawl." With regard to Philip of Spain, that
prince had been his sovereign for thirty-five years, and he desired,
he said, "to remain a true and trusty servant to his Majesty of
Spain, though I have to live and perhaps to continue in the court
of Rome. . . . I would wish that some of the council about his
Majesty in Spain might understand the same." In case Persons had
missed the point, Stapleton made it clearer:

> The favor of his Holiness toward me now seemeth great,
> but what it may be hereafter, when he shall see me and

52. Stapleton to Thomas Hurley, Jan. 20, 1597 (*DD*, p. 389).

know me better, is very uncertain, and I build not a jot thereupon. The dignity and favor which his Holiness hath offered me is a sufficient motive for me to come and try for a time, and a sufficient place of credit to do some good to the common cause, as long as I shall remain there; desiring nothing more than to return . . . to my studies again. Upon which hope I keep my lesson here and will leave my house in such very state as now it is [for eighteen months], which will be a time of sufficient trial both for his Holiness of me and for me of Rome. Many here have great imaginations of this my calling, but surely I have none such. Only the good Cardinal Aldobrandini . . . desireth to have me about him, somewhat for learning famous . . . and to accomplish his desire hath (I suppose) induced his Holiness to offer me the abovesaid dignity. . . . This I take to be the very root and ground of my calling and to look further, as it were a great folly in me, so it is an ungrounded imagination of others.[53]

During the spring and early summer of 1597 Stapleton went halfheartedly about the task of preparing for his Roman journey. He had insisted that, as a condition for his departure, the Roman authorities procure for him an eighteen-month leave of absence from his position in the university and supply him with funds for his travel expenses. He had also asked that he be allowed to delay his arrival until autumn to avoid the brutal heat of a Roman summer. By May, Persons had definitely given up the notion that any Englishman should be, for the time being, elevated to the cardinalate. There was nobody, he decided, who could take Allen's place, and he evidently communicated this view to Stapleton.[54] As a final word on this curious business of the red hat, Stapleton wrote Persons early in July what might have been, in a man more worldly-wise, a faintly sarcastic sentence: "For the point of preferment in [Rome], which hath been so much wrestled for, as I firmly and sincerely believe you that you pretend no such

53. Stapleton to Persons, April 16, 1597 (*DD*, p. 390).
54. Lechat, *Réfugiés anglais*, p. 180.

matter, but rather shunneth and avoideth it, so I pray you, believe me that I am of the same meaning, desire and purpose."[55]

Stapleton never embarked for Rome. By late August 1597, the leave of absence he had requested had not been cleared, and the travel money had not arrived. Autumn became winter, and still the reluctant prothonotary delayed his departure. Sometime before the new year 1598, he asked the Pope to excuse him once again, and Clement granted his request. On New Year's Day he gratefully acknowledged the receipt of an apostolic brief "given in kind recognition of my humble efforts."[56] Thomas Stapleton was by this time a dying man. He had been laid low the preceding June (1597) by a severe attack of gout from which he never completely recovered. Early in the summer of 1598 he took to his bed, never to leave it. His physicians prescribed cauterization, which painful treatment proved no remedy, and, after three months of painful lingering, he died on October 12, 1598.[57]

There was a congruity in the fact that Stapleton's death came only a few weeks after that of Philip II. If it is permissible to date the beginning of the Counter Reformation with the abdication of Charles V, the death of his son forty-three years later might well mark the movement's close. By that time the enthusiastic Catholic counterattack had about run its course. By that time two hostile camps faced one another, neither of them strong enough to drive its rival from an entrenched position. A few years before, the distinguished Anglican divine, Richard Hooker, had tersely summed up the religious situation: "Two things there are which trouble greatly these later times: one that the Church of Rome cannot, another that Geneva will not err." Thomas Stapleton, like Philip II, had played a role in the combat with Protestantism. His whole life had been framed by it, and he would scarcely have understood a world in which it was not the all-important activity. But the world by 1598 had changed. It was not true, as it had been when Stapleton began his literary career, that a large un-

55. Stapleton to Persons, July 6, 1597 (*DD*, pp. 391–93).
56. *Antidota apostolica,* p. 719.
57. "Vita Stapletoni," *Opera, 1.*

committed group remained to be persuaded. The keen interest which the educated man in the street had formerly taken in religious controversy was now directed to other concerns. No doubt a well-thumbed copy of one or another of Stapleton's books could still be found in 1598 hidden in an upstairs cupboard of an occasional English country house. But the urgency that had been felt over the issues was gone, never to return. A new era was dawning in which Stapleton would have been a stranger.

Chapter 3

THE WORK

Thomas Stapleton was buried in the Church of St. Peter in Louvain under a monument whose inscription read in part: "Relictis laborum suorum monimentis . . . quae quanta fuerit ejus industria, quanta animi pietas, quam accensum veritatis Catholicae propugnandae studium, omnibus ea lectura testatum facient."[1] The "monimenta" which came from his pen fall into three distinct parts. The first group he wrote during his second sojourn at Louvain —that is, during those six years (1563–69) immediately following his refusal to swear the Oath of Supremacy—and it included three translations from Latin into English, lengthy appendices to two of them, and two other independent controversial works. Stapleton, therefore, even as a "student in divinity," as he described himself at this time, made a considerable contribution to that dramatic flowering of English Catholic literature which took place in the sixties. The move to Douay (1569) resulted in a significant change in the kind of literary work he produced. During the twenty-one years he spent there, he wrote exclusively in Latin and for a more or less scholarly and professional audience. Though his target was the same, he appeared at Douay less the angry young man and more the erudite university professor of theology. This period saw the publication of his great books on the Church and on justification, the beginning of serious Scripture commentary, and the work for which Stapleton is perhaps best remembered, the *Tres Thomae*. Finally, a third category of contro-

1. Cardon, *Université de Douai,* p. 338.

versial work emerged when Stapleton assumed the chair of Scripture at Louvain (1590). In his lectures there he commented not so much on the sacred text itself as on the scriptural interpretations offered by John Calvin and his disciple Theodore Beza. From Louvain he also engaged another "homo Calvinianus," the Englishman, William Whitaker, again over scriptural matters. All this labor, he said, would satisfy him if it formed an "antidote" to the Calvinist poison.

The preoccupation with Calvin and Calvinism was a unifying thread woven through the work of thirty-five busy years. It can be detected in the very first piece of Stapleton's ever to be published, a slight appendix he wrote to his translation of a book by Frederick Staphylus: *A Discourse of the Translator upon the Doctrine of Protestants Which He Trieth by the Three First Founders and Fathers Thereof, Martin Luther, Philip Melanchthon and Especially John Calvin.*[2] Most of this short treatise was devoted to a refutation of the "Contradictions of Calvin," who, said Stapleton, had had much greater success in spreading his peculiar brand of heresy than had his intellectual forebears, Zwingli and Oecolampadius. In England the Calvinists had become so numerous and powerful that they had driven underground all the other sects, and they preached that Luther was virtually a papist. Therefore, Stapleton continued, since Staphylus' work concerned itself mostly with Lutheranism, it was fitting that an appendix should deal with the Genevan brand of Protestantism. Even in the few pages devoted to Luther, young Stapleton carefully noted that "Calvin had vomited out more blasphemies" than the whole school of Wittenberg combined. Melanchthon was dismissed in little more than three pages: "This friend of Luther, this chief defender of the Confession [of Augsburg], ultimately became a sacramentary, as the letters he wrote to the Count Palatine, published in 1560,

2. The translation was published at Antwerp in 1565. Stapleton's appendix was translated into Latin and included in the *Opera, 2,* 1603–53. Staphylus, born Stapellage (1512–64), had once been a disciple of Melanchthon.

clearly show." The author saved most of his opusculum to debate
Calvin's doctrines on the Eucharist, baptism, and free will. Perhaps
the most notable thing about this first plunge into the controversial swim was the wide acquaintance it exhibited with the
writings of John Calvin: in twenty-five pages he quoted the *Institutes* twenty-one times, referred to Calvin's commentaries on
St. John's Gospel, the Epistle to the Romans, and the first Epistle
to the Corinthians, and, for good measure, analyzed in some detail the "Consensus Tigurinus," the 1549 agreement signed by
the Protestant schools of Zurich and Geneva.

Of much greater length and certainly of greater importance
was the second of Stapleton's appendices. This was *The Fortresse
of the Faith*,[3] almost five hundred pages long, which he appended
to his translation of Bede's *Ecclesiastical History*. The most significant thing the *Fortresse* exhibited was Stapleton's grasp of the
use which the historical argument might have in the disputes with
the Protestants. The theme ultimately became a favorite with the
English Catholics. Allen made St. Bede's *Historia* required reading
for the students of the English College at Douay because it provided them with a "very telling argument."[4] Divided into two
roughly equal parts, the *Fortresse* attempted to demonstrate the
Church's permanence, for "to deny the continuance of the Church
in a sound and upright faith is to defeat the mystery of Christ's
Incarnation." In chapter 5 and throughout the first section of the
book, Stapleton, as he examined Calvin's ecclesiology, placed great
emphasis on the fact that the true Church must consist in a visible
organization if a man of good will is to recognize her. In the
second part he examined one by one the forty-six differences he discerned between "the late pretended faith of Protestants" and the
primitive Christianity which he "gathered out of the History of
the Church of England, compiled by Venerable Bede, an Englishman, about eight hundred years past." The translation of Bede

3. First published at Antwerp in 1565. The references to it here are taken
from the St. Omer edition, 1625.
4. This judgment was Allen's. See Hughes, *Reformation, 3,* 292.

and its lengthy appendix were meant to be read together, and taken together they made an impressive case.[5]

During the spring and early summer of 1566, Stapleton put the finishing touches to his contribution to the massive debate initiated by John Jewel and Thomas Harding. Jewel, Elizabethan Bishop of Salisbury, delivered his famous "Challenge Sermon" first at Paul's Cross, in London, on November 26, 1559, repeated it at court (enlarging it somewhat) on March 17, 1560, and repeated it again at Paul's Cross a few weeks later. In it he dared any Catholic to prove that certain doctrine and practice (e.g. universal authority of the pope, Holy Communion distributed under one kind) used by the Church of Rome had flourished during the first six hundred years of the Christian era. Harding wrote and privately circulated shortly thereafter *An Answer to Master Jewel's Challenge*. Early in 1562 Jewel published his *Apologia ecclesiae anglicanae*. An enlarged edition of Harding's *Answer* appeared in January 1565, and Jewel responded with his *Reply to Master Harding's Answer* (August 1565). This last book, Stapleton observed, was "esteemed to be learned and thought to be such a piece as the party impugned shall never be able to answer." He agreed that for one man to answer Jewel's work, "and that stich

5. Stapleton's translation of Bede into English is "of the best literature of its kind in the world," writes Bede Jarrett in his introduction to Venerable Bede, *The Ecclesiastical History of the English People,* trans. Thomas Stapleton, ed. Philip Hereford (London, 1935), p. xxxi. The comment of another translator, who based his work upon Stapleton's, is also of note: "Stapleton belonged to the age of the Book of Common Prayer and the Authorized Version of the Bible. The structure of his clauses is nearer akin to the Latin than the more choppy sentences of modern English, he has a dignity and nobility of style and a constant happiness of phrase which have deservedly kept his translation alive. And apart from the intrinsic merits of his work, it is probably better to read an author dealing with an age like Bede's, so different from our own in its thoughts and ways, through the medium of a translation which does not belong to our day. It gives an atmosphere in which we breathe more naturally; we see, as it were, the ancient building in a mellower and less garish light." J. E. King, trans., *Bedae opera historica, I* (London, 1930), xxiv. Southern (*Elizabethan Prose,* p. 93) thinks that "the familiar ease and picturesqueness of [Stapleton's] prose invites comparison with North's translation of Plutarch."

by stich (as the Replier requireth), both the time would be so long that many a soul in the meantime might perish, abused by that lewd piece of work, and also the book would be so great that few would buy it, fewer peruse it and not one among a hundred read it over." It was determined by the exiles at Louvain that several replies should be made to various of Jewel's articles, "everyone to follow as zeal pricked forward." Nicholas Sander and John Rastell each determined on a partial response, and "The Answerer," Harding himself, "hath not been idle, as by his *Rejoinder* it will well appear." For his own part, Stapleton wrote,

> I have thought good to justify the untruths which it hath liked the Replier to charge upon his adversary. . . . To this I was moved by diverse reasons. I ever thought . . . that the weak parts throughout the *Reply* should be those where such untruths were noted. . . . It seemed to me these presumed untruths being redressed or discharged the whole *Answer* [i.e. Harding's book] might go for good, godly and true. . . . Another cause was this: The Replier in all these four articles, the former half of his *Reply,* hath noted for untruths both the principal matters treated and proved. This is in effect to answer the whole. For other small matters neither so weighty as the Replier would cavil at them, neither so weak as he could find no color of untruth to set upon them, might well, for brevity's sake, in a full and perfect rejoinder be omitted.[6]

This was the plan behind Stapleton's *A Returne of Untruthes upon M. Jewelles Replie.* He proceeded by quoting the passage of Harding which Jewel challenged as untrue, then quoting Jewel himself, and finally making his own attempt to "return" the untruth. The first article of Jewel's *Reply* had dealt with the question of private Mass. In this section Stapleton entered fully into the Bishop's text in only two instances, "because Doctor Harding hath himself made a full and perfect rejoinder to this first article."

6. *Returne,* preface.

The second article, in which Jewel had attacked various of Harding's assertions about the Eucharist, occupied Stapleton's attention for a scant thirty pages, "as the untruths there noted require very seldom such labor but may shortly be justified." But "in the third and fourth articles, especially in the fourth, I have not left any whit of Master Jewel's *Reply,* were it ever so long and tedious, unanswered, in such places as untruths were noted."

Something of the matter discussed and the tone employed in the controversy can be gathered from this example:

> HARDING. The nations that have ever had their service in the vulgar tongue, the people thereof have continued in schisms, errors and certain Judaical observances, so as they have not been reckoned in the number of the Catholic Church: as the Christians of Moscovia, of Armenia, of Prester John his land in Ethiopia.
>
> JEWEL. The 86th untruth. For the service in the vulgar tongue never was the cause of schism or heresy.
>
> STAPLETON. Doctor Harding saieth not so much. Their vulgar service was not the cause of their schism. But their schism and other heresies were the cause of their vulgar service. For having once divided themselves from the Church in doctrine they chose also that order of service which was contrary to the Church. I perceive, Master Jewel, it is all one with you whether a man bid you drink ere you go or go ere you drink.[7]

In this instance Stapleton did not feel it necessary to quote Jewel any further. When he did (and this was the more common practice), the text became awkward to say the least, since each of the three combatants' statements was printed in a distinct type face, and each of them was quoting, a good share of the time, this or that passage of Scripture or patristic literature. At any rate, Stapleton, by the time he had finished, had not only "returned upon" Jewel 125 accusations of lying which the latter had made against

7. Ibid., fols. 123–24.

Thomas Harding, but had also laid at the door of the Bishop of Salisbury 562 brand-new "untruths." Sixteenth-century religious controversialists scorned half measures.

The same massiveness characterized the last of Stapleton's original English works, *A Counterblast to M. Hornes Vayne Blaste against M. Feckenham*. This tract of more than a thousand pages was Stapleton's contribution to a quarrel already well underway, and so it too involved the direct quotation of two other authors, one of whom, another Anglican bishop, was indicted for "untruths . . . to the number of six hundred, four score and odd." The genesis of *Counterblast* is described elsewhere, but a word must be said here about its arrangement. Robert Horne, Bishop of Winchester, had answered John Feckenham's objections to the Oath of Supremacy in a book of two parts. Stapleton described it thus:

> In the first and chiefest [part] he plaieth the opponent, laying forth out of the holy Scriptures both old and new, out of Councils both general and national, out of histories and chronicles of all countries, running his race from Constantine the Great down to Maximilian, great-grandfather to the Emperor that now liveth, taking by the way the kings of France, Spain and of our own country of England since the conquest, all that ever he could find by his own study and help of his friends, partly for proof of the like government of princes in ecclesiastical causes, as the Oath attributeth now to the crown of England, partly for disproof of the pope's supremacy, which the Oath also principally intendeth to exclude. In the second . . . part he plaieth the defendant, taking upon him to satisfy certain of M. Feckenham's arguments and scruples of conscience whereby he is moved not to take the Oath.[8]

Stapleton followed "the same order and course" as did Horne, though he complicated matters somewhat by replacing Horne's

8. *Counterblast*, preface.

two sections with four of his own: "Comprising in the first book
[Horne's] objections out of Holy Scripture, in the second his
objections out of the first six hundred years, in the third his objections out of the later nine hundred years." The scriptural part
of *Counterblast* included Horne's arguments (drawn, for example,
from the Books of Kings) which covered roughly thirty-five pages
and Stapleton's refutations (as he considered them), taking up
perhaps 140 pages more. The second and third books, Horne's
historical arguments and Stapleton's replies, occupied better than
six hundred pages. The fourth book stated verbatim the scruples
about the Oath pleaded by Feckenham, then Horne's denials and
counterexplanations, and, finally, Stapleton's observations.

The scope of this remarkable book has given rise to questions
about its authorship, and it is understandable to wonder how one
man could have brought its vast number of disparate parts into a
comprehensive whole.[9] Yet young Stapleton (who had celebrated
his thirty-second birthday a few months before completing
Counterblast) pulled together discussions of Bracton (fol. 380 ff.)
and Justinian (fol. 169 ff.); he "proved" that Pope Liberius had
not been an Arian (fol. 112) and that Marsiglio of Padua had

9. It seems to me that Southern states his case rather too strongly when
he says (*Elizabethan Prose*, p. 88) that *Counterblast* was written "in collabora-
tion with Nicholas Harpsfield." Nor is his appendix III (pp. 526–32), in
which he tries to prove Harpsfield rather than Stapleton responsible for
"the great body of the work," very convincing. It should be noted that Stapleton had hesitated (by his own testimony) to undertake Feckenham's defense
because the dispute covered "a number of such private matters touching the
state of the realm [to which] without further advice I could not thoroughly
shape an answer." Now the "great body" of *Counterblast* was not concerned
with "private matters," as the text, I hope, makes clear. Holland ("Vita
Stapletoni," *Opera*, Vol. 1) squares best with the internal evidence when he
asserts simply that Stapleton was its author. More significant still, less than
four years after *Counterblast's* appearance, Nicholas Sander, in *De visibili
monarchia ecclesiae* (Louvain, 1571), p. 688, credits Stapleton alone with the
"eloquent" and "copious" answer to Horne. This is not to say, of course, that
Harpsfield's *Historia anglicana ecclesiastica* might not have been of use to
Stapleton in the work of composition or that Harpsfield, still in England,
might not have contributed information to Stapleton. But that is a long way
from saying, as Southern does (p. 259), that "we should conclude . . . that
the great body of the work was [Harpsfield's]."

leaned toward heresy (fol. 314); he ridiculed the new English Protestant clergy as a group of "cooks, catchpoles and cobblers" (fol. 481); he defended Philip the Fair (fol. 329: "To be short, the dealing of this king proveth nothing like the regiment that now is in our realm"); he wrote with equal facility of David (fols. 47–48) and Josias (fol. 53), of Otto the Great (fol. 273) and Richard II (fol. 350), of the Council of Nicaea (fol. 101 ff.) and the Westminster Disputation (fol. 12), of Hildebrand (fol. 275 ff.), of the accidental good which heresy can do the Church (fol. 37), and of the collection of Peter's Pence in England (fol. 346). All this, and much more, Stapleton fashioned into a book not only brilliant in its clarity, erudition, and method but also alive with wit and humor and sometimes crackling with magnificent rhetoric.

Save for a final piece of translation, published also in 1567,[10] *Counterblast* marked the end of Stapleton's writing in his native tongue. The Belgian war which unsettled the exiles' printing operation, the move to Douay and the new duties which occupied him there, the increased vigilance of the English government, especially after the Rising of the North (1569), all contributed to Stapleton's exclusive use of Latin from this date forward. His decision clearly involved a loss to English letters, but Stapleton, for whom the combat against Protestantism was an all-consuming obsession, would hardly have thought of that. At any rate, there began at this point the second period in Stapleton's literary career, and eleven years passed before the first fruits of it appeared.

Principiorum fidei doctrinalium demonstratio methodica was published at Paris in 1578. It took Stapleton several years to write, having been in rough draft as early as November 1576. The language was Latin and the subject general, but the author's mind never strayed from England for long. He dedicated the work to Pope Gregory XIII, who "has supported with great liberality the seminary of our nation, located first in the famous Belgian University of Douay, and now, because of the disturbed times, trans-

10. Hosius, *Of the Express Word of God* (Louvain, 1567).

lated to the splendid French city of Reims," and he recommended
to the Pope his unhappy country:

> Indeed, for these many long years our nation has been
> afflicted for the sake of the Catholic faith. The greatest noble
> and the humblest peasant woman have endured the rapine
> of property, the squalor of prison, irksome exile, and some
> of our bravest brothers have suffered the cruelest and yet
> most glorius death. Still, in the midst of these great troubles,
> next to our love of God and the saints, we take greatest
> solace in the fact that at last we have been blessed with
> another Gregory in the person of your Holiness, given us
> by God, a fond father who will preserve and repair the
> orthodox faith among us. . . . For even so long and harsh
> a persecution has brought about nothing else but this, that
> after two decades of schism England still has more Catholics,
> counting those at home and those in exile, than she has
> serious practitioners of heresy.[11]

   Stapleton began his book by giving a list of the authorities he
intended to cite, more than a hundred names in all. Among the
"veteres" he included the great figures of the early Church, the
various ecumenical councils from Nicaea I to Trent, St. Thomas
Aquinas, Durandus, Biel, and Aeneas Sylvius; the "moderni"
counted in their number Dominic Soto, Melchior Cano, Cajetan,
Erasmus, Sander, and St. John Fisher. Stapleton divided the
Principiorum into seven controversies and twelve books. The first
controversy he considered the most important, because, he wrote,
"it deals with the first doctrinal principle of faith into which the
other matters ultimately resolve themselves. And so the first controversy concerns itself with the true Church of Christ *in se,* what
it is and how and among whom it is found. Because of the various
lies and cavilings of our adversaries, the irrefutable demonstration
of so important a point is set out in four books." After he had
discussed the various Protestant positions in Book I, he devoted

---

11. *Principiorum,* dedicatio, n. p. In the *Opera omnia* this work was given
the title *De principibus fidei doctrinalibus.*

the next three books to a demonstration of the catholicity and perpetuity of the true Church and the presence in it of the other necessary properties unavailable to the Protestants. The second controversy (Books V and VI) treated of the subject of ecclesiastical power, particularly the "subjectum primarium," the successor of St. Peter. Each of the next three controversies took one book. Book VII treated of the Church's use of her teaching power, Book VIII the formal nature of her authority, and Book IX the canon of Scripture. The sixth controversy (Books X and XI) discussed the Church's authority to interpret Scripture and her procedure in doing so. The subject of the seventh controversy (Book XII) was the Church's function as guardian of tradition, the "dogmata non scripta." All this covered, in the first volume of the *Opera omnia* 452 pages, of which the first controversy occupied 159 and the seventh 34. A 14-page "Admonitio ad lectorem" brought the work to a close. Stapleton felt that he had in this work demonstrated to his readers that the Catholic and Roman Church had on its side the testimony of Scripture and the Fathers as well as the best arguments provided by human reason, and he hoped that they could, after reading it, more confidently "hold in contempt the arrogance, repress the boldness and indeed show to all who care to see the stupidity" of the heretics.[12]

It was always Stapleton's view that the Protestants had coined their new doctrines about the nature of the Church because they needed to posit an authority other than the traditional one, which had rejected their ideas about justification. Therefore, his *De universa justificationis doctrina hodie controversa,* which appeared in 1582, must be considered as carefully as the *Principiorum* if Stapleton's full criticism of the Reformation is to be understood. Everything else he wrote might well be thought of as an appendix to one or the other of these two books. In them, he came to grips with the issues he took to be fundamental.

---

12. Ibid., p. 452. Later editions, beginning with the third (1582), included a 13th Book, in which Stapleton undertook to rebut William Fulke (1538–89), Master of Pembroke Hall, Cambridge, and a prodigious pamphleteer (see Southern, passim), who challenged Stapleton in the matter of the visibility of the Church. Bk. XIII was about 50 pages long.

In the first few sentences of *Justificationis* he set out the root
difference separating Protestant and Catholic:

> The ruin of the human race by the sin of our first parents,
> the terrible lapse and fall into a lower state of nature, whether
> with regard to man himself or to his use of other created
> things, all this was a grave matter. Man fell a long way from
> that rectitude in which he was created; all at once a mist
> enveloped his understanding, a palsy seized upon his will.
> And as part of the complete inversion of the order of things,
> as if a mistress were dominated by and subjugated to her
> servant girl, the flesh of man began to issue commands to his
> mind. Then the custom of sinning, the example of it, the
> apparent impunity of the sinner, gave increase to this evil
> growth. Nevertheless, the corruption of man's nature was
> not so great that every good natural thing perished as a
> result of it or that no glimmer of virtue and reason survived.[13]

Stapleton divided *Justificationis* into twelve books and these
were subdivided into 191 chapters. The discussion ranged from
original sin and the "errores moderni circa peccatum vel ab
haereticis defensi vel Catholicis falso impositi" (Bk. I, chap. 1) to
the distinction between mortal and venial sin (Bk. XIII). The
eleven chapters of Book III were concerned with "concupiscentia
in renatis" and aimed at refuting the position of the Lutheran,
Martin Chemnitz. Book VIII, dealing with the notion that justification is by faith alone, was the longest of the twelve (36 chapters, 68 pages). It contained a minute analysis of the Calvinist
definition of justifying faith and an attack on "various cavilings
of Flacius Illyricus over the condition, efficacy, and necessity of
good works."[14] Book IV dealt with the problem of grace and free
will, Book IX with the certitude of grace, and Book X with
merit. On the last page of the work Stapleton added a short appendix in which he listed, with citations from the *Institutes*,

13. *Justificationis*, p. 1.
14. Ibid., pp. 278–81.

thirteen "lies" Calvin had told about the scholastic doctrine of justification. He had, for example, constructed this straw man: "Circa cooperentem gratiam, quod doceat hominem naturae suae viribus et facultate naturali concurrere cum gratia."[15] A caricature of Catholic doctrine, Stapleton concluded, was much easier for the heretics to overturn than the genuine article.

As an active teacher and lecturer, Stapleton did not restrict his work during these years to lengthy and formal treatises, but he aimed all his activity, public and private, at contributing in some way "to the illustration of the Catholic faith or to the refutation of the various impieties of contemporary heretics," and almost all the short "orationes" he delivered at Douay and, later, at Louvain expanded or embellished the positions assumed in the two great books. Typical of those addresses which found their way into print were the nine delivered at Douay and published in 1580 under the title *Speculum pravitatis haereticae per orationes ad oculum demonstratae*. All of them pointed an accusing finger at Protestantism. For example, three lectures which Stapleton gave at the Collège de Marchiennes in December 1578 attempted to discover "whether the heresies of our times are a proximate preparation for Antichrist," "whether there is any certain or constant doctrine among contemporary heretics," and "whether there is in today's heretics any religion at all." Another considered the line of conduct to be followed by a "pious man" living among heretics.[16]

The longest and best of these discourses, also delivered before a distinguished audience at the Collège de Marchiennes, dwelt upon the Protestants' proudest claim, that they had reformed the Church. Stapleton began his oration by pointing out that, to find what true religious reformation consists in, one must examine the various functions of religion. "The universal religion by which God is properly served has to do with the doctrine of faith divinely transmitted, with the external and public cult prescribed by God, and, finally, with the moral life ordered according to God's laws;

15. *Institutes*, II.6.20.
16. *Speculum*, pp. 415 ff.

for without these three there is no true religion." The true re-
former finds one of these avenues closed to him: doctrine, given
by God to men, remains, as Tertullian said, "immobilis et in-
formabilis," and so the heretic can never claim to have reformed
doctrine but only to have discovered or restored it. The peculiar
feature of Protestantism, Stapleton continued, is that in defense
of its doctrine of imputed justice it denies the possibility of reformation in the area of morality. For this reason the Protestants
have spent most of their energy calling down curses on the
Roman Church, because, they say, in her cult she has reverted to
the superstitions of Judaism and paganism. The Protestants have
set up, therefore, a form of public worship which they claim to
be consistent with the doctrine as well as the example of the
primitive Church. But upon close scrutiny, said Stapleton, all this
comes to nothing, for, when pressed by the antiquity of practices
like prayer for the dead or the sacrificial use of the Eucharist, the
Protestants desert the Fathers and even the Apostles and take
refuge under the wing of privately interpreted Scripture. The
carefully documented argument ended with a peroration which
even in translation retains something of its force:

> If those who today try to pawn themselves off as reformers
> of the Church . . . preserving unity and peace, had wanted
> to apply themselves with zeal and prudence to a certain
> reformation, together with the leaders and doctors of the
> Church; if their doctrine had supported an inquiry in a
> Christian and holy fashion into the cleansing and renovation
> of the interior man, which is the foundation of all true
> religious reformation; if they had deigned to recognize, to
> follow and to embrace in their reformation of divine cult
> the example and practice of the early Church; if finally they
> had not snatched away the substance of the Catholic faith,
> abolished the Christian sacrifice, denied the sacraments and
> altogether confused and upset due order and polity; had they
> instead proposed to criticize and correct the abuses and
> superstitions which had sprung up in various places on ac-

count of the crass negligence of certain pastors: then the Church of God would neither have called into question their zeal nor have repudiated their counsel. . . .But since they want to be taken for new apostles or, at the very least, for new evangelists, it follows that what they are talking about is not a reformation but a transformation, that these men ought to be called transformers, not reformers, and indeed the most audacious and noxious of their kind who ever lived. For they are preaching a gospel other than the one we have received: it is not really a gospel at all, because it perverts the only true gospel of Jesus Christ. And so with reason the whole Church of God says to them, "Anathema."[17]

Another of the numerous public lectures Stapleton gave at Douay deserves special notice, because ultimately it became part of his best known work, the *Tres Thomae*. In 1586 he preached a eulogy in honor of his patron, St. Thomas the Apostle, on his feast day, December 21, dwelling mostly on the saint's activities as an intrepid missionary, who "had preached the gospel of Christ even in the new western world, America itself."[18] Two years later a small book appeared which included this short sermon as well as a description of the "res gestae" of two other Thomases, the twelfth-century Archbishop of Canterbury and the sixteenth-century Lord Chancellor of England. The treatment of St. Thomas of Canterbury[19] consisted of a collection of documents prefaced by an "apologeticum breve" in which Stapleton tried to point out the "true cause" of the Archbishop's martyrdom. This seemed especially appropriate at a time when St. Thomas was so violently hated by the English heretics because he had dared to resist the interference of Henry II in matters of ecclesiastical jurisdiction.

17. Ibid., p. 394.
18. *Tres Thomae*, 4, 941. As an authority on St. Thomas the Apostle's activity in Brazil, Stapleton cited one Emanuel Nobrega, who, in a book written in 1552, claimed that the Indians knew of an apostle they called "Zome." It was clear, observed Stapleton, that they had changed the theta in Thomas' name to a zeta.
19. Ibid., pp. 944–88.

Thus, said Stapleton, it has come about that the name of St. Thomas of Canterbury has been reduced on English calendars simply to "Becket the traitor."[20] "The liar Foxe, in his pseudo-martyrology," claimed that the Archbishop had not been at all interested in "matters of faith, religion, true doctrine or sincere discipline" but only in "worldly possessions, exemptions, preroga-tives, and things of that kind." The "image of him which was on London bridge was thrown down before any of the others in all England, as I find in the English works of Thomas More." What appeared to Stapleton more alarming, however, was the spread among continental Catholics of the calumny that St. Thomas had died simply to defend the Church's temporalities.[21] This conclu-sion had been propagated with great success by "that swinish heretic, John Bale, who had published a catalogue of English writers."[22] There followed Stapleton's analysis of the Archbishop's death as a martyrdom in behalf of doctrine, drawn from contempo-rary reports and buttressed, in the best manner of the scientific historian, by twenty-four pages of manuscript sources.

It is the last section of *Tres Thomae*, "The Life and Illustrious Martyrdom of Thomas More, Sometime Lord Chancellor of Eng-land," that has gained for Stapleton the slight attention posterity has chosen to pay him. This work was of considerable size[23] and,

20. For centuries St. Thomas of Canterbury had been the most popular of all the English saints, Chaucer's "holy, blissful martyr."

21. Among the continental Catholics who held this unfortunate view, Stapleton cited Colchaeus, "surely a most learned man and an excellent Catho-lic."

22. The adjective Stapleton used (*Tres Thomae*, 4, 944) was "spurcus." John Bale (1495–1563) was an ex-Carmelite who became Bishop of Ossory (Ireland) in 1553. He wrote and produced morality plays with an anti-Catholic slant. In and out of trouble with successive governments, he lived out his last years in England without influence. His *Illustrium Majoris Britanniae scriptorum in quinque centurias divisum* was first published in 1548. Of all the Protestants, Stapleton detested Bale with a special fervor. "Bawdy Bale," for example, was a constant target in *Fortresse*. Froude, who was certainly not unfriendly to Bale's theology, nevertheless considered him a "foul-mouthed ruffian."

23. *Tres Thomae*, 4, 988–1057. The work was divided into 21 chapters and roughly half of it dealt with More's trial, imprisonment, and martyrdom.

as Stapleton noted in his preface, was based on a variety of sources: the Latin and English works of More himself, the correspondence of Erasmus, the personal recollections of John Harris, once More's secretary, and of his wife Dorothy, once Margaret Roper's maid (still living in 1588, and in Douay),[24] and of many others of the onetime chancellor's friends and relatives, like John and Margaret Clements, John Heywood, and William Rastell.[25] Stapleton also searched contemporary writers who might have had reason to mention More and "his ergo omnibus praesidiis instructus, de Thomae Mori vita rebus gestis, ac potissimun illustri martyrio, non brevem mode commentarium, sed forte etiam justam quandam historiam conficiam."[26] It is significant that this, "justa historia" went through several editions in the original Latin and that in more recent times it has been translated into French and Spanish, but that not until 1928, 330 years after its author's death, did an English translation appear.[27] In the light of that fact, there is something of the pathetic in the words with which Stapleton closed his essay:

> Habes, amice et candide lector, quae de Thomae Mori viri clarissimi et praestantissimi vita, moribus, rebus gestis atque illustrio martyrio colligere potui et collecta describere. Deus

24. Dorothy Colly Harris gave Stapleton her late husband's manuscript collection, which included letters in the martyr's own hand.

25. All of these people Stapleton would have had the chance to know in the early years of Elizabeth's reign, because all of them, like Stapleton, settled in the Low Countries.

26. *Tres Thomae*, 4, 991.

27. *The Life and Illustrious Martyrdom of Sir Thomas More*, trans. Philip Hallett (New York, 1928). The greatest modern authority on More writes: "Stapleton was master of a beautiful English style, as his translation of Bede's *Ecclesiastical History* shows. It is to be regretted that his boyish enthusiasm did not lead him to compile his Life of More earlier, and in English, when he was in constant communication with the friends of More. . . . [In the evidence of Dorothy Colly and the reminiscences of other intimates over half a century] we have to thank Stapleton for having preserved what, but for him, would almost certainly have perished." R. W. Chambers, *Thomas More* (London, 1935), p. 39. For an extensive use of Stapleton's study of More by a modern historian see G. Constant, *The Reformation in England, 1* (London, 1934), 200–84.

patet misericordiarum afflictissimae genti nostrae, in hor-
rendo schismate et haeretica tyrannide tricesimum (uno
minus) nunc laboranti annum, merito sanguinis dilecti filii
sui, et tot in Anglia martyrum, atque imprimis Thomae
Mori, sanctis precibus; clementer tandem propitiari digne-
tur; et ad communem Catholicae Ecclesiae gremium aber-
rantem reducere: cui fit omnis honor et gloria in omnem
aeternitatem. Amen.[28]

A final word must be said about a series of works begun by
Stapleton during his last years at Douay and continued after he
had returned to Louvain. These were the various *Promptuaria,*
commentaries he prepared for the gospel texts appointed to be
read at Mass throughout the liturgical year. The *Promptuaria
moralia super evangelia dominicalia,* first published at Douay in
1589, occupied no fewer than 541 pages of the fourth volume
of the *Opera.* Each *promptuarium* is devoted to a Sunday gospel.
Each begins by quoting the text in full and is followed by a
"Pericope moralis hujus Evangelii" and then by Stapleton's im-
mensely learned, verse by verse comment, which might run to
as many as ten pages and never less than five. These *Promptuaria*
were not directly controversial.[29]

Of quite a different character were the *Promptuaria catholica
super evangelia dominicalia,* which appeared a year earlier. Stapleton hoped this book of commentaries would provide a useful
manual for popular preachers who had to deal with congregations
exposed to heresy.[30] It covered the same ground as the *Promptuaria moralia,* but the commentaries were much shorter (two or
three pages each at most) and much more pointed. For example,

28. *Tres Thomae,* 4, 1057.

29. *The Tablet* (London), Oct. 27, 1888, published a letter from a sub-
scriber who suggested that the translation of the *Promptuaria moralia* be
undertaken as a joint exercise. "As a *sermonnaire* for priests," wrote Canon
Henry Cafferata, "no book can equal it." In the journal's next few issues some
interest was manifested by other correspondents, and by Nov. 10 Cafferata
could report that one party had already contacted him about the project.

30. *Opera,* 4, 547.

Stapleton opens his comments on the gospel for the second Sunday after the feast of the Epiphany with this remark: "This passage provides an excellent occasion to explain to the people the petulance, ignorance, and impiety of today's heretics and to defend against their attacks the glory and innocence of the Virgin Mother of God."[31] A twofold appendix to this work eventually appeared, though not until its author had left Douay for Louvain. Published in 1592 was the *Promptuaria catholica in evangelia festorum totius anni,* which contained commentaries for many of the feast-day gospels, and, among other things, explained the proper notion of vocation (as opposed to the heretical one) on St. Andrew's day (November 30) and on St. Martin's day (November 11) "one of the many ways in which Calvin contradicts Christ." In 1594 Stapleton completed the last of this series. Dedicated to Owen Lewis, it provided short and controversial comment on the gospel of the Mass for each weekday of Lent from Ash Wednesday through Maundy Thursday.[32]

At the same time as he prepared for the press the last two of these popular manuals, Stapleton was embarking on another kind of scriptural work which made altogether different demands on him. With his assumption of the chair of Scripture at Louvain, he began a third distinct period of literary activity. He had to lecture on the text of the New Testament to theological students of high caliber, and do so with a scientific rather than an ascetic or homiletic objective in mind. Yet, one does not, at fifty-five (which Stapleton was in 1590), change the intellectual habits of a lifetime or brush aside deep emotional commitments. For nearly a generation Stapleton had devoted all his strength to the battle against Protestantism, and, both as an Englishman and as a long-time resident of the Low Countries, he saw no reason, in

31. Ibid., p. 575. The text is St. John's Gospel, 2:1–11 (the wedding feast at Cana).

32. In 1610 the third Synod of Antwerp directed that pastors possess in their personal libraries Stapleton's *Promptuaria moralia* and *Promptuaria catholica,* both of which had been recently translated into Flemish. See Lechat, *Réfugiés anglais,* pp. 200–01.

the last decade of the sixteenth century, to relax his efforts. "In the study of the Bible," he wrote, "two things chiefly must be sought: the literal and genuine sense of the sacred text, and, secondly, the use of Scripture most necessary for the times in which one lives." These two objectives, he believed, meshed nicely: if the Scriptures were to be properly understood, the perversion of them popularized most successfully by Calvin and his "lackey," Theodore Beza, had to be swept away. Nothing, he submitted, was more necessary for the times than that. Stapleton never doubted that he was equal to the task. When the Anglican controversialist, William Whitaker, wrote that "in Calvin's little finger there was more solid doctrine, wisdom and genius than in the whole of Stapleton's mind and body," the latter replied without a trace of false modesty.

> These commentaries of mine will, I think, make clear if not to Whitaker at least to the indifferent reader that there is not so vast a difference between Calvin and me. In any case I do not take upon myself this literary task nor have I ever done so in order to gain a reputation for wisdom, doctrine, or genius. . . . Out of my zeal for the true faith I have been satisfied to struggle against the pestilent heresies of these times to the best of my ability. I only hope that by God's blessing all those who read this work of mine may be satisfied that by whatever doctrine, wisdom, and genius (which really amount to a cunning brashness and a dissolute craft) Calvin managed to pervert the Holy Scripture, doctrine, wisdom, and talent have not been lacking to me to refute his distortions convincingly.[33]

Stapleton considered the lectures he was giving at Louvain "antidotes" to the "poison of Calvin and Beza" or simply "to the heresies of our time." When they came to be published, they formed two distinct parts, the *Antidota evangelica,* which included a study of each of the four gospels, and the *Antidota apostolica,*

---

33. *Antidota apostolica,* p. 517.

which was made up of commentaries (published in 1595) on Acts and Romans and commentaries (completed in the autumn of 1597) on I and II Corinthians. Stapleton wanted to "explain those places in Scripture which today's heretics (and particularly Calvin and Beza) have distorted in their attempt either to establish their own frivolous doctrines or to weaken those of the Catholic Church." He passed by without comment any passage he judged to have been left undisturbed by the Protestants. Thus, for instance, he made no mention of the first chapter of St. Matthew's Gospel. These commentaries varied greatly in size. In the *Antidota evangelica* the study of St. Matthew took up 135 pages and St. John 157, leaving scarcely fifty pages in which to consider the other two Synoptics. The first volume of the *Antidota apostolica,* which dealt with the Acts of the Apostles, was almost exactly the same length as the earlier treatment of St. John's Gospel, while the longest single commentary of all was, understandably, that on the crucial Epistle to the Romans. The study, thirty pages long, of this Epistle's fourth chapter was exactly three times the length of the study of the whole Gospel of St. Mark.

Stapleton followed the same method in all the *Antidota.* After stating the particular verse, he quoted directly the commentaries of Calvin and/or Beza in connection with it and concluded with his own consideration of their arguments. The following short example will give some idea of Stapleton's procedure and objective. After quoting the first part of Romans 12:6,[34] Stapleton commented:

> Calvin's commentary on this passage is pleasant to read, because the truth in this instance rings out more clearly from the mouth of the adversary. "Here," he says, "we have the chief objective at which the Apostle has been aiming; he does not intend to make all the gifts of God apply to every individual but to have them distributed so that everybody might have a limited share. So it is needful that each individual be zealous in the use of that gift given to him for the

34. "And having different gifts, according to the grace that is given us."

building up of his own function and pass on to something
else." Now this is a very good and useful observation, but
it stands clearly against the position taken by Calvin, Beza,
and all the other sectaries. For all of them have left derelict
their own functions and instead have seized upon that
properly belonging to others. When the Bishop of Geneva
had been driven from his see, Calvin, together with his ac-
complices Farel and Viret, intruded himself into the Bishop's
place. Afterwards, both he and Beza attempted to impose
the consistorial form upon all the other reformed (to use
their phrase) churches, whether English, Scotch, Polish, or
French. Up to the present day in England the ancient form
and polity is not free or immune from the complaints of the
Puritans, who never cease in their demands for consistories,
and this is one cause of the interminable and passionate
quarrels which separate them and the other Anglocalvinists.
However, many sectaries there are today who, without legitimate ordination in the one Catholic Church, have taken to
themselves the offices of teaching or ministering. They are
the ones who have abandoned their own functions and have
passed on to something else.[35]

In England, the later literary activity of the sometime fellow
of New College did not go unnoticed, and if Bishops Horne and
Jewel had some years before passed to a land where controversy
plays no part, they had left behind them a number of hardy
champions no less prepared to do battle for the gospel's sake.
Among these was William Whitaker, Master of St. John's College, Cambridge, since 1580, Regius Professor of Divinity, who
in 1588 published his *Disputatio de Sacra Scriptura* which he
directed "against the papists of our time, especially Bellarmine
and Stapleton."[36] Whitaker was anxious to demonstrate that the
authority of Scripture stood independent of the Church's judg-

35. *Antidota apostolica*, pp. 705–06.
36. *A Disputation on Holy Scripture*, trans. William Fitzgerald (Cambridge, 1849), title page.

ment: "Of all the popish writers, Stapleton hath treated this question with the greatest acuteness. . . . With him, therefore, we will
engage, as well because he is our fellow countryman as because
he seems to have handled this subject most accurately of them
all." In order to prove that the "Roman popish synagogue"[37]
had no business meddling with the Scriptures, Whitaker subjected
the ninth book of Stapleton's *Principiorum* to the closest scrutiny.[38]

Four years passed before Stapleton had either the time or the
inclination to engage with this latest and last of his opponents.[39]
Not until early in 1592 did his response to the *Disputatio* appear.
He called it *Autoritatis ecclesiasticae circa S. Scripturarum appro-
bationem defensio,* and he wasted no compliments on Master
Whitaker:

> I find it shameful and disgusting, Whitaker, that in this one
> section of your book you have sinned so much, told so many
> lies, made so many paralogisms, contradicted yourself and
> refuted yourself so often, fabricated so many foolish, im-
> pudent, and impious charges, and, in short, proved yourself
> to be so perfidious, lazy, and ignorant an opponent. You
> claim you want to debate with the papists of our day, with
> Robert Bellarmine and myself, to discuss Sacred Scripture,
> the number of its books, its authentic editions, its authority,
> its interpretation, its perfection. Let me warn you, you have
> chosen adversaries who do not lack perception and who, in
> this wrestling in controversy, are not easily knocked about.[40]

Stapleton divided his *Defensio* into three books which discussed
in turn the "status quaestionis" (for it was Stapleton's contention

37. Ibid., pp. 14, 280, 285.
38. Bk. IX of the *Principiorum* (*Opera, 1,* 309–33) treated "of the first
and particular object of the Church's authority, the Canon of Scripture."
39. *Autoritatis ecclesiasticae, 1,* 854. Stapleton explained that he had not
seen Whitaker's book until a friend sent it to him from Frankfort in June 1590.
A month later had come the appointment to Louvain, and so he had not found
the opportunity to answer sooner.
40. Ibid., p. 851.

that Calvin and his followers had "inverted" the proper order in this matter), the arguments which established the Church's authority with regard to Scripture, and, thirdly, the merits of Whitaker's contrary arguments.

Two years later the appearance of *Pro autoritate atque autepistia S. Scripturae contra T. Stapletonum* proved at least that Stapleton had overshot the mark when he had labeled Whitaker an "adversarius ignavus." This time Stapleton did not wait so long to answer, and in the summer of 1595 he put the finishing touches to his *Relectio scholastica et compendiaria prinicipiorum fidei doctrinalium . . . adversus Gulielmum Whitakerum anglocalvinistam.*[41] This work constituted Stapleton's major contribution to the controversy, and, as its title suggests, it differed completely in form from the *Defensio*. Instead of quoting Whitaker and then fashioning an ad hoc reply, Stapleton divided the whole discussion of the Church's authority into six ordered parts ("Controversiae capitales") which he broke down again into smaller "quaestiones" and "articuli." The first Controversy dealt with the "Ecclesia in se" and treated of the nominal definition of the word "Ecclesia" (q. 1), of the Church's membership (q. 2), and of the marks of the Church (q. 4). "Controversia capitalis tertia," which explained the functions of the Church's visible head, makes up the longest section of the book. It includes a consideration of whether Christ had indeed set up for the Church any one head (q. 1) and, if he had, whether that head possessed the power of excommunication (q. 10). Stapleton covered in this manner the whole range of problems with which Whitaker had confronted him. For example, he plunged into the tricky question of the various biblical editions and versions (Cont. 5, q. 3), and he even raked the coals, still not quite cold, of the conciliar theory (Cont. 6, q. 3, especially art. 5).

Even so, Stapleton a year later was not satisfied that he had made his position as clear as he might have. At the heart of Whitaker's criticism of the Church's authority, he wrote from Louvain in March 1596, was an inversion of the proper order of discussion

41. See *Opera, 1,* 507–838.

which made an understanding of the relationship of Scripture to the Church exceedingly difficult. To remedy this, Stapleton offered "per modum appendicis" his *Triplicatio incohata adversus Gulielmi Whitakeri anglocalvinistae duplicationem.*[42] In twenty-three short chapters the author explained how Calvin and his followers had so changed the "status quaestionis" that what the Roman Church really taught about the authority of Scripture had become obscured.

If compared to Stapleton's great books on the Church and on justification, to his various Scripture commentaries, or even to the efforts of his youth such as the *Fortresse of the Faith,* the *Triplicatio* can claim only modest importance. Yet even in this slim volume appear those elements which made Thomas Stapleton a contender (to use his own metaphor) in the intellectual wrestling match of his time. The prime functions of what Catholics have come to call Positive Theology were to combat the genuine doctrinal challenge presented by Protestantism, and, no less importantly, to disassociate the Church from that caricature of Catholicism which the Reformers, in their polemic, had created. Stapleton proved himself a particularly skillful practitioner of this new art because he possessed a combination of gift, training, and conviction whereby the attainment of this twofold objective could be more readily accomplished. The *Triplicatio* gives a hint of this by the very fact that it calls for an orderly discussion of the matters controverted; its author believed that questions of the faith are intellectual questions which must be approached by a sound methodology. As a son of the Counter Reformation, he further believed, all too optimistically, that victory in argument, like victory on the battlefield or in the Parliament house, would lead ultimately to the cessation of the unseemly religious quarrels.

The old faith had been challenged fundamentally as a corruption, and so the Protestants needed to make out a case that would show their doctrine to be, on the whole, consistent with that of the primitive Church. The good opinion of St. Jerome

42. Ibid., pp. 1115–1293.

and the assent of St. Augustine became great prizes to be won,
for if they and the other Fathers had been on Luther's side, who
could have stood against him? What obscure second- and third-
century divines had to say about prayer for the dead or about the
Eucharist suddenly took on great importance, as the Centuriators
of Magdeberg ransacked libraries in search of historical support
for their doctrine.[43] In such an atmosphere a simple obiter dictum
from, say, Hosius of Cordova, carried far more weight than did
the careful distinctions of the *Summa theologica*.

Stapleton could not long have survived in this arena without
vast erudition, a wide acquaintance with patrology, history, and
philology "in an age and a century," as he put it, "most distinguished for knowledge and restoration of Christian antiquity."[44]
Rhetorical talent to spare, in two languages, helped considerably.
But it mattered no less vitally that his intellectual equipment also
included a solid grasp of the best of scholasticism. What a later
critic has referred to somewhat contemptuously as his "subtlety
of logic"[45] was in Stapleton's hands a weapon of no little utility.
His understanding of Aristotelian modes of argument may not
have saved him from verbosity, but it did rescue him from the
crime and folly of rhetoric for its own sake and made it possible
for him to make the right distinctions. He would readily grant,
for instance, that disciplinary regulations about the reception of
the chalice by the laity or the use of vernacular in the liturgy

43. *"The Centuries* took the Catholics by surprise. . . . Up to the appearance
of the volumes of Flacius the past of the Church belonged to the Catholics.
The general attacks brought against the papacy were of a rather superficial
nature. The Catholic writers were confident that they were more than holding
their own. They had not even been forced to consider how they would accord
their humanism with the medieval historical conceptions. *The Centuries* put
them on the defensive." At least so thinks E. A. Ryan, *The Historical Scholarship of Saint Bellarmine* (New York, 1936), pp. 12–13.

44. *Speculum,* p. 397.

45. Fitzgerald, *Disputation,* p. xi. "There is a prolixity in Whitaker's style
which contrasts unfavorably with the compactness of his great antagonist,
Bellarmine: though he trespasses far less upon the student's patience than
Stapleton, whose verbose rhetoric made him admired in his own day, and
whose subtlety of logic cannot save him from neglect in ours."

admitted of modification, but in the next breath he demanded of the Reformers why they wanted these particular changes introduced. Was it because the Apostles had understood Aramaic and had consumed both Elements at the Last Supper, or was it, in fact, because heretics wanted to introduce into the daily lives of the people a new Eucharistic doctrine or a new conception of worship?

The integral approach which Stapleton took in his controversial work can be seen from a glance at a typical list of his Catholic sources. In eight pages at the beginning of his treatise on justification,[46] he cited St. Augustine ten times,[47] St. John Chrysostom twice,[48] St. Basil twice,[49] and St. Jerome,[50] St. Gregory Nasianzen,[51] St. John Demascene,[52] St. Ambrose,[53] and St. Irenaeus[54] once each. In the same space, he also called upon St. Thomas Aquinas a dozen times,[55] Cardinal Cajetan three times,[56] Hugh of St. Victor[57] and Gabriel Biel[58] twice each, and St. Anselm,[59]

46. *Justificationis*, pp. 23–31.

47. There are three references to *De civitate Dei* (J. P. Migne, *Patrologia latina*, Paris, 1857–66, 41, 13–804), two to *De peccatorum meritis* (ibid., 44, 109–200), one to *Enchiridion* (ibid., 40, 231–91), one to *De nuptiis et concupiscentia* (ibid., 44, 413–74), one to *Contra Julianum haeresis Pelagianae defensorem* (ibid., 44, 671–874), one to *Epistola LXXXIX* (ibid., 33, 310–13), and one to *De Genesi ad litteram* (ibid., 34, 245–486).

48. *Homilia XVI in Gen.* (J. P. Migne, *Patrologia graeca*, Paris, 1857–66, 53, 125–34) and *Homilia IV in Epist. I ad Cor.* (ibid., 61, 34–40).

49. *Homilia in Psalmum XLVIII* (ibid., 29, 431–59), and *De Spiritu Sancto* (ibid., 32, 87–218).

50. *Contra Jovinianum* (ibid., 23, 211–338).

51. *Oratio XLV in Sanctum Pascha* (ibid., 36, 623–64).

52. *De orthodoxa fide* (ibid., 94, 781–1228).

53. *Hexaemeron* (ibid., 14, 123–274).

54. *Adversus haereses* (ibid., 7, 437–1224).

55. There are references to the *Summa* (8), to the *Contra Gentiles* (2), and to the *De malo* (2).

56. The references are to Cajetan's commentary on the *Summa*, Ia IIae, q. 71 and q. 79.

57. *De Sacramentis christianae fidei* (Migne, *Patrologia latina*, 176, 173–618).

58. *Collectorium sive epitome in magistri sententiarum libros IV* (Tübingen, 1501).

59. *De conceptu virginali* (Migne, *Patrologia latina*, 158, 431–64).

St. Bonaventure,[60] and Scotus[61] once each. Stapleton, it would seem, considered the doctrinal tradition a single defensible whole. He appeared convinced that if he could show what Protestantism meant essentially, if he could push aside those secondary issues over which so much ink (and blood) had been spilt and reveal the principles which lay behind them, choice might be confidently left to the ordinarily sensible man. It was not hyperbole when Stapleton used the word "mendaciter" in describing his opponents' arguments. He could not believe that these men did not see what he saw, that their position was illogical. This point of view left little room in Stapleton's work for chivalrous compliments to his adversaries, but, at the same time, it made for lively controversy and, more important, for clarity. He hounded them over their lack of precision; he demanded they state their principles and give order to their arguments (as e.g. in the *Triplicatio*). Nor did he spare those of his fellow Catholics who had panicked in the face of the Protestant onslaught and had as a result muddled their arguments. John Eck, he thought, had done the Catholic cause serious disservice by throwing over the Thomist for the Scotist position on original sin, not because he had been convinced by the latter but because he had found the former difficult, or inconvenient, to defend against Luther.[62] Pighius and Dominic Soto, with opinions on original sin which, Stapleton wrote, "can scarcely be excused from Pelagianism," had to his mind stimulated rather than refuted the innovators.[63]

St. Thomas Aquinas had once devoted considerable space to an attempt to elucidate Aristotle's deceptively simple description of a principle as "that from which something flows." Whether or not Stapleton was familiar with that passage, he was certainly aware of St. Thomas' own constant preoccupation with the search

---

60. *Comentarii in quatuor libros sententiarum Petri Lombardi.*
61. Ibid.
62. *Justificationis*, p. 42.
63. Ibid., p. 52. "Haec sententia a Pelagianismo excusari vix potest, nec . . . cum S. Augustini vel cum Conc. Trid. sententia et doctrina concordat." Stapleton cited Soto, *De natura et gratia*, Bk. I, cc. 3, 13.

for principles. He knew that all the distinctions and syllogisms and citations aimed only at laying bare that from which the thing under discussion flowed. Stapleton viewed the heresy at hand in the same way. There must be, he thought, an essential cause or principle for the disagreements which had in a generation spilled out into civil war in one place and moral collapse in another, which had overturned ideals and institutions cherished for more than a thousand years. There could be no simple explanation for such a cataclysm, but the wise man, to explain it at all, had to look first for the first principle. "Sapientis est ordinare" is a dictum as ancient as Western civilization itself, and in its spirit Stapleton maintained throughout his controversial career a conviction that the religious quarrels of the century were not essentially about the Eucharist or Latin or indulgences, not about avaricious prelates or incontinent priests, but were, rather, reducible to a first cause with a double character: an error about justification and a concomitant error about the nature of authority.

Chapter 4

THE QUARREL OVER JUSTIFICATION

The religious quarrel which agitated the sixteenth century eventually concerned itself with many issues. It was modified, too, by extraneous elements: economic and political considerations led it down some strange and highly untheological paths. But whatever tangents it took and however it swerved under the impact of secular interests, it nevertheless remained radically what it had been from the beginning, a quarrel about justification. Martin Luther raised his cry not fundamentally against the Mass as such or even against the papacy but rather against a doctrine which explained God's relationship to his human creatures in such a way that the Eucharist became the Christian community's supreme good work and the pope a necessary instrument of mediation.

European intellectuals of the sixteenth century were preoccupied with matters religious to a degree unapproached by any intellectual community since. Once, therefore, we of a later time, absorbed by more mundane concerns, have become used to the idea that in those quaint days politicians of the highest rank wrote books in defense of the seven sacraments, that best sellers were, almost without exception, religious tracts, it will surprise us very little that a considerable amount of learned ink was spilled over the basic problem of justification. The forging of the two positions and the defense of them engaged the attention of Europe's finest minds for three or four generations. The theologians of the Counter Reformation were not exceptional in this regard. Sooner or later, if they were worth their salt, they had to abandon peripheral controversies, however important, and face squarely the issue around which everything else swung.

By 1582, when Thomas Stapleton finished his great book on the subject, both sides were securely entrenched. The Protestants had demonstrated that their theory was viable and that it could win acceptance in every section of contemporary society. The Catholics had responded in the first stormy sessions at Trent thirty-five years before and had produced an authoritative, carefully worded definition which had, in its turn, inspired an intellectual counteroffensive. Stapleton worked within the framework of this latter movement. He wrote not in serenity but in the midst of a struggle which he, like his friends and adversaries, presumed would go to the death. In this conviction he and they were mistaken; as it turned out, neither side had strength enough to destroy the other, whether with pen or sword, and so each side had ultimately to accept, however distasteful it may have been, coexistence with the other. If this result appears inevitable to us who look back on the events, it was not at all clear to the generation of the 1580s. Thomas Stapleton expressed the view of his contemporaries and also the timeless and futile optimism of the intellectual when he opined that "once certain doctrinal problems have been reduced to their principles, then might men hope for an end finally to this vast controversial chaos."[1] Here no doubt was an unrealistic sentiment, but without such rising hopes and great expectations there never would have been a Counter Reformation.

How does a human being pass from the state of unrighteousness in which he is born to the state of justice which he must attain if he is to see God? This is the question that a Christian doctrine of justification attempts to answer, and it takes but little reflection to see how grave a question it is. Justification, as the construction of the word suggests, means a process, an activity that produces a change in him who experiences it. No sixteenth-century Christian would challenge the absolute need of such a process, because he believed that every man had come into the world under God's ban, bearing within himself the dreadful taint of original sin. But unanimous agreement that the human spirit suffered from a criti-

1. *Principiorum*, p. 39.

cal malaise had never prevented Christians from debating heatedly the manner in which health could be restored, nor did it in the
first half of the sixteenth century, when two new statements of
justification appeared, each claiming to represent the genuine
Christian revelation. As Newman put it, "Few but will grant that
Luther's view of justification had never been stated in words before his time, that his phraseology and positions were novel,
whether called for by circumstances or not. It is equally certain
that the doctrine of justification defined at Trent was, in some
sense, new also."[2]

In the opening chapters of his Epistle to the Romans, St. Paul
says in forceful language that neither the natural law of the
Gentiles nor the revealed law of the Jews suffices for him who
would walk pleasing in God's sight. What must be done is to
grapple to oneself the redemptive work of Christ, to participate
in it in some way and thus to become numbered among those
"friends" for whom the Son of God laid down his life. The process
called justification, therefore, must involve the achievement by
the individual of a participation with Christ. Only in this way can
one pass from death to life. The theology of the Middle Ages,
which reached its summit with St. Thomas Aquinas, explained
this participation by giving a strict determination to the biblical
word grace. "Gratia gratum faciens" was that quality which really
resided in the human soul and which rendered it genuinely de-
lightful (*gratum*) to God.[3] Included in this spiritual presence, so
the teaching went, were two elements, logically distinct: the remission of the guilt and penalty due to sin and, simultaneously,
the infusion of supernatural charity which in turn directs the
faculties of the human personality toward an Object otherwise
infinitely beyond their native capabilities. Grace (as the etymology
of the word makes clear) was a free gift of God which, in His

2. J. H. Newman, *Development of Doctrine* (New York, 1949), pp. 53–
54.

3. This is what Catholics usually call "sanctifying grace." It must be distinguished from "actual grace," which is the action of God aiding the individual in this or that supernatural situation.

inscrutable fashion, He might dispense to whom He would. But whoever received it did so because of Christ, the perfect Mediator, the Son of God made man, who became "partaker of our humanity that we might become partakers of his divinity."[4] The choice of the word "partaker" was no accident; it had its scriptural root,[5] and it underscored the notion that justification involved a breathtaking mystery, that men and women, even in this valley of tears, can share in the very life of God.

Christians could enter into this intimate relationship with the Divine, could receive the grace which sanctifies, through faith and the sacraments. Neither would do without the other because, according to the theory, faith without works, particularly without those works which placed the believer in direct contact with Christ, was dead, and the sacraments without faith were empty gestures. The Church existed for the sake of the faith and the sacraments, to preserve the former and to administer the latter. A human being joined his act of faith to baptism and the other sacraments and became thereby incorporated into the Church which, setting aside valid but less essential definitions, was the extension of Christ into time and space. As a member of the Church, he bore within himself the glow of God's life and shared a unique fellowship with others in the same happy condition. This presence that transformed him, that lifted him and his powers to a plane far above themselves, might be called charity or sanctifying grace or a lively faith; what mattered more than its name was the fact that it really did inhere in the human person. As a living thing, it admitted of growth and dimunition; as a free gift, it could be lost and then regained. It could coexist with weakness and trouble, with any kind of temperament, with any social position. It might manifest itself at white heat in the reckless courage of the crusader or in the flights of the mystic. More ordinarily (and not always less heroically) it showed itself as that element

4. These are the words of the Offertory of the Mass.
5. "By whom he hath given us most great and precious promises: that by these you may be made partakers of the divine nature, flying the corruption of that concupiscence which is in the world." II Peter 1:4.

which kept the mother devoted and the merchant honest even under trying circumstances. Because of its presence, a man could be literally holy, so that his activities, even unspectacular ones like the offering of a glass of water to a thirsty neighbor, took on a divine character worthy of God's attention and reward. The only thing "gratia gratum faciens" could not abide was the evil choice in an important matter, the sin called mortal because it snuffed out the soul's spark of divine life and destroyed with it the human capacity to achieve supernatural results.

It has often been asserted, and with much scholarly support, that the medieval statement of the doctrine of justification reached Martin Luther only in a form garbled by nominalism and obscured by the inexact terminology of the Augustinian tradition. Some have gone so far as to suggest that had Luther understood the scholastic or, more specifically, the Thomist explanation he would never have constructed his theology of grace, because he would have found in the pages of the *Summa theologica* and the *De malo* his fundamental positions fairly stated, clinically examined, and dismissed. But the inadequacies of Luther's professional training, and speculation about what his views might have been had he received a better education, are really quite beside the point. His theory of justification possessed an intuitive character which not even the most rigorous syllogistic reasoning could have penetrated. Just as irrelevant, in the last analysis, was the activity of the ecclesiastical racketeers, unfortunately so common in Luther's time, who for personal gain turned the delicate sacramental system into a faithless machine dispensing salvation like piece goods on a quid pro quo basis. That Luther abhorred and castigated these men goes without saying; others of equally good will did the same. But in a very real sense he did not quarrel with the Dominican Tetzel, the indulgence hawker with the stench of simony upon him, or even with the Dominican Cajetan, who might stand as the finest representative, intellectually and morally, of orthodoxy. In his doctrine of justification, Luther did not attack a corrupt Catholicism or a Catholicism he did not understand. He did not from one point of view attack Catholicism at all.

He went outside it and beyond it to fashion a novel idea about the kind of being God is and the kind of relationship he has established with mankind.

The Lutheran vision of justification had about it a grandeur and a simplicity both of which contributed to its appeal. Over the spirit of every human being, it began, lay the shroud of original sin which had maimed his nature beyond hope of repair. Neither the waters of baptism nor any other instrument could set right what was amiss in him. As early as 1515 Luther had made, at least implicitly, his fundamental commitment: "All the virtues," he said, "coexist in the soul with their contrary vices. . . . The just man is always standing in sin with his left foot, that is, by virtue of the old man, and in the state of grace with his right." It is not a long step from this paradox to a complete denial of the presence of grace, insofar, at any rate, as grace is a positive something rendering the soul "gratum" in God's sight. What, then, the alarmed Christian might ask, will become of me? Will I ever pass from unrighteousness to justice? "Because we are carnal it is impossible for us to fulfill the law; but Christ has come to fulfill it . . . and he communicates his accomplishment to us. . . . He makes his justice mine and my sin his. But if he has made my sin his then it is mine no longer and I am free of it."[6]

This freedom from sin (which is Luther's way of saying "this justified state") can come to the Christian only through God's mercy working through the act of faith.

> Faith is the one principle which God's grace makes use of for restoring us to his favor and image. Born in sin and the heir of misery, the soul needs an utter change of what it is by nature, both within and without, both in itself and in God's sight. The change in God's sight is called justification, the inward change is regeneration; and faith is the one appointed means of both at once. It is awakened in us by the secret influences of the Holy Spirit, generally cooperating with some external means, as the written word; and as em-

6. Martin Luther, *Werke* (Weimar, 1883), *4*, 664; *1*, 35.

bracing the news of salvation through Christ, it thereby also appropriates salvation, becoming at the same time the element and guarantee of subsequent renewal. As leading the soul to rest on Christ as its own savior, and as the propitiation of its own sins in particular, it imparts peace to the conscience and the comfortable hope of heaven; and, as being living, spiritual and inseparable from gratitude towards Christ, it abounds in fruit, that is, in good works of every kind.[7]

By means of this definition of faith, Luther solved to his own satisfaction, and to that of countless millions of others, the age-old riddle of man who is at once image of God and debased criminal. Christian justification in the new theory was to have primarily a forensic meaning: it declared a man righteous, it did not make him so. After it had touched him, he still remained what he had always been, a helpless sinner faced by a law he could not possibly keep. And yet, at the same time, he became a new creature, serene and blessed, not because of anything he had accomplished or because of some internal change in himself but solely because of what Christ had done for him. If, moved by God's mercy, he believed, if he truly accepted Christ as his personal savior, if he combined in his act, thoroughly useless in itself, that confidence and apprehension which constituted a lively faith, then he already lived justified. It did not matter any more that his damaged nature inclined him relentlessly to sin, that his lower powers responded to the commands of his higher only with the greatest difficulty. In order to give witness to the faith abiding in him, he lived, of course, as upright a life as he could. But his failures did not damn him and his successes did not save him. For Christ had succeeded beyond all measure, and now, through faith, Christ's victory was imputed to him.

The theory, beautifully simple, struck a responsive chord in every human heart. What Christian is there who has not been

7. J. H. Newman, *Lectures on the Doctrine of Justification* (London, 1924), p. 5.

appalled at the chasm between the sublimity of his vocation and his constant failure to measure up to it? "For the good which I will," St. Paul cried out, and every Christian with him, "I do not; but the evil which I will not, that I do. . . . Unhappy man that I am, who shall deliver me from the body of this death?"[8] Here, in Lutheran justification, appeared an explanation which seemed to reconcile two contrary facts, the sinfulness of men and the all-sufficient redemptive work of Christ: "He makes his justice mine and my sin his." Besides this psychological appeal, those who proposed the theory could seek support in the words of Scripture. Numerous texts point out the absolute gratuity of salvation, the corruption of human nature, and the unique connection between faith and the attainment of justice. Finally, there was no doubt that Christ had demanded of His followers, first of all, faith, by which, according to the theory, was not meant simply intellectual assent to a creedal list but, more important, a commitment to a person. When Our Lord asked the blind or the halt whether they believed in Him, His primary intention was to elicit from them a personal acceptance of himself and then, incidentally, of what He taught. It was this apprehensive power of faith which made it so important. By means of it, one can catch hold of the Object and bind oneself to it with hoops of steel. Away, therefore, with indulgences and pilgrimages and relics; religious vows can have no place in this new dispensation nor can fasting and abstinence. Most significant, however, was the new theory's elimination of the need for sacraments in the traditional sense of that word. Christ has died once for all, and contact with His saving sacrifice will come only through God's gift of faith, never through material things joined to verbal formulas which will serve at best as signs and stimulators of faith and which all too easily disintegrate into blasphemous magical incantations.

The Catholic prelates who gathered at Trent in 1545 had their work cut out for them. A generation had passed since Luther had first given publicity to his views on justification, and during those

8. Romans 7:19, 24.

years his persuasiveness and that of the other Reformers, all of whom agreed with him on this pivotal issue, had led to a profound change in the religious lives of many thousands of Christians. There was plenty of raw material to occupy the bishops and their theologians, for, if the Protestant version was new, the debate about precisely how the process of justification operated was at least as old as St. Augustine's controversy with the Pelagians. Each of the great theological schools, Thomist, Scotist, and Augustinian, had its position, and within the schools the subtleties and distinctions ran on almost ad infinitum. Then, too, in the heat of recent controversy, some Catholic writers had protested their enthusiastic opposition to Luther by slipping off the deep end of optimistic Pelagianism, while others had given far too much ground to the Reformers' arguments. Add to this, finally, the fact that the Church's supreme teaching authority had remained virtually silent about the problems of justification raised by Luther, and the difficulty of the task at Trent can be better appreciated.[9]

To have overcome this multitude of intellectual obstacles (not to mention the awesome political ones) and to have arrived at unanimous agreement marks an achievement for the Fathers of Trent with hardly a parallel in the history of the Church. On January 13, 1547, they gathered in solemn session to issue their decree. They were proud but weary, for their great hour had not arrived without sweat and turmoil. Throughout the summer and autumn of 1546, in congregation and commission, the arguments had raged. One draft after another had been drawn up and discarded as each adverb and each punctuation mark received exhaustive attention. Every possible point of view had been advanced, this one representing the Scotist or Thomist position, that one hardly distinguishable from Lutheranism, still another obviously aiming toward compromise. Christmas came and went, and they worked on. What is meant by "twofold justice"? they asked one another. Has the Christian Church ever taught that one can be certain of salvation? If not, can one be sure at any given mo-

9. See Hubert Jedin, *A History of the Council of Trent*, 2 (London, 1961), 166 ff.

ment that he is in the state of grace? Not a chapter of the decree, not one of the attached canons escaped the most rigorous scrutiny.

The Tridentine decree on justification, the result of this labor by the Church's official teachers and by the best professional theologians available, provided an authoritative answer to the fundamental Protestant doctrine.[10] It was new in the same sense that the anti-Arian Christological statement at Nicaea had been new—that is, it claimed to reformulate the divine revelation made originally to the prophets and apostles in a way which would meet the heterodox theories of the time. This, the Fathers solemnly proclaimed, is the traditional Christian teaching about justification: that no sinner is capable of saving himself, although he must prepare himself and cooperate with God's mercy by use of his free will; that he must believe what God has revealed, acknowledge his sin, and "resolve to receive Baptism and to begin a new life"; that justification includes not only the remission of sin but also "a sanctification and renewal of the whole man" and a communication to the individual of "God's justice—not indeed the justice whereby he himself is just, but the justice by which he justifies us"; that the fulfillment of God's commandments is a duty, not merely a sign of one's justified state; that once the grace of justification (which neither faith nor works can merit) has flooded the soul of the Christian, he can gain eternal life as a gift and as a reward because he has been joined to Christ in an intimacy which makes his observance of divine law a meritorious act; that the Christian ordinarily grows in the divine life within him (as he gained it in the first place and will recover it if he should lose it) through the instrumentality of the sacraments.

The guidelines laid down at Trent for succeeding Catholic controversialists proved useful both in the limitations they imposed and in the latitude they allowed. As one distinguished student has put it, the Council was "clear and precise" when dealing with the essence of justification, "ambiguous and obscure from

10. See DB, pp. 284–99. The decree was divided into 16 chapters and attached were 33 canons (i.e. the short statements of condemnation, always worded, "If anyone should say such and such, let him be anathema").

sheer caution" when treating of particular details.[11] The theologians of the Counter Reformation, therefore, secured a marked advantage over the writers prior to 1547 simply by being able to differentiate the matters open to discussion from those not. With a copy of the decree before them, Thomas Stapleton and his colleagues could presume a measure of unanimity unattainable before the Council: wherever their reasonings took them in detail, they all began and ultimately returned together to the same certain point of departure. But, at the same time, ample room was left for the opinions of the schools; Thomist and Scotist could continue to advance their respective theories as long as they did not contradict the "clear and precise" statement contained in the decree. The ecclesiastical scholar was free to employ not only the classical scholastic arguments but also the modern techniques of history and philology. In skillful hands like Stapleton's, these materials could be used to build an impressive structure.

11. F. Loofs, *Leitfaden zum Studium der Dogmengeschichte* (Halle, 1906), pp. 667 f., quoted by Jedin, 2, 309.

Chapter 5

THE GHOST OF PELAGIUS

If the modern reader shoulders his way through Stapleton's vast and sprawling tract on justification, he will find a complete statement of the kind of argumentation employed by Catholic controversy in the generation after Trent. He will also find a bewildering amount of repetition and a verbosity not at all to his taste. But its enormous bulk (roughly 350,000 words), though it poses a difficulty, does not in the end detract from the book's considerable merits, including the almost compulsive care which the author gave to its proper order. This means, of course, that Stapleton's treatment of justification begins with a lengthy consideration of original sin; the degree to which human nature had been damaged by Adam's fall was crucial to an understanding of the passage to righteousness.

There is a refreshing candor to Stapleton's opening remarks on this subject. Certain scholastics, he writes, either through carelessness or downright misstatement, have given occasion to the primitive Lutheran view that original sin effected total and irremediable corruption of the human personality. Some Catholic writers have maintained that original sin is "the least of all the sins, less serious than a venial sin," and some that, strictly speaking, it is no sin at all because there is lacking in it the essential note of guilt. Still others, without consciously intending to minimize the effects of original sin, have done so nevertheless through an indifferent use of terminology; these latter have so defined "concupiscence" that for them the physical side of man only, and not his spiritual, has been damaged by original sin.[1]

1. *Justificationis*, p. 23.

In making this accusation Stapleton did not hesitate to name names, some of them eminent and some of them belonging to his own contemporaries. The chief villain was Durandus of Saint-Pourcain, the fourteenth-century Dominican nominalist, dubbed "Doctor Resolutissimus" because of the strenuous way he expressed certain of his views. Not far behind, in Stapleton's judgment, were Albert Pighius, the Dutch controversialist who wrote extensively in the 1530s and whose works were a favorite target for the English Protestants,[2] and Dominic Soto, one of the imperial theologians active at the first session of Trent. Stapleton lumped these writers together as "almost Pelagians" who provided the Protestants with priceless ammunition. Soto, for example, taught that by original sin man reverted to a natural state marked by a natural sensuality which had been happily curbed by the grace given to Adam. Thus, to use Soto's image, the present human condition is like a man stripped naked; he differs from the man who has never worn clothing only in that once he was dressed and ornamented and in the process of stripping he has incurred some guilt. Durandus arrived, without the benefit of metaphor, at the same conclusion: man's state after the fall is no different from what it was before except for the absence of grace. He can therefore fulfill the precepts of the law and avoid sin, although he cannot perform meritoriously. Pighius, for his part, proposed that original sin had been the unilateral rupture of a pact drawn up between God and Adam.[3] As a result, the justice which God had guaranteed the human race has now been lost, but that is the extent of the damage. What law, asked Pighius, can be advanced by which Adam or his descendants are bound to preserve original justice? Even if there were such a law, nobody but Adam could be accused of sinfully breaking it, because only he voluntarily did so.

The sanguine description of fallen human nature which these

2. Jewel, for example, referred sarcastically to Pighius as "the papist captain, the greatest learned man, as it is supoosed." John Jewel, *Works, 1* (Cambridge, 1844–45), 7.

3. This pact, Stapleton observed tartly, is a "fabula." *Justificationis,* p. 34.

theories share can no longer be held by a Catholic. Indeed, said Stapleton, they are no more than disguised resurrections of the ancient heresy of Pelagianism, refuted so completely by St. Augustine. The Council of Trent uncovered it in its new trappings and condemned it as unequivocally as its Protestant opposite number. Original sin (as Stapleton paraphrased the Council) is literally a sin which like other sins can be remitted or not. Sanctity, given freely by God to men, was lost through original sin by the man who committed it and by all his posterity. "It would be heretical," he went on, "and not simply erroneous to defend the opinion of some scholastics that original sin is not properly a sin but rather a state of punishment due to the sin of another . . . or a state of fault."[4] The darkness and disease in which the human spirit labors must be acknowledged if ever they are to be overcome.

Pelagian optimism among certain Catholic theologians had provided Luther and his friends with a decided apologetic advantage, but this was not the only mischief the intellectuals had bequeathed to later foes of Protestantism. Take, for example, said Stapleton, the great John Eck, Luther's first adversary, who had had rhetorically the better of it at the famous disputation of Leipzig in 1519. Presented with the choice between the Scotist and Thomist explanations of original justice (i.e. the question of precisely what had been forfeited by Adam's sin), Eck had chosen to defend the former not out of conviction but out of expediency. The Scotists maintained that Adam's original grace had been a kind of charismatic gift or what one might call an actual grace. The Thomists, on the other hand, taught that the first man had been blessed by a "gratia gratum faciens," a sanctifying grace which included the infusion of supernatural virtue and the elevation of his powers. Now as Luther talked of original sin filling the soul with vice and hatred, Eck, an extremely clever debater, saw at once that St. Thomas' doctrine, superficially at least, might play into his opponent's hands: if original sin meant the privation of sanctifying grace, it meant the concomitant loss of the virtues as well, and the opposite of virtue is vice. Therefore, Eck, instead

4. Ibid., p. 54.

of thoroughly examining the Thomist position, abandoned it at first sight and took up the Scotist, because he then could argue that the loss of original justice did not necessarily imply the loss of virtue. This, to Stapleton, was a shoddy maneuver which resulted at best in Pyrrhic victory.[5]

Stapleton dealt severely with Eck on this point because he felt strongly that St. Thomas' argument, if rightly followed through, provided the best defense against the Protestant theology of original sin. "Certainly," he wrote, "the Protestants wish to include in the spiritual damage done by original sin not merely a privation of original justice, insofar as that means the gift of a rectified nature, and not merely the privation of all the virtues which follow upon such rectification; they are most interested in establishing the positive presence in the soul, really inhering and existing there, of the whole troop of contrary vices. And this is the genuine point of controversy between them and us today."[6] To unravel the problem, particular care had to be taken with the term "privation." The Aristotelian-Thomistic tradition, which Stapleton followed closely here, taught that evil is essentially a negation, the absence of some good. Poor health, for example, means the absence of the proper balance among the various constituents of the body. Moral evil, or sin, is negation also, but it is the absence of a good which ought to be present by reason of divine law and which has been lost through the sinner's free choice. It is therefore a privation. Lust means the absence of chastity, but, since proper control of sexual activity is something dictated by God's law and right reason and is sacrificed voluntarily by the lecher, lust is, strictly speaking, a privation.

Original sin, Stapleton maintained, must be viewed the same way. It is not the positive presence of evil; it is rather the absence of a good which should be present, the good called original justice by the scholastics. It is essentially the privation of God's friendship and the possibility for meritorious action on the part of mankind. Adam, acting for the race he founded, deprived, by

5. Ibid., p. 42.
6. Ibid., p. 41.

his crime, himself and his descendants of the justified state, and all men have been burdened ever since with a "caecitas mentis," a moral and intellectual blindness plunging them helplessly into the void. But here, as in every scholastic explanation, there had to be a material element to accompany the formal. "Caecitas mentis," or the privation of original justice, was teamed with "concupiscentia" to describe the total havoc wreaked by original sin. Concupiscence includes in its definition that classic "weakness of the flesh" experienced by every human being, but, Stapleton warned, only the naïve would restrict it to the simply carnal or sexual context. It means rather the endemic inability of man's higher powers to dominate his lower; individual appetites tend to seek individual satisfaction without regard to the good of the integral personality, discoverable only by reason, and the mind itself responds only feebly to the touch of God's actual grace. Concupiscence, so to speak, fleshes out the spare concept of privation of original justice, but it, too, refers to evil and therefore it, too, is negation and denial.[7]

The picture thus drawn of man's native plight was bleak indeed, but not bleak enough for Luther, who dismissed the carefully structured position as "a dream of Sophists." Look within yourself, he invited, and see if you discover a "caecitas mentis," a "carentia justitiae originalis." Do you really find an abstraction in the midst of your soul, and a negative abstraction at that? Is it a privation which lies at the root of all the contradictions which plague the human spirit, of the pettiness which weighs it down, of the crime of which even the just man is guilty at least seven times daily? Surely, it is a snare for the mind and heart to explain the evil within us in terms of privation, when the image of a rabid animal, uncontrolled in its rush toward a merited self-destruction, would be more appropriate. Is it of privation that the psalmist sang?

> There is none that doth good, no, not one. Their throat is an open sepulchre; with their tongues they acted deceitfully;

7. Ibid., pp. 31, 46 ff.

the poison of asps is under their lips. Their mouth is full of cursing and bitterness; their feet are swift to shed blood. Destruction and unhappiness in their ways; and the way of peace they have not known; there is no fear of God before their eyes. (Psalms, quoted in Rom. 3:12–18)

Original sin, said Luther, if it means anything, means the total corruption of the human personality. If one would employ the scholastic division into formal and material elements, let him take care to use the terms properly: "caecitas mentis" is the positive hatred, contempt, and anger for God, and "concupiscentia" is the total domination of the higher human powers by the lower.[8]

Essentially, Luther, in order to posit the total damage done human nature by original sin, proposed to substitute a metaphor for an abstraction. Stapleton did not fail to see the direction of the attack, nor did he underestimate its potential. The metaphorical approach could marshal some powerful weapons to go along with its natural attractiveness. In facing the problem of human depravity, Stapleton wrote ponderously, "we immediately plunge into the [Protestants'] first line of battle; we strive herein against the phalanx and cohort of all the arguments they are accustomed to advance in this matter."[9]

The Protestants appealed to logic, Scripture, and the Fathers. They put forth first of all a logical argument based on opposition. Even if the Catholic explanation is true to the extent that virtuous operation did indeed follow upon the state of original justice (granted, in other words, a scholastic distinction between Adam's status and the working of his faculties in such a state), the fact remains that the corruption of man's powers involves the introduction of contrary vices. As Stapleton read the Confession of Augsburg, he found the point clearly asserted: if in original justice a man were able to observe both tablets of the law, in original sin he cannot do so. If man were made originally in God's image, he has, since sin, taken on Adam's image and been struck im-

8. Ibid., pp. 56 ff.
9. Ibid., p. 46.

potent with regard to accomplishing good. Various scriptural citations, they continued, will confirm this view. As Stapleton described them, several distinct kinds of passages might be invoked:
those, for example, "which impute sin to nature itself" or "which
appear to posit the mind and will and heart as the subject of sin."
And other parts of the Bible testify to the same thing when they
speak "of the depravity of human nature positively, not privative-
ly," or when they speak of the depravity of the whole man "from
the moment of his conception, in all his parts and members."
Finally, the Protestants turned to the Fathers, to St. Augustine
especially, whose gloomy opinion of sinful mankind was, they
claimed, but a foretaste of their own.[10]

When Stapleton framed his replies to these assertions, he took
care, as a good controversialist must, to say no more than a refutation of his adversary's position demanded. He did not attempt on
each occasion to state fully what he conceived to be the traditional
doctrine but was, rather, content to point out either that the
Protestant argument in question erred in some way or else that it
was no better than one of several possible explanations to hand.
Behind this tactic lay Stapleton's conviction that the Protestants'
greatest intellectual sin and their greatest intellectual weakness
was oversimplification. Thus, with regard to the argument from
opposition, he charged that the Protestants had leaped to a hasty
conclusion. "The injustice originally contracted is not opposed to
original justice as a contrary or a contradictory but only as an opposed alternative." It is not necessary to conclude, therefore, that
the loss of original justice involved the automatic infusion of an
opposite viciousness. And could it not be, he added, as "the fathers
teach clearly and consistently," that the divine image in us "consists in the power of free choice and in the use of reason through
which we excel the beasts" and which, though diminished by
original sin, have not been extinguished?[11]

The same moderate method was employed when Stapleton came
to examine the scriptural arguments brought forward by the

10. Ibid., pp. 46–47.
11. Ibid., p. 61.

Protestants. Indeed, he observed, the Bible imputes sin in many passages to human nature; anyone who can read realizes this. However, the problem is to discover what precisely that expression means with regard to the baptized Christian. Is it not used, and has it not always been used, because, had the rectitude of original justice not been lost, men would not commit sin? Damaged nature is "the remote cause and root" of every moral evil, but the real culprit remains the individual of bad will who chooses to do the evil. Natures cannot commit sin; only persons can. In the same sense, concupiscence burdens the lower human powers and drags a man away from the greater good by dangling before him the particular good. This could not have happened (and in Adam's case did not happen) in a nature rectified by original justice. Even so, it is still the selfish intention, the bad will, which consents to the pull of concupiscence and is the agent of evil. Various scriptural passages describe the spiritual faculties as the subjects of sin, the Protestants maintained. True enough, answered Stapleton, the ignorance of the mind and malice of the will are realities which set up a proclivity toward sin. Such is the clear teaching of St. Paul in many places like, for instance, the fourth and fifth chapters of Ephesians. But a proclivity toward sin is one thing, a necessity to sin quite another. How can the Protestant exegete claim that his interpretation of St. Paul rules out all other possibilities?[12] This question formed part of a tune Stapleton never tired of playing. As he wrote in another context: "We all embrace Scripture. . . . The question today is not about Scripture, nor has this question ever separated Catholics from heretics. Rather, the question is, from whom ought we to receive the Scripture and through whom ought we to understand it?"[13]

This sentiment, shared by all the Counter Reformation theologians and basic to many of the positions they assumed, was very strong in Stapleton. He did not, however, thereby fail to appreciate the biblical scholarship of his opponents. In fact, on this issue of original sin's relationship to human depravity, he paid tribute to

12. Ibid., pp. 61–62.
13. *Relectio*, pp. 508–09.

Calvin and to Martin Chemnitz,[14] who "use the Scriptures in their discussion (of this matter) with the most scrupulous accuracy."[15] So much could not be said, he added quickly, about their appeal to the Fathers. The Protestants had drifted, in his opinion, from a vague attempt to identify themselves with patristic tradition at the time of the Confession of Augsburg to a specific rejection of it, at least on this point, thirty years later. Of all the Fathers, protested the preface to the *Fifth Century* of Magdeburg, only St. Augustine had kept his doctrine of the total corruption of human nature unsullied. But to win St. Augustine, the *Doctor Universalis* who was worth, in the controversial scales, any ten ancients, was to win the war, as Stapleton well knew.[16]

The Protestants, he observed, left only with the testimony of St. Augustine, must approach the writings of that great doctor without refinement and blur their meaning if they are to be of any use. Accordingly, they pounce upon the Augustinian phrase that "man through sin has lost the possibility of accomplishing good." This is literally true, but does it apply, asked Stapleton, with equal force to the unregenerate sinner and to him who has been born anew through Christian baptism? Why do not the Protestants ever fully explain the word "bonum" and why do they not couple with the phrase above another like the following, in which Augustinian literature abounds: "The precepts of justice cannot be fulfilled in their entirety unless we are aided by God." Another favorite Protestant error (and, hinted Stapleton, an error born in malice) was to employ St. Augustine's arguments against the Pelagians as though they had been constructed to oppose traditional Catholic doctrine. Surely, and on every opportunity, the Bishop of Hippo denied the possibility of accomplishing good in the insanely optimistic Pelagian sense. Man cannot merit his own redemption or observe the commandments without special

---

14. One of the most distinguished Lutheran theologians, Martin Chemnitz (1522–86) spent ten years composing his massive *Examen Concilii Tridentini quadripartitum* (1563–73). See *DTC*, 2, Pt. II, cc. 2354–57.

15. *Justificationis*, p. 47.

16. Ibid., p. 106.

divine help, and, said Stapleton, to maintain these things is to be as hopeless (though opposite) a heretic as Luther. The identification of Catholicism with Pelagianism is a myth, exploded long ago, and to attempt to make it in these latter days, Stapleton charged, stems from a slothful reluctance to come to grips with the real issues, a maneuver to set up a straw man which will topple to the ground with a single Lutheran breath.

Stapleton was never a more characteristic sixteenth-century controversialist than when he chided his opponents for their misuse of St. Augustine. As a matter of fact, the saint's vast and unsystematic work, highly influenced by rhetorical considerations and abounding in ad hoc argumentation, provided ample ammunition for Catholic and Protestant alike. Only the Bible, it seemed, could be quoted with more facility on both sides of a question. Witness, for example, the crucial matter of free will. Those who held for the total corruption of human nature could cite Augustine to the effect that "free will has no value except for sinning," while their Catholic adversaries had only to turn a few pages in the same source until they found a statement like this: "A man condemns himself by using his free will badly." Whatever twists and turns the disputants engaged in in their use of sources, it was true that their views about the measure of freedom left to a man infected by original sin lay at the heart of the controversy.

In the Protestant teaching on free will Stapleton discerned an uneven evolution which, to his mind, had still a long way to go.[17] Luther, to employ one of Stapleton's least felicitous expressions, had "consumed the vomit of Wycliff and the Manichees," had constructed a theory which denied free will altogether, and had ironically dubbed that faculty "a title without real foundation."[18] Calvin had tended to parrot this extreme position, and some Lutherans, like Flacius Illyricus, maintained it still, although Melanchthon had softened it a little by "introducing certain subtleties." In any case, said Stapleton, they all agreed that the

17. Ibid., pp. 93 ff.
18. Trent noted this expression in its fifth canon on justification. See DB, p. 296.

Catholic doctrine of merit, connected as it necessarily is to the idea of man's freedom of choice and his cooperation in the process of salvation, should be assailed as Pelagianism. Man, as they saw it, receives grace only passively, and this opinion Trent had explicitly condemned.

The next generation produced a moderate Lutheran party anxious to mitigate the "horrors" (the word is Stapleton's) of the primitive Protestant view without, however, striking the polemically useful anti-Pelagian banner. It counted among its ablest and most articulate spokesmen the German theologian Martin Chemnitz, whom Stapleton described as "singular in cunning and deceit." This phrase, when translated out of the controversial jargon of the day, was a rare compliment, a testimony to the writer's high regard. Chemnitz and his friends proposed a distinction between the first conversion of a man to God and the "new obedience" under which, once converted, he operates. In the former activity the subject remains completely passive; in the latter free choice has its part to play. This theory, observed Stapleton, marked a considerable advance over Luther's, but it was based upon the fallacious assumption that half a heresy is not quite so bad as a whole one. It abounded in double talk. Chemnitz appeared to want to identify his doctrine with Luther's and at the same time free himself from it. In order to do so, he blandly and "impudently" claimed as his own the views of the first Reformers and in the next breath gave away half of their position. Did he do this, Stapleton asked sarcastically, so that he might avoid the anathema of the Council of Trent?[19]

As long as he stubbornly refused to grant free human participation in man's first conversion, Chemnitz was just as heretical, if not quite so barbarous, as the older Protestants nor could the ramifications of this refusal be hidden behind a flurry of words. For Chemnitz had been careful to point out that the passivity of the human being in his reception of grace was not comparable to the functioning of an inanimate instrument. "The mental and volitional activities," he wrote, "which God stirs up in conversion

19. *Justificationis*, pp. 93–94.

are not like the marks left by a seal upon hot wax . . . nor is conversion violent like the hurling of a stone. . . . In one way does a
carpenter employ his lifeless tools, in quite another does the Holy
Spirit work conversion in the mind and heart of man." What was
all this, commented Stapleton, but a rhetorical façade, behind
which lurked the classical Protestant pessimism about sinful human nature. It was moreover an evasion, a grand attempt to turn
the whole controversy over justification from its proper course.
Nobody, neither Luther nor the Fathers of Trent, had quarreled
with the idea that genuine conversion let loose certain "mental
and volitional activities." But the disagreement swirled around
the "quomodo." "How does divine grace excite the mind and will
of man to these movements and activities?" Does it happen solely
through God's action or is some room left for human cooperation?
Here lies the issue which divides us, Stapleton maintained, a
delicate problem, a riddle which touches at once the most human
and divine mysteries.[20]

The Revelation of God in this matter, guarded through the
centuries by his Church, is opposed, Stapleton claimed, to the
Protestant notion with or without Chemnitz' distinction. To say
that God provides aid in the initial conversion of the sinner does
not mean, as the Protestants would have it, that he deprives the
human being of free choice, for to do so would amount to a denial
of his own creative act. A man differs from a horse fundamentally
because, in Augustine's words, "he is free to bend this way or that."
He may choose to cooperate with God's grace or he may choose to
resist it. But there was more to the controversy, as Stapleton well
knew, than a simple statement of differences. In discussing free
will, as well as in almost every related topic, a Catholic had to
beware a tactic as favored by Chemnitz as by Luther. If one denied
the total corruption of human nature and the servility of the will,
did one not thereby commit oneself to their opposites—that is, to
the heady optimism of Pelagius? Consistent with his "cunning,"
Chemnitz tried to involve contemporary Catholicism with ancient

20. Ibid.

Pelagianism, once removed but Pelagianism nonetheless.[21] The dogma defined at the Council, he wrote, repudiated the notion that the will unaided could achieve salvation through a series of good choices, but did it really repudiate Pelagianism? Not at all, said Chemnitz. It merely took a step in the right direction and then stopped. For it declared that once God has stirred and aided ("excitare" and "adjuvare" were Tridentine terms) the human will, the individual can go forward and seize the prize of eternal life. This is what the papists mean when they quote Our Lord, "The kingdom of heaven suffereth violence and the violent shall carry it away," and this is why the papists, all the more since the shallow definitions of Trent, must bear the Augustinian assaults against the Pelagians.[22]

It can be readily seen from this that "papist" polemic in the late sixteenth century had the task of keeping two balky horses abreast of one another; there might have resulted an impossible tangle if the positive statement of Catholic doctrine had outrun the refutation of the Pelagian charge, or vice versa. Stapleton began this arduous business by advancing what he called "solid proofs" that the salvation of man, even in his first conversion, depended upon a balance between grace and free choice. He shrewdly made use of Scripture as interpreted by St. Augustine, the ancient foe of Pelagius. First he noted that Scripture's habit of command is itself a testimony to the freedom of the human will. "As often as the Bible orders us to do something, so often is our free will moved to action," so often have the alternatives of good and evil action been presented to us. Scripture provides another argument because it speaks so frequently of reward and punishment. As St. Augustine wrote in response to certain "extremists" who, in combat with the Pelagians, had denied free will (and Stapleton must have smiled as he made this citation): "If there

21. "By this dark maneuver they obscure things for the eyes of the inexperienced, and by devices and deceits like this today's Protestants alter the orthodox doctrine. And among them nobody is better at this than that proud Censor, Martin Chemnitz." *Justificationis*, p. 91.

22. Ibid., p. 96.

is no grace of God, then how will He save the world? If there is no free choice, how will He judge the world?" There is no explaining reward and punishment in the Bible without free will, said Stapleton, except to make God (and not perverse human choice) the author of every evil. And this blasphemy Luther, Calvin, and Chemnitz have been guilty of. Finally, human nature dictates the same conclusion. If God dealt his grace out by force instead of offering it to us made in his image and likeness, we would be no different from sheep.[23]

Stapleton did not claim any particular originality for these arguments, and he realized that none of them was new to Chemnitz. It did not surprise him that he had immediately to meet the charge that he (together with those who argued as he did) was a crypto-Pelagian. So long as the words of the Bible were the only authority, he could do little more than repeat wearily over and over: a Pelagian argument can indeed be constructed from these texts, but it is not our argument; we maintain the cooperation between grace and free will, not the independence of one from the other. He faced at the same time the almost endless list of texts brought forward by the Protestants to demonstrate the mortal sickness of the human will. "What have you that you have not received?" St. Paul demanded of the Corinthians. "No one can come to me," Our Lord said, "unless my Father drag him." And the God of Israel proclaimed through the Prophet Ezechiel: "I will take away your heart of stone and give you a heart of flesh." Stapleton shrugged at these impressive biblical citations. They are all very well, he wrote, and useful and true, and if we were Pelagians they would surely render our position untenable. But only (and here he addressed the Protestants, and Chemnitz in particular) if you can verify the false accusation of Pelagianism, can you use these texts against us. You have marshaled your forces against an enemy defeated and discredited by the Bishop of Hippo a thousand years ago. "You have proved the infirmity of nature; you have proved nothing against its liberty."[24]

23. Ibid., pp. 96–97.
24. Ibid., p. 99.

The freedom of the Christian man, and therefore the true measure of the damage wrought upon his will by original sin, must be viewed, Stapleton explained, in relation to the manifold works of God. There are three distinct types of divine activity which relate directly to human justification. "First are those works which precede . . . even in time our justification, and thus are properly God's so that our liberty plays no part in them, neither by way of consent nor by way of cooperation." Included here, and shrouded in deepest mystery, are the eternal and immutable decrees of predestination and vocation. Also under this heading are acts whereby God "sometimes" reveals things to individuals, whether extrinsically through the senses' natural grasp of phenomena (Hopkins' "The world is charged with the grandeur of God. It will flame out, like shining from shook foil.") or intrinsically through inspiration. With regard to these activities, Stapleton said, we are wholly passive. They are gratuitous graces; they represent a "divine motion" and are what St. Augustine had in mind when he wrote: "God so works that we will without ourselves." Together they make up what is called prevenient grace, and they bring us to the point at which it is possible for us to choose in a "holy fashion, without any anticipatory activity of our will" or, to use a phrase Stapleton personally disliked, without any prior merit. But, lest one imitate Chemnitz and leap from this to an unwarranted conclusion, Stapleton spelled out carefully what was involved:

> It might be mistakenly gathered that first conversion is accomplished by God alone and then afterwards a new obedience or observance of the commandments comes about with God aiding and ourselves cooperating. This is not the case. Rather the doctrine of prevenient grace means that if one who formerly willed badly should now choose well, this is God's work and his alone.[25]

25. Ibid., pp. 105–06.

Stapleton advanced another set of divine works which were just as completely God's own. Habitual or sanctifying grace and the infused theological virtues through which, he said, we are rendered truly pleasing in God's sight or, in the technical language of the schools, through which we are "formally justified," do not depend upon human choice. Grace in this sense (*gratia gratum faciens*) means the participation in the divine life which God imparts to the spirits of individual men, and only the Giver of that life can determine what it will be and how it will operate. Again, the human response can be only passive and humble in the face of this inestimable gift. No man shapes the faith and charity within him nor does he direct the faculties now raised to a divine level, "for they," as Stapleton put it simply, "are purely supernatural."[26]

There is, finally, a third kind of divine activity which, as it aims toward our justification, calls forth a concomitant human activity. Our cooperation, Stapleton explained, is not involved in God's predestination, but it is necessary in the multitude of choices of means presented to us once God moves us toward himself. God chooses us; we do not choose God. But as befits the intellectual nature of man, we stand at a perpetual crossroad, forced to select the avenue which will lead us to Him and to the happiness only He can give. The Pelagian was confident that he could choose the correct way unaided and unerringly. The Protestant (according to Stapleton) did not want to choose at all; he was prepared to forfeit the greatest dignity of his nature in exchange for the certainty that, after all, there was only one road. The Catholic, on the other hand, abandons both these illusions and, to make the proper decision, he puts into play his precious freedom and, at the same time, calls upon God's special help, "gratia cooperans." He will never be as sure of himself as either the Pelagian or the Protestant, but this is the great risk involved in freedom, the price one must pay for one's human nature. Likewise, sanctifying grace is a free gift of God in which our cooperation remains nil, but, as the principles of meritorious acts, habitual grace and the in-

26. Ibid., p. 106.

fused virtues call upon free will and cooperating grace for fulfillment. "With our free will," said Stapleton, "we believe and love in act; and the same is true of the other infused virtues."[27]

As he tried to unravel the thorny problem of the relationship between omnipotence and freedom, Stapleton aimed primarily at maintaining a delicate balance. Not one factor was at work, he said, but two, and, to his mind, only an explanation which took account of both would satisfy all the scriptural texts (and not just isolated ones) as well as the ancient and traditional teaching of the Church. The Pelagian, with his sunny disposition, upset the equilibrium from one side and the gloomy Protestant did the same from the other. One minimized the effects of original sin and the other exaggerated them, but neither acted out of bad will (though Stapleton, for rhetorical purposes, pretended to think they did). Rather, they missed the mark, one to the right and the other to the left of true center, because of an understandable intellectual failing. This, leaving aside the invective, is the heart of Stapleton's charge against them both. *Deus solum simplex.* Life outside God is a complicated business, and the human spirit longs for simplicity. In the realm of thought this means that a man automatically prefers the explanation which explains everything in one fell swoop. He avoids, if he can, distinctions and subtleties which draw him into long and dreary labors. He is impatient to see the truth, and he wants to see it now. His gravest intellectual temptation, therefore, is to brush away complicated arguments and plunge headlong into the intoxicating waters of intuition. As long as truth reflects life as we know it, however, it will be made up of propositions, of subjects joined to predicates. The human condition being what it is, the whole truth cannot be expressed in one glorious shout, nor can even a small part of it. To tip the balance, to oversimplify, is a sin crying to heaven for vengeance.

27. Ibid., p. 107.

Chapter 6

SOLA FIDES

The "principium proprium et propinquum controversiarum," to use Thomas Stapleton's expression, was the new doctrine of justification. The Protestants had begun by confusing original sin itself with its effects. This had led to the theory that original sin amounted to nothing less than the total perversion of human nature, that man was corrupt body and soul. After awhile it became a commonplace with the Protestants to assert that original sin is a corruption so deep and so all-pervading that it could not in any sense be considered accidental. "It is the very heart of man, his reason and all his powers, as Flacius Illyricus said was Luther's view."[1] The "fear of that justice by which God punishes sinners" had started Luther down his tortuous path; the doctrine of total depravity was a natural consequent of a desire to be free of such fear. A man could hope for nothing from his helplessly sinful self, but what might he not attain in the merits of God's own Son? Perhaps God would pretend he was "as just and obedient and holy as Christ himself was."[2] Salvation came as a result of the imputation of Christ's merit to the human spirit, not through any amelioration effected in that spirit. The technical language, in this instance at least, is illuminating: the process called justification had, in the new theory, an extrinsic, not an intrinsic, significance. And the instrument that made it work was faith and faith only.

We for whom the theological quarrels of the sixteenth century (and perhaps theological quarrels as such) have become largely

1. *Justificationis,* p. 40.
2. Ibid., pp. 6, 9.

academic might well judge the gulf between the two sides, created
by their divergent doctrines about original sin, too vast for further
meaningful debate. It did not appear so to those engaged, and
Stapleton, like the other disputants, pressed his arguments forward
to what he called, curiously enough, "that noblest and most excellent consideration of all," justification by faith alone.[3] Characteristically, he began his treatment with distinctions, always so
dear to his scholastic heart:

> There seem to me to be three headings under which this
> material can be discussed. First is the meaning of faith as
> understood by the various sects when they maintain that we
> are justified by only faith and also in what orthodox sense
> faith is said to justify. Secondly, inquiry should be made into
> the degree to which the various sects eliminate the need for
> good works. And finally something must be said about the
> heretical as well as the orthodox teaching about the manner
> in which faith justifies.[4]

To grasp the enemy's definition of faith struck Stapleton as of
the first importance. Luther had proposed a simple one to begin
with: "for him faith was equivalent to a firm belief in God's
promises and a good opinion of God's truthfulness, etc." In their
debates with Catholics, Luther's disciples had brandished the
master's statement like a weapon, and, if they phrased it differently
on occasion, it remained substantially the same, enshrined in the
fourth article of the Confession of Augsburg: faith is "not simply
a knowledge of past events, but also the assent to a promise in
which for Christ's sake remission of sins, justification and eternal
life are guaranteed us." But, said Stapleton, "this definition did
not satisfy these new teachers for long." In order to shore it up,
they introduced the notion of "acceptance" of the promise made
by God, a subtlety for which Philip Melanchthon was chiefly
responsible. There is at work, therefore, in the act of faith not
just the intellect but also the will. Stapleton recognized that this

3. Ibid., p. 235.
4. Ibid., p. 241.

did not alter Luther's original idea essentially; it was really, he observed, a clarification of Luther's chronically careless terminology. The task of framing for the theory its "fullest" definition of faith was likewise left to the scholarly author of the *Loci communes:* "Faith is the assent to every word God proposes to us and, what is more, to the promise of gratuitous reconciliation given us on account of Christ's mediation, and it is also trust [*fiducia*], for the same reason, in the pledge of God's mercy." This accent upon the fiduciary element—that is, upon the part played in the act of faith by the will—appeared to Stapleton as the position of "almost all the Lutherans who today call themselves Confessionists," nor did he discern any but minor verbal differences in the position taken on the subject by the old-line "Stoical" Lutherans like Flacius Illyricus or by the moderate revisionists led by Chemnitz.[5]

This distinction between the intellectual and volitional reaction to faith possessed an immediate controversial importance. The Protestants agreed that faith meant in part an assent of the mind. As an example, Stapleton quoted Flacius Illyricus: "True and justifying faith is knowledge." More explicitly, they agreed that this was a "knowledge of past events," as the Confession of Augsburg expressed it, an historical knowledge of God's dealing with men. "When they come to divide faith into its parts," Stapleton explained, "they do not treat it as a genus divisible into species but rather as an equivocal expression which can signify variously this historical faith or faith in miracles or faith in God's promises." Whenever they speak of a "general assent to the word of God," it is historical faith that they have in mind, and they object to the Catholics' definition of faith, because it restricts itself, they claim, to this factor alone: "they would persuade their hearers that Catholic faith is nothing more than the historical knowledge of Scripture and of other matters accepted intellectually on the testimony of the Church, much in the way one accepts the historical work of Titus Livy." From this poverty-stricken notion the Protestants piously insisted they must flee. "Our adversaries,"

5. Ibid., pp. 236–37.

sniffed Melanchthon, "imagine that faith is a knowledge of history." Or as Calvin put it: "A large proportion of Christians, when they hear the word 'faith,' think it only a sort of vulgar assent to evangelical history."[6]

Stapleton branded this accusation a "calumnia putidissima." All the world knows, he said, that, for Catholics, faith is a theological virtue, having God himself not only as object but as bestower as well. Catholics have always held to the "celebrated" division of faith into infused and acquired, "the one divine and Christian, the other human and historical." "Perhaps," he added, one could argue "that the calumny is really an error," because those intellectual villains, Durandus and Gabriel Biel, taught a fantastic doctrine that a Christian without the infused virtue of faith could still "firmly believe all that had been revealed by God through the sole testimony of the Church." Yet the universal repudiation of these authors on this point, a hundred years before Luther, led Stapleton to suppose that Melanchthon and Calvin knew better than to identify this fable with genuine Catholic doctrine. The charge of calumny, he asserted, must stand. Besides, did not all the Protestants admit intellectual assent as part of their definition? Then why did they maintain that for Catholics it was "vulgar" while for them it was divinely inspired? They did so, said Stapleton, answering his own question, in order to calumniate the orthodox position and to render it ludicrous.[7] As these men turn everything topsy-turvy, he commented in another context, they ought to be called not reformers, a grand and prestigious title, but transformers.[8]

Most polemical invective is beside the point, and so it was in this instance. Whether the Protestants cynically caricatured the Catholic explanation or simply misunderstood it mattered much less than their own assertion that "general assent to the word of God" was in any case insufficient. The faith which justifies, they said, is a special act with a special object. Indeed, it presupposes

6. Ibid., pp. 249–50.
7. Ibid.
8. *Speculum*, p. 394.

(as Stapleton read the Protestant line of argumentation) a more general assent, and it exists within a "universal" framework which by itself, however, stands empty and useless. Martin Chemnitz explained it this way:

> Faith . . . embraces the whole range of God's word, but nevertheless it discovers in Scripture . . . an object which is certainly and peculiarly its own . . . and in respect of which it accomplishes justification. . . . [This object] is the gratuitous promise of mercy and remission for the sake of Christ. In this object alone does faith truly justify; in the other objects or articles of faith this is not so. They however are not unimportant, because the absolutely necessary article of redemption in Christ could not be perfectly grasped without them, and because, if faith in them were weak, then faith in it would suffer too.[9]

Chemnitz' statement, said Stapleton, could be found in the other prominent Protestant authors in other words. And they shared arguments advanced to prove a point like the following one, scrutinized by Stapleton. There are many objects of belief, enumerated in Scripture, which have nothing to do with justification. The gospel narrative, for example, which describes comings and goings together with the most solemn events, those parts of the Bible which talk about sin and punishment or which demand obedience—none of this, though truly the Word of God, relates directly to our reconciliation with Him. Now obviously faith cannot find in Scripture what is not there, and so it follows that not every object which faith embraces brings about justification, but only that which, by assenting to it, makes the divine mercy operative. "Even the history [of Christ's passion]," Philip Melanchthon wrote in the *Loci communes,* "only increases the desperation . . . of the sinner as it does of the damned. For what more terrible sign of God's wrath could there be than that the death of no other

9. Chemnitz' *Examen Concilii Tridentini quadripartitum* as quoted in *Justificationis,* p. 251.

victim but his Son could placate him."[10] With regard to the passages in the Bible which excoriate men for their sins, what do they, asked Chemnitz, "but set before us the wrath and hatred of God for sinners?" The faith that truly justifies must stand aside finally from those passages which prescribe obedience to the commandments, "because [in Stapleton's words] the condition of perfect fulfillment is attached to the promises of the law, and this, with our injured nature, cannot be accomplished." It must be concluded, therefore, that justifying faith has to do only with assent to "reconciliation with God, peace of conscience, and eternal life."[11]

It will come as no surprise to learn that for Stapleton this line of reasoning fairly bulged with error. At the root of it lay the Protestants' bland assumption "that the whole problem of justification is solved by the initial act of reconciliation with God" which, as a matter of fact, is "only the beginning of our justification or, more precisely, a part of that operation by which one takes the first step from impiety to righteousness; they propose therefore that justifying faith has force and function only in this one step" and so they deny, without discussing the point, that it really operates throughout the various steps of one's religious experience. Just as argumentative, said Stapleton, is the assertion that the process of justification does not work any interior change in the subject, that there is, in other words, no such thing as "inherent justice." What a weird and fantastic structure has been raised upon these foundation stones. Protestants, Stapleton maintained, must relapse into Manichaeism and teach that "Christian man is always in a state of mortal sin, always locked in the struggle between sin and conscience and thus (!) always saved so long as he apprehends, through faith, the mercy of God, always confident of salvation, even when mired in sin and vice." How different is this doctrine from the wholesome (and traditional) fact that the faithful "labor through their sins of infirmity constantly in need of the remission which comes from Christ." In Stapleton's view,

10. Ibid., p. 252.
11. Ibid.

the Protestants had oversimplified even their major oversimplification: "They err also in this, most gravely, that they do not consider the different functions of justifying faith even in the first justification, which is the only one they admit, and they are satisfied merely to repeat that Christ died for our sins." Finally, Stapleton lodged his basic complaint about the Protestant distinction which gave a special and unique place to justifying faith.

> Faith by nature is one, whether it embraces the word of God as the history of things accomplished or threats of retribution or promises of mercy. . . . The Protestants destroy the real meaning of faith by introducing the notion of a special as opposed to a general faith, the former concerned with God's promise of redemption and the latter with everything else. For faith by nature and species is one virtue which has all these things as its various objects. And all of them play their parts in the business of justification. Thus, for example, if the Protestant notion is allowed to stand, faith in miracles will disappear. For faith accepts the miracles of Christ and the Church in the same way it accepts other objects. And the faith which works miracles is not a distinct or special faith. . . . It is greater and more acute, more intense of course, but it does not differ from the common faith in its object or in its assent.[12]

"Who will deliver me from the body of this death?" Justifying faith, chorused the Protestants, is the only instrument of deliverance, and by this they meant, in a severely limited way, a trustful acceptance of God's promises of mercy and reconciliation. They shrugged at Stapleton's charge that they had "lacerated" the genuine Christian notion of faith, and, when he noted that their position involved the severance of virtuous works from the plan of salvation, they rapturously agreed. A man cannot be saved through observance of the law, because to be saved thereby he cannot break even the slightest of the commandments. As a matter of fact, nobody has ever kept the most important precepts of the law, much

12. Ibid., p. 253.

less the picayune. How, therefore, can good works be the vehicles of justification?

According to the Protestant polemic, the two most patent instances of the law's impossibility of fulfillment were, first, the injunction to love God "ex toto corde" and, secondly, the solemn conclusion of the decalogue, "Thou shalt not covet." Who is there, the Protestants asked triumphantly, who has not preserved at least a small corner of his heart to love something other than God and who is there who has not for even a passing instant wanted his neighbor's lands or house or wife? The same impossibility extends also, the Protestants maintained, to other, less august, of God's commands; none of them obliges in this life, but, rather, each in its own way shows us our weakness and bids us flee to Christ to find righteousness. In his commentary on the "great commandment," Calvin expressed the common doctrine: "From this summary [of the law and the prophets] it appears that God in the precepts of the law does not regard what men can do but what they ought to do. For in the infirmity of the flesh it is not possible that perfect love of God should win for us the kingdom. We know how prone are all our senses to vanity." Stapleton's reply to this piece of exegesis was direct and, for him, unusually terse: "This is a pernicious and pestilential teaching, expressed crudely and obscurely. God does not indeed in the precepts of the law demand what men can do of themselves, by their own strength, but what they can and therefore ought to do, perfected by the aid of his grace."[13]

Stapleton contended that the Protestant error to which could be traced any number of "calumnies" was "not that the just God demands from the human race the most exact obedience to his law, for this is true. . . . If God were to judge man with a severe judgment, no human justice could stand in the face of it." But it is also true, he continued, that this exact obedience is not violated by venial faults, "because such transgressions are perpetually condoned; and therefore (what the Protestants do not want to admit)

13. *Antidota evangelica*, p. 83.

all remaining obedience to the law, whereby mortal sin is avoided and the other commandments which produce rectitude if not perfection are observed, is the kind of justice which can stand in the face of God's judgment."[14] Whatever scriptural citations the Protestants might advance to prove the universality (and hence the nonobservance) of the law,[15] the fact remains, said Stapleton, "that we should see our weakness and learn to flee to Christ . . . in this sense, that we implore the grace of Christ by which the law, even in this life, can be fulfilled."[16]

Certain scriptural passages gave the Protestants not a little difficulty in defending their notions in this regard, and Stapleton was quick to point them out. He quoted, for example, the following comment of Calvin on Our Lord's direction to the rich young man to "keep the commandments":[17]

> One must take note of the form which the young man's question took. He does not simply ask how or what he should follow to find life, but what good he can do to acquire it. Therefore, he is thinking unrealistically of merits by which eternal life will be handed to him, as if of due compensation. Wherefore, Christ appropriately refers him to the observation of the law. . . . These words have been badly interpreted by some of the ancients[18] whom the papists have followed, as if Christ were teaching here that we can attain eternal life through the observance of the law. But Christ did not consider what men can do; he answered the question as though it had been asked: what would the righteousness of works be, or, what does the law define?

14. *Justificationis*, p. 200.

15. In *Justificationis*, pp. 196–98 Stapleton listed some of the favorite Protestant texts: Deut. 27:26, Gal. 3:10, Matt. 5:18, James 2:10.

16. *Justificationis*, p. 191.

17. Matt. 19:16–17. "And behold, one came and said to him: Good Master, what shall I do that I may have life everlasting? Who said to him: Why askest thou me concerning good? One is good, God. But if thou wouldst enter into life, keep the commandments."

18. "He ought to say all of them unanimously," Stapleton interpolated at this point in the quotation. *Antidota evangelica*, pp. 64–65.

Calvin, as Stapleton understood him, tried to ease his way out of the difficulty imposed by Our Lord's clear expression by juggling the passage in such a way that the answer "Serva mandata" would be directed simply to the young man's "What good shall I do?" and not to the additional, troublesome phrase, "that I may have life everlasting."

Pressed by the language of Scripture in this fashion, the Protestants, said Stapleton, set down the second foundation of their doctrine of the impossibility of justice: nobody can make proper satisfaction in this life because whatever renovation might be accomplished therein cannot be perfect or complete but only "incohate."[19] The Protestants introduced this "new distinction" in order to explain scriptural citations about good men and their good works; good works indeed had a measure of justice but an "incohate" and highly imperfect justice, because they did not and could not adequately reflect the true justice, that of Christ, imputed to them.[20] Stapleton believed the expression of two kinds of justice, used by some of the Fathers in their Scripture commentaries, gave the Protestants occasion to employ this "fictitious distinction"; they studiously pointed out the difference between the "forum iudicii divini" and the "forum approbationis hominum," between the "forum severae justitiae" and the "forum gratiae," and between the "forum operum" and the "forum personae." Whichever pair of names was used, the former meant that divine judgment whereby the most exact obedience to the whole law is demanded, while the latter referred to "the grace and favor of God," given as a reward. All this apparatus, Stapleton maintained, "has been invented out of their own minds" in order to "elude the sane doctrine of the Church and the Fathers." His complaint was consistent: the Protestants in this matter had again oversimplified a complex problem and attempted to separate what cannot be separated. There is mercy and justice in God, a fundamental gratuity in his relationships with men, but there is also a just reward for merit, and all these factors play a part in the "unique tribunal"

19. *Justificationis,* p. 172.
20. Ibid., p. 200.

of God. So Flacius Illyricus displayed great foolishness when he charged Catholics with "ignoring the judgment and justice of God, and extenuating the severity of the law." It is not, submitted Stapleton, so simple as that.[21]

The Protestant position rested upon the obvious failure of human beings to accomplish perfect justice through good acts of their own doing. Does this not imply, then, Stapleton asked, the need of a perfection of that faith with which the justice of Christ imputed to us is apprehended? This must have been the kind of faith which Philip demanded of the eunuch.[22] If such is the case, what happens to the Protestants' sacramental theology, with its contention that the sacraments have value only "to sustain, confirm and strengthen the weakness of our faith?" What about Calvin's flat assertion that "no one of the sons of men ever attains the perfection of faith in this life?"[23] This confusion originated in the heretics' failure to recognize the true nature of the New Covenant. "I agree," Calvin had written, "that since God promises the reward of eternal life to those who observe the law, this path must be followed, unless some infirmity of our nature should prevent it. . . . And if anyone objects that it is in vain to propose righteousness to us in a law which nobody can master, my answer is that the law is by no means superfluous, because it is the beginning by which we are led to a precarious kind of justice." Thus, said Stapleton, Calvin makes it appear that mankind is still under the law promulgated to the Jews, which was indeed a beginning, a "rudimentum" in man's search for grace. But now grace has come in the person of Christ, and the law, as fulfilled by him, lies before his followers, "a direct road to eternal life." Calvin's presupposition (his frame of reference, one might say) that human frailty made observance of the law impossible prompted him to

21. Ibid., pp. 198–99.
22. Acts 8:36–37. "And the eunuch said, See, here is water; what doth hinder me from being baptized? And Philip said, If thou believest with all thy heart thou mayest. And he, answering, said, I believe that Jesus Christ is the Son of God."
23. *Justificationis*, p. 200, citing *Institutes*, IV.14.7.

see that law only in its Mosaic context, unblessed by the grace of Christ. For this fallacious view of the inadequacy of the good man's good works, Stapleton found an ancient parallel:

> This preposterous affectation of the Protestants has some similarity to the madness of the Stoics. For the latter would not admit that a man advancing in wisdom was in any sense wise until he had entirely perfected himself in it. . . . So also the Protestants say that the baptized advancing in justice do not really have justice until they are perfectly just, until, that is, they observe most exactly the whole law. Since they do not see perfect observance accomplished in this life, they want us all to be clothed instead with the imputed justice of Christ, through only faith apprehending it, and thus to be justified.[24]

Stapleton found it difficult to keep patience with men who feigned to see no difference between a pang of concupiscence and an act of adultery.

If any Catholic were asked to describe precisely what the process of justification involved, he would answer that as far as the human soul is concerned a twofold change is effected: the remission of sin and the concomitant infusion of grace. Central to the Protestant theology, Stapleton explained, is a denial of the second factor. Justification meant "remissio peccatorum tantum," and the existence in the soul of a quality inherent or infused is a fable. The Protestants claimed that Scripture clearly supported their view. The Publican had gone "down to his house justified" not for any good he had done or even was capable of doing (for by popular definition his office made him a bad man) but simply because he had owned himself a sinner and had asked for mercy.[25] St. Paul wrote to the Corinthians that "God indeed was in Christ reconciling the world to himself, not imputing to them their sins."[26] Therefore, since reconciliation occurs solely through the

24. *Justificationis,* p. 199.
25. *Antidota apostolica,* p. 525.
26. II Cor. 5:19.

remission of sins, so only through that same remission does justification take place.[27]

This line of thought had, as Stapleton clearly recognized, staggering practical consequences, and it provided the Protestants, he said, with their "argumentum potentissimum." Man's injustice to God is a debt, and so justification will be a remission or condonation of the debt of sin, which has nothing at all to do with the infusion of virtue into the soul. This condonation must include the debt of guilt as well as the debt of punishment. Christ accomplished through his passion and death, through his obedience and his other virtues, man's reconciliation. In other words, the debt described in Scripture has been condoned through the earthly activity of God's own Son. It is therefore blasphemous to deny that man's justice is anything less than that most perfect righteousness of Christ himself.[28] "The most grave and the most characteristic error of the heretics of our time," wrote Stapleton, "is to teach that the justice of the Christian man, through which he is accepted into eternal life, is only that most perfect justice and obedience of Christ himself, imputed by God, and through this imputation made proper to anyone believing." Through confidence in God's promises, or faith in the Protestant sense, the wonderful works of Christ become our works, and so much is this taken for granted as the heart of Protestant doctrine, Stapleton said, that the condemnation of it at Trent brought forth the "incredible charge that Catholics have robbed of its efficacy the death of Christ."[29]

Here, then, was the *raison* of justification by only faith. No man really changed by reason of it; formally—that is, in his own essential constitution—he remained exactly as he had been before, a helpless criminal faced with a law he cannot possibly keep. Reconciliation meant only that God overlooked his sins or, one might say, condoned them and regarded as sufficient satisfaction

27. *Justificationis*, pp. 146–49.

28. Ibid., p. 147, quoting Flacius Illyricus "fere ad verbum," as Stapleton put it.

29. Ibid., p. 215.

the sacrifice of his Son. But most important of all, a man really was just (hence Stapleton's use of the technical word "formaliter") because he had found a way of seizing upon the justice of Christ and applying it to himself: the instrument he used to do this was faith. "Faith," Luther had said, "apprehends Christ, who is the form which distinguishes and informs it, like color does a wall. Thus, our formal justice . . . is our faith in something we cannot see, Christ Himself."[30] Whatever doctrinal differences might separate the various Protestant sects, they agreed at least on this. In commenting on the first chapter of Romans, Theodore Beza made clear that he did not distinguish the expression "justitia Dei" in any way: the two words mean that "integritas summa" whereby God is himself holy and just. If this, wrote Stapleton, the "justice of God," is communicated to us through Christ, if this is what formally makes us righteous, "then imputation follows of necessity or some other like pretense." The germ of divine life really inhering in the human soul, that quality called grace which admits of growth and diminution, of loss even and recovery, the formal cause of justification (as Catholics had always believed, long before they made use of that technical term) certainly did not pretend to transmit the "integritas summa" of Almighty God.[31]

The new theory of justification explained for Stapleton many of the events of his time which at first glance might seem to bear little relationship to it. What had the burnings at Smithfield or the riots in Antwerp to do with the subtleties of "remissio peccatorum tantum" or "gratia cooperans?" The answer, a gloomy one for both sides, was woefully clear. If there were no possibility (and, indeed, no necessity) for the gradual but real renovation of the human spirit, the delicate machinery of the old Church was a fraud, its sacraments meaningless, its discipline (save as a purely accidental phenomenon) useless. If what the Protestants taught about justification were true, Christians had dwelt, for a thousand years or more, in unspeakable superstition and under unparalleled

30. Ibid., p. 132.
31. *Antidota apostolica,* pp. 523–24.

tyranny. If, on the other hand, the Protestants were indeed what Stapleton called them, "a few apostate friars and monks" who had infected Christendom with their "upstart news"[32] and had thus deprived countless Christians of their birthright, they had to be resisted with every possible weapon. Arguments might rage about the canon law or liturgical ceremonies, or even about the matters most sacred to a Christian, such as the doctrine of the Eucharist. At the root of them all lay the quarrel over justification. Stapleton, for one, never doubted that this was the central issue, that nothing else would be settled until it had been settled: "[The Protestants'] pestilent doctrine has denied the reformation of the interior man, making this unnecessary for salvation; they have as well fallen into . . . terrible schism by daring to judge the Church from outside, instead of deliberating with it and within it."[33]

32. *Fortresse*, pp. 130, 285.
33. *Speculum*, p. 396.

Chapter 7

THE NEW ECCLESIASTICAL POLITY

The problems surrounding the mystery of Christian justification
do not admit of easy solution, and no one can be surprised when
in any era of the Church's history complex debates arise in connection with them. The difference between debate and schism,
however, is enormous. The Protestants, wrote Thomas Stapleton
in 1565, "be all at variance and defiance one with another. Not
as *concurrentes* do in Italy for learning's sake, but as heretics do
among Catholics for honor and glory's sake. Not upon quirks
and subtleties in matters indifferent as schoolmen that hold positions, but upon the weightiest articles of our belief, as heretics are
wont to hold opinions."[1] The Reformers had rejected what had
been heretofore a generally accepted final court of appeal, which,
if it could not in these complicated and mysterious matters supply
an entirely satisfactory answer, could nevertheless be counted
upon to decide in complete conformity with the doctrine Jesus
Christ had revealed to his apostles. The profound changes worked
in the Christian's life by the theory of justification by only faith
were accompanied by a new notion about the nature of the Church
and, more specifically, about the authority exercised by the Church.
However often the Protestants denied it, it remained a basic assumption among Counter Reformation Catholic polemicists, like
Stapleton, that the new churches had been founded solely to
provide a refuge for the new justification theories.

This was, needless to say, a simplistic view of Protestant ecclesiology, but in Stapleton's case it was a view relentlessly ad-

1. *Fortresse,* p. 260.

hered to. Why else, he demanded, did the Reformers put the Scriptures to a use never before dreamed of? What else could explain their bickering and their fragmentation into new parties and institutions at the slightest disagreement? Martin Luther, that "monachus scrupulosus,"[2] had solved his personal problems with a new definition of the relationship between God and redeemed mankind, and, when his ecclesiastical superiors had chided him, he had reacted by burning the books of the canon law. In effect, Calvin, Bullinger, and the others had done the same thing. Wherever Stapleton looked, he saw the same small clique repeated over again, university people mostly and clerics for whom celibacy was an intolerable burden. He saw "a few apostate friars and monks, Martin Luther, Peter Martyr, Bucer, Barlow, Barnes,"[3] an "unhappy brood of fellows" spawned by "grandsire Luther and the heavenly conjunction of him and a nun together."[4] These frivolous men founded the new churches, preached "the ragged new gospel," "erected the kingdom of sin." They threw off the traditional authority because it disagreed with them, and they proceeded whimsically to set up new ones to satisfy themselves.

Central to Stapleton's thesis was a chronological argument: only when the new justification theories had been advanced did a readjustment of ecclesiastical polity appear necessary. Luther in the beginning (as Stapleton understood him) "had been so impressed by the authority of the Church that it seemed to him impossible to contradict this singular fact."[5] As his theories developed, however, and as he met with increasing resistance to them, he set aside this scruple, and, as he explained to Erasmus, concluded that error had never indeed infected the Church, but error

2. This phrase (*Justificationis*, p. 5) Stapleton employed in his summary of Melanchthon's famous account of Luther's conversion. It is surely more sympathetic than Peter Canisius' description of Luther as "porcus subans." See James Brodrick, *Saint Peter Canisius* (New York, 1935), p. 756.

3. *Fortresse*, p. 130. Aside from the charm of alliteration, which Stapleton could seldom resist, one might conclude that Barlow was listed because, as Bishop of Chichester, he had been instrumental in Stapleton's deprivation.

4. *Counterblast*, fol. 420.

5. *Principiorum*, p. 5.

had very much corrupted the institution which men habitually called the Church. "The essential definition of the Church," so Stapleton quoted him, "is this: the Church is that gathering of people where God dwells so efficaciously that he makes us enter through it into the kingdom." Out of this vague description, said Stapleton, one could deduce the three characteristics of all Protestant thinking on the nature of the Church: that the Church is composed only of the Elect (or, in the theory's most extreme statement, only of the Perfect), that the Elect include only a few of the world's inhabitants at any one time, and that, finally, the Church and its members are indiscernible to ordinary observation.[6]

Stapleton once described how this idea had worked itself out in various Protestant practices when confronted with a scriptural text which appeared to vest in a definite ecclesiastical organization a very definite power of decision. Our Lord had instructed his disciples in the method to be followed in the delicate matter of fraternal correction. He had said that after discreet use had been made of ordinary and private counsel, and in vain, witnesses should be summoned and an attempt at correction made in their presence. If this too should fail, Our Lord had said, "tell the Church. And if he will not hear the Church, let him be to thee as the heathen and the publican."[7] "Everybody understands," wrote Stapleton, "that Christ in this passage has established ecclesiastical discipline and censure, but what ought to be understood by the word 'Ecclesia' has certainly not been rightly grasped by all. Today's heretics, in order to subvert ecclesiastical discipline, which they see is exercised by prelates, and thus keep themselves immune from censure . . . have prepared new interpretations for this passage." Some of them, he went on, attribute this authority to the whole congregation, both because the word "Ecclesia" means a group or a congregation, and, more importantly, because these verses have reference to a public censure. "For Christ (they say) ascended step by step from a private exhortation to the use

6. Ibid., p. 15.
7. Matt. 18:15–18.

of two or three people, and from the witnesses to the Church."
Unless the Church included more than two or three people, there
would be a retrogression rather than an advancement in publicity.
The congregation of the faithful referred to here, Stapleton noted,
was "not indeed that dispersed throughout the world, but that
which is found in the place or parish to which the brother who
needs correction belongs." This was the opinion of the primitive
Lutherans, so much so that some of them even changed Christ's
words to read, "Dic Reipublicae," as Beza reported in commenting
on this passage.[8]

For Calvin and his followers, Stapleton continued, "Dic Ecclesiae" meant "Dic senioribus populi." "It is clear," wrote Calvin
in his commentary, "that the legitimate governing of the Church
has been assigned to the elders, not only to ministers of the Word,
but also to those of the populace joined with them as censors of
morals." Stapleton found the same doctrine in the *Institutes* and
in Beza's commentaries. The latter, both in his *Confessio fidei* and
in the preface to the Helvetic Confession, "urged that for this
senate of elders (or consistory as they call that body now) the important men of the neighborhood and the nobles, those, that is,
who enjoy authority, should be chosen.[9] . . . To implement their
doctrine the Calvinists set up their consistories all over France
and Holland, and with these groups, made up of both laymen and
pastors, lay all ecclesiastical power, not only with regard to discipline and censure, but as well to financial matters, moral prescrip-
tions, liturgical ceremonies and the elucidation of doctrine."[10]
But the consistorial system had by no means found universal approval among Protestants. The prominent Lutheran theologian,
Musculus, had attacked it bitterly, and some non-Lutherans, such
as Gualter of Zurich, had expressed grave reservations about it.
In England, Stapleton noted contemptuously, where Puritans
quarreled with other "Anglocalvinists," "Dic Ecclesiae" had come
to mean simply, "Tell the magistrate."

8. *Antidota evangelica,* p. 55.
9. Ibid.
10. *Principiorum,* p. 180.

"However various and confusing are the opinions of today's heretics about these words of Christ," and whatever conflicts arose among their rival ecclesiastical organizations, the differences in Stapleton's simplistic and jaundiced view were only of detail: "One thing there is upon which all of them agree, that the word Ecclesia here should on no account be understood of the prelates of the Church, whether pastor or bishop or supreme pontiff himself."[11] This was why the whole Protestant chorus, so discordant on so many things, could sing out together in denial of the sacrament of Holy Orders. "[The Catholics] say that the right of creating presbyters belongs to them alone," Calvin observed in the *Institutes*. "But in this they corrupt the ancient constitution, because they create by their ordination not elders to feed the flock of Christ but priests to offer sacrifice."[12]

At the same time, the overthrow of the priesthood presented the Reformers with a practical dilemma. Though their theory of justification (not to mention what Stapleton gladly mentioned as often as possible: their personal ambition) demanded it, few of them were prepared to face the logical consequences such a revolution involved. Sacrifice as a meaningful good work had of course to be eliminated, but the authority wielded by sacrificing priests under the old order could not be dispensed with under the new lest anarchy prevail. Stapleton remembered a Calvinist conference held in France in 1559 among whose articles was one which demanded "the imposition of hands by the old upon the new ministers." Only three years later, at the famous confrontation at Poissy, Theodore Beza had declaimed at length upon the extraordinary nature of his vocation, comparable, as he put it, to that of Elias and Eliseus. "Later, when [the Calvinists] had grown into a larger group, with their own cities and provinces, the ordinary vocation became more to their liking, controlled as it is by those already pastors." Calvin himself, in well-organized Geneva, insisted that no one assume any office in the Church "without being publicly called, lest turbulent or restless men take it upon themselves to

11. *Antidota evangelica*, p. 55.
12. *Principiorum*, p. 180, citing *Institutes*, IV.3.4.

rule and to teach." Even imposition of hands was to be retained, not now indeed with sacramental significance but as a practical expedient for those men who "would play the pope themselves."[13]

In the imposition of hands, in this formal "traditio" of ministerial power, Stapleton sensed he had an issue:

> Thus I say of Protestants, if they can show any succession of bishops in the time of the Albigenses in Provence, of Berengarius in Angers, of the poor brethren in Lyons, of Huss in Bohemia, of John Wyclif or Oldcastle in England, before the days of Martin Luther, they shall name but a few, and those few without succession, suddenly arising and soon broken off. . . . As Victor among the Donatists, so Luther among the Protestants of Wittenburg, so Zwingli among the sacramentaries of Zurich, so Calvin among those of Geneva, so Bernard Ratman among the Anabaptists, so now M. Jewel, Grindal and Horne, and such other false bishops in England have risen and started up suddenly, without Fathers, without predecessors, without masters at home, in any right and lineal succession.[14]

This was an objection which could not be expected to tell with an Anabaptist or with a radical Puritan, neither of whom regarded any religious authority except the instantaneous inspiration of the Spirit experienced by the individual believer; but, addressed to the Calvinists and to most of the Lutherans, who were neither fools nor fanatics, it had, at least speculatively, considerable relevance. Could they demonstrate that their teaching authority and hence their doctrine stretched back, through the imposition of hands, beyond Luther and Zwingli? They knew that, if they and their doctrines were to survive, they had to establish an organized Church which could rival the traditional one. When they admitted the practical necessity for the imposition of hands, how-

---

13. *Principiorum*, p. 180 and *Fortresse*, p. 350.
14. *Fortresse* p. 249.

ever (the necessity, that is, for an ecclesiastical estate within the Church possessed of real and inalienable authority), could it not be reasonably demanded of them to show with whom their "traditio" had begun?

Stapleton found that most Protestants avoided this discussion as best they could, and he cited as typical the able Lutheran theologian Johann Brenz: "In this controversy about succession one should not so much inquire whether it is licit for anyone to come into the ministry of the Church without a legitimate and ordinary calling, but rather determine whether the bishops of the Roman Church, since they are the enemies of apostolic doctrine, really constitute the true Church."[15] Stapleton was fully satisfied that there had been no "body of faithful ones, no uncorrupted remnant before [1517]. Luther had no elect scattered across the world, as the Protestants pretend to have hidden, to whom he could join himself. Rather, those who joined him were our apostates and those who left us, not some pre-existing evangelicals or Protestants."[16]

Protestant attacks upon the Roman primacy also revealed the uneasy association of the reluctance to give too much weight to succession and tradition with the need to create an ersatz papacy. Beza wondered, for example, if Peter's name stood first in the evangelical lists of the apostles because it had been placed in that position by "someone" who wanted to set up the primacy. It struck him as "mysterious" that Peter should head each list when the order among the other apostles was not constant. Calvin explained that Simon had been renamed Peter "because he retained his firmness as one stone in the temple of God. . . . Moreover, even granted that Peter was given something more than the others . . . the papists have no right to infer that he was given a primacy which made him universal head of the whole Church. For dignity is quite a different thing from power, and there is a difference,

15. Brenz' *Prologomena contra Petrum Sotum,* cited in *Principiorum,* p. 101. Brenz (1499–1570) was one of the most colorful figures of the time. For a sketch of his brilliant and controversial career see *DTC,* 2, Pt. I, cc. 1128–30.

16. *Principiorum,* p. 101.

too, between enjoying the highest rank of honor among a few and collecting under one's thumb the whole world."[17]

In the controversies, the Protestants had taken considerable advantage of the argument that all they intended was the restoration of the ancient Church. If the pope would consent to the doctrines of St. Augustine and St. Cyprian, they proclaimed, the quarrels would be over. In practice, however, as Stapleton noted many times, the Protestants had actually picked and chosen among patristic witnesses, claiming this piece of literature as a blueprint of their own teaching and rejecting another as "inconsistent with scripture."[18] In practice, too, they had to be content with a tradition which went back only to the beginning of the sixteenth century:

> In 1561 there was published at Leipzig in Saxony a large work called *The Corpus of Christian Doctrine,* in which appear the Confession of Augsburg . . . certain of Melanchthon's writings and things of that sort. In the "Admonitio" to the reader, the Lutherans describe their Church this way: "The doctrine of those churches which are in the lands subject to the Prince-Elector of Saxony is not doubtful, variable or flexible. From the beginning it has been sincere, harmonious, and constant, conserved and made use of now for thirty years by all parties, wholly consistent with the Confession of Augsburg." This is the definition of the Protestants' Church. You hear of "these churches." You hear of the "Saxon dominion." You hear of "thirty years." You hear finally of the Confession of Augsburg. You hear nothing of the Catholic Church dispersed throughout the world or of the communion of all nations, or of a Church derived from Christ himself through the apostles to us by a continuous succession. Clearly, Jerusalem for these people is the Confession of Augsburg.[19]

17. Quoted in *Antidota evangelica,* pp. 29, 49.
18. See *Speculum,* pp. 385 ff.
19. *Principiorum,* p. 145.

Stapleton's point in all this was clear enough. What had the Protestants made of the idea of the Church of Christ, he asked, but "a veritable nothing"?[20] To escape the censure which in his judgment they deserved, "they bind the Church to the written word of God, so that the Church is present only where one hears the written Word." If this were so, could there ever be an end to controversy? Among the illiterate masses could any faith survive? But Stapleton never believed for a moment that the ambitious men who led the rebellion against the Church really accepted this "impossible doctrine," for he knew of dozens of remarks like this one of Calvin: "The papists are foolishly superstitious to seize so tenaciously these words of Christ [i.e. *Hic est Sanguis meus*]. Indeed," retorted Stapleton, "you ought not seize too closely upon the words of Christ. And why? So that you can cling fast to the words of John Calvin. This is the cursed impiety of the man." The problem, he added, was not, and had never been, Scripture versus the Church but rather Scripture as used by this or that individual versus Scripture as used by the Church.[21]

"Who does not know," Stapleton wrote in 1578, "that with today's heretics it is held most constantly, as the firmest principle, not otherwise than as an article of faith, that Scripture alone is the entirely sufficient norm and rule of faith, and this they defend unanimously as the head and arch of their religion."[22] Here then was the "principium commune" of the Reformation; here, as he wrote eighteen years later, was the most fundamental enemy of all:

> As it was with ancient heretics, so also with those who are at work today in this unhappy century. They have cast aside impiously and audaciously ecclesiastical authority as often as they decided it stood in the way of their own opinion. They have tried in every way to oppose it with testimonies of Scripture and thus to conceal their wolfish madness beneath this cover: that Scripture can neither deceive nor be deceived,

20. Ibid., p. 15.
21. *Antidota evangelica,* p. 108.
22. *Principiorum,* p. 24.

that in it all sacred truth is plainly contained, that outside
it the truth is sought in vain, lost in human doubt and un-
certainty. This specious if cunning argument, which they
impose upon simple minds, with which they deceive the unlearned or the unstable, appears clearly to firm and true
Christians as linked to the most inane deceit. The ancient
Church of Christ . . . believed, held to, and understood the
divine Scripture. Her faith, tradition, and doctrine were always either drawn from Scripture or else entirely consistent
with it. Posterity judged that this derived from the fact that
the Holy Ghost acted through her leaders in directing the
Church.

There was no reason for Catholic Christians to suppose
that Arius, Nestorius, Eutyches, and the other inventors of
new dogmas understood, held to, and preached Scripture
and that the Church's official teachers did not. The same line
of reasoning holds good today against the sectaries of our
time. We all embrace the Scripture, but, in determining
what Scripture means, shall I follow the ancient Church or
some new sectary who accuses the Church of error? Neither
the Catholics of former times nor we today will tear asunder
the judgment of the Church from the Word of God, for we
receive the Word from the Church, we understand it through
the Church's mouth, we learn its lessons from the Church
interpreting it. The sectaries cry out for the Scripture, but
only the parts which they want to recognize and only in the
sense in which they want it to be understood. Thus the question today is not about the Word of God or the Scripture,
nor has this question ever separated Catholics from heretics.
Rather, the question is, from whom ought we to receive the
Scripture, and through whom ought we to understand it?[23]

For Stapleton the proof of Protestant error lay in what he considered the abominations of Protestant practice. Here he stood on
slippery ground indeed, for Catholic closets rattled loud with

23. *Relectio*, pp. 508–09.

skeletons in an age in which, as Robert Bellarmine expressed it, "religion had become almost extinct."[24] The generation of Catholics after Trent, Stapleton's generation, had, compared with its predecessor, little to be embarassed about, but one wonders at the airy way in which the whole matter was dismissed: "We read no promises in Scripture of continuance of uprightness of life, of virtue and holiness to continue in the Church universally."[25] When he argued with the Protestants, Stapleton did not blush over the Tetzels and the Wolseys. He would admit that certain people had been "offended with the dissolute life of the clergy, some for malice at their wealth, some desirous indeed of a reformation . . . and, to follow the trim trade of that loose liberty that Luther preached and practiced both, became Lutherans." One finds here no beating of the breast nor even a decent apology. Those who had espoused Luther's "loose liberty," Stapleton jeeringly concluded, had masked their real intention, for the sake of convenience or respectability, behind a pretended horror of the Tetzels and the Wolseys: clerical abuse "was the pleasant . . . bait that poisoned and choked a number."[26] This was Stapleton's stubborn view, and he never swerved from it. The discussion, he said, is beside the point. "Though evil manners have corrupted good ordinances, though some abuses have blotted holy decrees . . . shall we therefore condemn for the pride, ambition, sluggishness, ignorance of some, though of the clergy itself, the Church of Christ throughout all parts of Christendom, condemn the faith of our forefathers?" The question was rhetorical, and the answer was obvious: "Our superiors . . . were they as bad as the Pharisees, or worse, yet . . . are to be obeyed by the commandment of our Savior in such things as they say, though not to be followed in their doings."[27]

24. "According to the testimony of those who were then [i.e. in 1517] alive, there was an almost entire abandonment of equity in ecclesiastical judgments; in morals no discipline, in sacred literature no erudition, in divine things no reverence. Religion was almost extinct." *Opera,* 6 (1617), 206.

25. *Fortresse,* p. 95.

26. Ibid., p. 174.

27. Ibid., pp. 95, 50.

To emphasize the weaknesses of his own side is never part of
the controversialist's craft, and Stapleton turned with much more
zest to a consideration of the practical difficulties encountered by
the Protestants in the establishment of their evangel. He employed in this congenial task all the rhetorician's tools, ridicule,
hyperbole, dramatic contrast, and the rest. He did not refrain on
occasion from a strident tone and a manner of expression which
sank well below the level, even, of bad taste. The Marian martyrs,
for example, excited neither his admiration nor his pity. Foxe's
Acts and Monuments, devoted largely to an account of those who
had suffered at Smithfield, was "a mad martyrology,"[28] "a dunghill heaped [with] a number of miserable miracles to set forth the
glory of their stinking martyrs."[29] Such remarks grate on the ears
of us who live in more polite times, when nobody gets very excited
about religion. But for Stapleton, and for Foxe, the struggle was
a matter of life and death, with little room for the amenities. They
had in any case entered the discussion at a relatively late date
when its penchant for coarseness and invective had been long
established, canonized, so to speak, by that master of crudity who
had initiated it.

"Protestants, by the liberty of their gospel, have broken [the]
order and array of their forefathers, and placed in their room a
headless disorder of their own invention."[30] This statement might
well stand as a summation of Stapleton's accusations against the
Reformers. The scandal of a splintered Christendom, an appalling
ignorance, the overturning of ancient Christian practice, all these
had grown out of the "headless disorder" invented to keep alive
the doctrine of justification by only faith. What have they done,
he asked over and over, these men of God, what have they accomplished except to compound divisiveness with destruction? If
I should become a Protestant, he once mused mockingly, I would
not know to which sect to go:

28. *Counterblast,* fol. 108.
29. *Fortresse,* p. 61.
30. Ibid., p. 362.

I would not know in what branch of their pedigree I should place myself. I see such sweet sops in their whole gospel that, fearing the sour sauce which will follow, I dare not put my lips unto it. I see such horrible fruits to have ensued of this late alteration: so many churches pulled down, so few set up; so many monasteries, hospitals and alms-houses taken away [and] none erected; such notorious rebellions . . . so much hatred bred, so little charity used, with diverse the like, that I am not yet fully persuaded with such slender suspicions to believe that the Church hath erred so many hundred years.[31]

Stapleton delighted in pointing out the notorious intellectual inadequacy of the new Protestant clergy. This tactic served a double controversial turn: it hit the enemy in one of his most vulnerable spots, for the conversion of priesthood into ministry remained, understandably, a critical problem for generations, and it deflected attention from the dreadful educational preparation of the ordinary Catholic priest before Trent. He usually assumed a jocular tone in this matter. The English Protestant bishop and the country gentleman were riding one summer afternoon (so the story went) when the prelate asked his friend why his boots and saddle were in such sad disrepair. "Marry, quoth [the gentleman], my lord (and bound it with an oath), ye have taken up all our saddlers and shoemakers, promoting them to your ministry, that (swearing once again) there be scarce any left in the country that will work for money."[32] And this riot of alliteration Stapleton addressed directly to a real Anglican bishop:

And wherein, I pray you, resteth a great part of your new clergy but in butchers, cooks, catchpoles and cobblers, dyers and dawbers, felons carrying their mark in their hand instead of a shaven crown, fishermen, gunners, harpers, innkeepers, merchants and mariners, potters, pothecaries and

31. Ibid., p. 234.
32. Ibid., p. 371.

porters of Billingsgate, pinners, peddlers, ruffling ruffians, saddlers, sheermen and shepherds, tanners, tilers, tinkers, trumpeters, weavers, wherry men et cet.[33]

But, on the same subject, he was capable also of sharper words and solemn denunciation:

> Learn, ye ministers, which from your shops get to pulpits and maintain a schism which ye know not, preach heresies which ye understand not, and divide yourselves against the Church which ye esteem not, learn, I say, of Holy Scripture that you sin herein most grievously, and are not to be punished of God more sharply than if ye committed idolatry in your own persons, where the harm should extend to yourselves only.[34]

Stapleton insisted that the great mass of ministers (and so much more the people) had no idea of the complexity of the problems upon which they declaimed so confidently. "May this [not] be said not only to a number of unlearned craftsmen, never acquainted with learning, rashly presuming to the high office of preachers and pastors, but also to many young scholars which suddenly became preachers and planters of a faith which they understand not?"[35] The new ministry, then, was simply the engine by means of which the heresy of justification by faith alone was to be spread among Christians. This, said Stapleton, was their gospel:

> What is all your preaching but down, down, down with holy bread, holy water, with all holy ceremonies in Baptism and in other sacraments, with fasting, with night prayer, with all prayer to be made for our fathers' and friends' souls, or to the Blessed Virgin Mary or to other hallows, with all altars, with Mass, yea, and with the blessed Body of Christ in the Sacrament, which hath been most villainously defiled,

33. *Counterblast,* fol. 484.
34. *Fortresse,* p. 375.
35. Ibid., p. 28.

not only by blasphemous books and sermons, but most wickedly taken from the altar and most horribly . . . conculcated by the wicked feet of . . . your gospelling preachers. . . . No, no . . . for all your peacock's tail glittering with goodly and scripturely talk, we perceive your filthy heresy well enough when we look upon your foul feet. Away, away with these painted words wherewith men will not always be made fools.[36]

It was the persistent claim of the Protestants that they had formed religious associations of their own because they could not abide the superstition which flourished in the Roman Church. Stapleton never met this charge head-on, and for this failure he deserves both censure and credit. On the one hand, insofar as widespread popular superstition had been at least an occasion for the Reformers' movement, he responded with a yawn and a bit of sarcasm; he reacted, in other words, precisely as he did when the subject, say, of clerical avarice or any other abuse was brought up. But on the other hand, he kept his gaze fixed with admirable consistency on the fundamental issue involved in the great sixteenth-century brawl, and he was never blinded by the sand the Protestant polemicists kept throwing in their opponents' eyes. The issue, he never tired of saying, is justification and nothing else. However much the Reformers may nag about indulgences or relics or private Masses, they are really arguing about justification. Stapleton never gave up the principle he enunciated early in his career: "Such things which . . . in the doing are but ceremonial, yet both in the assertion do pertain to doctrine and in the condemning of them do make in heresy."[37] If this were true in con-

---

36. *Counterblast,* fol. 484.
37. *Fortresse,* p. 324. In this connection Henry Cole, Dean of St. Paul's at Elizabeth's accession, wrote cogently to John Jewel in March 1560. "One thing . . . I long much to be answered in, why ye rather offer . . . to dispute in these . . . points than in the chief matters that lie in question betwixt the Church of Rome and the Protestants. It seemeth to me far the nearer way . . . if ye began not with such matters which we deny not but a general council might take order that they should be practiced as ye would have it." The debate, Cole continued, should center upon matters like justification,

nection with peripheral matters such as pilgrimage or the use of Latin in public worship, it applied as well, and with more force, to the sacramental system. In the wearisome and technical debates over merit and grace, here lay the reason for struggle. Thus, for instance, few quarrels between Catholics and Protestants (and among the various Protestant sects) reached the dimensions of that over the Eucharist. Yet for Stapleton, who never wrote a tract *de Eucharistia,*[38] most of this argument was merely verbiage. The Protestants believe as they do about the Eucharist, he said, because of what they believe about justification. Since they are wrong about justification, they are wrong about the Eucharist, too. When an opponent raised a ceremonial or even a sacramental point, a reader of Stapleton can almost sense the author's impatience to return to the really critical discussion. John Jewel, the distinguished Anglican Bishop of Salisbury, voiced the usual Protestant complaint about reception of Holy Communion under only one species, and Stapleton hardly seemed to take him seriously: "That Christ is wholly received under one kind seemeth an untruth to M. Jewel. And why so? Forsooth, because it procedeth of the gross error of transubstantiation. Thus he salves one sore with another, and defends one heresy with another."[39] And behind all the heresies, he might have added, is that one which denies the possibility of meritorious human acts.

In this regard, at least, Stapleton is a valuable witness of the Reformation. He never thought the religious difficulties of his time could be explained in terms of simple reaction against Catholic sacramental practice or abuses, and surely he was right. The

---

good works, and the sacrificial character of the Mass. "I ween if ye had the upper hand but in one of these questions the world might well think we were smally to be trusted in all the rest. For we make a plain answer to them, without 'if' or 'and.' So do we not whether the service ought to be in English or not, or whether the people ought to receive in both kinds or no, or whether private Masses ought to be said in the Church or no." See Jewel, *Works 1* (Cambridge, 1844), 26.

38. The subject of the Eucharist did, however, come up incidentally very often. See for example *Antidota evangelica,* pp. 108 ff.

39. *Returne,* p. 41.

Protestants had positive things to say about the nature and destiny of man, and they meant to say them come what might. If they shrank from the Mass, with the people "tooting and gazing at that thing the priest held in his hands,"[40] it was because the Mass purported to be an effectual means of salvation whereas, according to their theory of justification, this was clearly impossible. Luther, Calvin, and their friends and followers did not need to seek out abuses in Catholic practices relating to the Eucharist. The doctrine itself was abuse enough for them.

40. These contemptuous words are Cranmer's. See *Writings and Disputations* . . . , *1* (Cambridge, 1844), 229.

Chapter 8

THE OATH OF SUPREMACY

"We yesterday received a letter from England in which the death of Mary, the accession of Elizabeth and the decease of Cardinal Pole is [sic] confirmed." Edwin Sandys was writing, from Strassburg, a hurried note to his friend and patron Heinrich Bullinger, Zwingli's successor as leader of the Reformation in Zurich:

> We have therefore nothing to fear from Pole, for dead men do not bite. . . . The queen has changed almost all her counsellors and has taken good Christians into her service in the room of papists; and there is great hope for her promoting the gospel and advancing the kingdom of Christ to the utmost of her power. . . . [Certain] persons of distinction have begun their journey this day; I, with God's blessing, will follow them tomorrow. . . . Entreat God in behalf of the Church of England, and of us, miserable ministers of the gospel, upon whom a heavy and difficult burden is imposed.

The future Bishop of Worcester noted that the midnight hour had struck, but, if it crossed his mind to apply the fact metaphorically to the new era that had begun, he did not write it down. He contented himself with the remark that he was "to quit this place early tomorrow morning" and with his signature, written "in haste, Strasburg, Dec. 20th, or, if you choose, the 21st, 1558."[1]

And so the pendulum had swung again. Mary the Catholic was dead, and dead with her was the possibility of a Catholic restoration in England. Her half-sister would, in the next four decades,

1. Hastings Robinson, ed. and trans., *The Zurich Letters* (Cambridge, 1842), pp. 3–6.

build an ecclesiastical system that would manage to be all things to most Englishmen: Protestant and yet episcopal and Erastian. From a political point of view it would occupy the center and would be attacked by Puritans from the left and by Roman Catholics from the right. The Queen would disclaim any intention to look within her subjects' souls, but at the same time she would exact from them a minimal ecclesiastical conformity. She might shift her emphasis right or left as pressures upon her grew from one direction or the other, but she would never be pushed outside the limits she had set for herself. Those limits were determined by political, not theological, considerations, and judged in these terms her creation was a remarkable achievement.

Not everybody, however, looked at the Elizabethan Settlement as a more or less successful experiment in political practice. Edwin Sandys and the other Marian exiles, who eagerly packed their bags and headed back to England during the winter of 1558–59, viewed it as a providential chance to preach the pure gospel at home once more. Thomas Stapleton, on the other hand, considered it simply an instance of doctrinal departure from the traditional Christian revelation. The word "doctrinal" might well be underscored here. For Stapleton the Act of Supremacy established the peculiar English version of the new ecclesiastical polity, and this, he maintained, was a matter not of politics but of theology. The heresy of justification by faith alone had been accompanied everywhere by a rejection of the traditional sources of ecclesiastical authority. What had happened in Saxony and Geneva had happened in England. As an Englishman, he was of course much more interested in the Act of Supremacy than he was in Calvin's Ecclesiastical Ordinance, but he did not see any essential difference between the two. In other words, Stapleton, who was always very impressed by consistency, judged Elizabeth's church within the general framework of his critique of Protestant ecclesiology. His rigid adherence to this point of view involved him in some strange theories about the Reformation in England, but, as he confronted his Protestant opponents with it, he forced them into the open with some curious opinions of their own.

Not a few of Sandys' fellow exiles received, as he did, high preferment in the Elizabethan Establishment. John Jewel, for example, became Bishop of Salisbury, Edmund Grindal went to London and Robert Horne to Winchester. There was never any doubt, however, that their elevation was precisely that—a "preferment," which brought with it certain theoretical drawbacks: these men took their spiritual leadership from the hands of the Queen and their legal position within the Church by virtue of an Act of Parliament. The sun of the new evangelical era had barely risen, however, when some of the exiles spied the cloud of unseemly royal interference on the horizon, a threat, they thought, to the proper diffusion of the gospel's light,[2] and during the early months of the new Queen's reign their fears had not been resolved.[3] In the end, Sandys and his friends had to accept the fact that the ecclesiastical framework within which they must work was not to be of their own making, that the Establishment of 1559 "was a thing devised by laymen—the Queen and her ministers—behind closed doors; put through parliament in the face of much opposition; sanctioned finally by parliament—the whole body of bishops, and convocation too, voting *contra* to the end—and then introduced to the country through the agency of a very small handful of clerics who saw that the thing was as much as they were likely to get of what they had dreamed."[4] There needed to

2. Thomas Sampson, writing (ibid., p. 1) on Dec. 17, 1558, asked Peter Martyr, his "excellent father," "How ought we to act with respect to allowing or disallowing the title of 'after Christ supreme head of the Church of England' etc.? All scripture seems to assign the title of head of the Church to Christ alone. . . . I cannot take upon myself the government of the Church until, after having made as entire reformation in all ecclesiastical functions, [the Queen] will concede to the clergy the right of ordering all things according to the word of God." Even Stapleton had a grudging respect for Sampson's integrity. See *Counterblast,* fol. 459.

3. "At present," Jewel wrote on May 22, 1559, "we are so living as scarcely to seem like persons returned from exile; for to say nothing else, not one of us has as yet had even his own property restored to him. Yet, although this long waiting is very tiresome to us, we doubt not that in a short time all will be well. For we have a wise and religious Queen." Robinson, pp. 32–33.

4. Hughes, *Reformation, 3,* 36.

be in these men, whose principles stemmed from their mentors in Geneva and Zurich and Strassburg, a certain flexibility if they were to swear that in conscience they held Anne Boleyn's daughter to be the supreme governor of England in spiritual as well as temporal matters. This may explain why the "small handful of clerics" included a bench of bishops which, even for Froude, was redeemed by only one name from "entire insignificance."[5]

The same events that brought the Marian exiles scurrying home sent Thomas Stapleton abroad, first on a prudent sabbatical and then permanently into exile; the same regime to which they rallied he repudiated. Though he displayed bitterness enough in the years which followed, he directed it not at the regime itself but at the "small handful of clerics" on whom he fixed the full responsibility for the settlement of 1559. He had them specifically in mind when he wrote that "the light wavering of a few, following the dissolute trace of that wedded friar, drew a greater number after them and broke the uniform array of Christ's Church."[6] It was a curious line to take, given the political realities, but it must be seen as part of a larger conviction of Stapleton's that all the Protestant churches had been established to support the new justification doctrine.

If (let us grant for the sake of the argument) a case could be made for this simplistic notion of Protestant ecclesiology with regard to the Lutheran and Calvinist congregations on the continent, the same could hardly be said about the Reformation movement in England. Here, in Stapleton's homeland, the political and economic factors counted for much more than they did elsewhere. The founders of the continental reformed churches were theologians whose primary interest, whose obsession, indeed, was religious. It is clear that Cranmer and Jewel, as theologians, had little to do with the final triumph of Protestantism in England.

5. *History of England*, 7 (New York, 1872), 179–80. Froude commented further: "Cecil laid hands on [Parker] as the one sensible man within reach who was religious without being a fanatic, and a Christian without being a dogmatist."

6. *Fortresse*, p. 211.

This was the accomplishment of Elizabeth and her ministers. To conceive therefore of the Anglican Church as merely a home for those with odd opinions about justification is to go wide of the mark.

Precisely this misconception appears to run through all of Stapleton's published work on the subject. Whether he really did not understand or whether he feigned not to understand the essentially laic character of the English Reformation is a matter for conjecture. At any rate, he ignored it. He advanced the fantastic explanation that Elizabeth, "that godly lady and meek lamb,"[7] had been somehow captured by the apostate friars. "We have made a king over us in spiritual causes," he cried, "and induced our sovereign, not desiring it, to unlawful government." This pious observation was almost as grotesque as the rhetorical question that followed it a few pages later. "Will [the Protestants] persuade us that the queen's majesty holdeth the Sacramentary, Lutheran, Osiandrin or any like heresy?"[8] Good Queen Bess and her doughty father ("your highness' most noble progenitor, Harry the Eighth"),[9] according to Stapleton, had assumed the supreme governance of the Church "not desiring it." Papists at heart, they had done no more than artlessly play the roles assigned them by men like Cranmer and Horne.

Perhaps at the bottom of this tactic lay a sixteenth-century man's reverence for monarchy or a political exile's exaggerated sense of patriotism. It may be that Stapleton indulged in the vain hope, especially before 1570, that the Queen would come to her senses and take up again the Catholicism she had practiced during her sister's reign. After all, it was the age of "cujus regio, ejus religio," and to identify Elizabeth closely with Protestantism might have struck Stapleton as an occasion for alienating her permanently. It is, however, perfectly credible that Stapleton, notorious for

---

7. This phrase was coined by Christopher Goodman, *How Superior Powers Ought to Be Obeyed* . . . (Geneva, 1558), fol. 54. He was a Calvinist who, as Stapleton was to point out, rejected the notion of the royal supremacy.

8. *Fortresse,* pp. 393, 397.

9. Ibid., p. 21.

his naïveté about the world of practical politics, simply failed to see the untheological issues which dictated the course of the English Reformation. The principle upon which he built was sound enough. The continental Reformers, in his view, had had at least the virtue of originality. Not even this much could be credited to the "miserable clawbacks" of England. None of the new theories had an English origin; all of them had been imported through the Lutheran books smuggled into the kingdom as early as 1520 or through the likes of Bucer and Peter Martyr lecturing in the universities in King Edward's days or, more lately, through the Marian exiles returned with their heads and notebooks crammed with the ideas of their continental mentors. It follows, argued Stapleton, that, when they accepted justification by faith alone, the English clerics accepted at the same time Lutheran or Calvinist notions about Church government.

Whether he acted out of expediency or simplicity, the fact remains that Stapleton was as fully deceived in his domain as William Allen in his. It did their cause no more good to absolve Elizabeth from her responsibility for the religious settlement of 1559 than to try to overthrow her regime, because each of these positions reflected a massive misunderstanding of the facts. For this reason the new Anglican hierarchy possessed a decisive advantage over the Catholic exiles. They knew exactly what had happened; they knew exactly where they stood. "Truly," Stapleton wrote, hoping the Queen would read it, "experience hath too well shown that the Protestants obey until they have the power to resist. When their faction is the stronger side, as they resist both prelates and popes, so they lay at both kings and kaisers."[10] The events which convulsed England a generation after Elizabeth's death give this statement the ring of prophecy, but so long as that shrewd lady wore the diadem (a time which included all of Thomas Stapleton's active life), logical or even inevitable as it may have been, it did not apply. Elizabeth cared less than her father about religious matters as such, but she agreed

10. Ibid.

completely with him that layman should never be subject to cleric again. The English Reformers could function quite freely if they did not forget that cardinal part of the public policy. Most of them swallowed hard, wrote apologetic letters to their confreres on the continent, and gratefully remembered the old saw that half a loaf is better than none.

With his villains clearly identified, Stapleton could move on to describe the evil they had done. "The faith of Protestants, which was first planted in England, is now in many points changed. ... I report me to the first communion [book] in King Edward's time, to the first preaching and lessons of Peter Martyr in Oxford to the first false martyrs, Frith, Barnes and others. For all these confessed the real presence in the Blessed Sacrament, acknowledged more sacraments than two, and were not so deep in predestination as the Genevans are now."[11] Prior to that first planting, however, when Henry VIII banished the Pope's authority out of England, neither he nor the Parliament had any intention of introducing into the country "the other errors of the Lutheran or Sacramentary religion which [they] then no less abhorred than they did Turkery." Cardinal Wolsey, "homo ambitiosus," piqued at the Emperor's failure to support vigorously enough his candidature to the papal throne, resolved to throw over the Hapsburg alliance in favor of one with France, to be sealed by Henry's marriage to the sister of Francis I. With this scheme in mind, the Cardinal persuaded the King's confessor to insinuate to Henry the possible invalidity of his marriage with Catherine of Aragon. But Wolsey, thanks to his own evil suggestion, reaped a whirlwind: "Novae nuptiae non iam cum Galla, sed cum Bolenia; Wolsaei primum posteaque totius status ecclesiastici et religionis in Anglia interitus fuit."[12]

The moment Henry VIII had thrown off the Pope's primacy, "immediately books came so thick abroad, as well of the Lutheran as of the Zwinglian sect ... that the king was fain to make diverse

11. Ibid., p. 266. Peter Martyr might have objected to the suggestion that he advocated the Real Presence.

12. *Tres Thomae*, 4, 1029.

strict laws and acts of parliament for the repressing of heresy, yea, and to forbid the common people the reading of the Bible." Henry himself authorized no alteration in these matters of faith, yet "after his death, and in the minority of his son, King Edward, all the laws that he had made touching matters of religion (saving against the supremacy) were repealed and abolished, and a new religion was throughout the realm set forth."[13]

Stapleton could see much similarity between this Edwardian Protestantism and the religion established by law in 1559, but, he pointed out, there were areas of difference, too. The marriage of priests, for instance, "which . . . had some color in King Edward's days by Act of Parliament, now [has] both the church law and the law of the realm against [it].[14] . . . Again, in the first year of our gracious queen, the Act of Parliament for making and consecrating bishops, made the 28 of King Henry, was revived. And yet the bishops were ordered not according to this Act, but according to an Act made in King Edward his days, repealed by Queen Mary, and not revived the said first year."[15] Finally, there

13. *Counterblast,* preface.

14. Stapleton raised a valid point here. Edward's Parliament had legalized the marriage of priests (2 and 3 Edward VI, cap. 21) and, while Mary had repealed this statute (1 Mary, Statute 2, cap. 2), Elizabeth had not re-enacted it. Stapleton chose to ignore, however, that Elizabeth took clerical marriage for granted and regulated it by virtue of her Injunctions of 1559. See GH, pp. 366 f., 378, 431.

15. Stapleton must have had in mind here the Ecclesiastical Appointment Act (25 [not 28] Henry VIII, cap. 20), which was repealed in 1554 (1 and 2 Philip and Mary, cap. 8) and revived in 1559 (1 Elizabeth, cap. 1). The second Edwardian Act of Uniformity (5 and 6 Edward VI, cap. 1), which provided the "adding also a form and manner of making and consecrating archbishops, bishops, priests and deacons" to the Book of Common Prayer, was of course repealed by Mary (1 Mary, Statute 2, cap. 2). As Stapleton pointed out, the 1559 Act of Supremacy (i.e. 1 Elizabeth, cap. 1) stated that "all other laws and statutes . . . repealed and made void by the said Act of Repeal, made in the time of the said late King Philip and Queen Mary, and not in this present Act specially mentioned and revived, shall stand . . . repealed and void." This Act of Edward's, since it was not "specially mentioned," was not revived. So, Stapleton argued, why had the ordinal of 1552 been used in the consecration of Parker and his fellow bishops when, in 1559, it had no legal existence? The trouble was that according to the law in force (i.e. 25 Henry VIII, cap. 20)

was a difference which Stapleton regarded as of the utmost importance:

> It is also to be considered that the words of the Oaths now tendered for the maintaining of the prince's supremacy are other than they were in King Henry's or King Edward's days, and such as to a civil prince, specially to the person of a woman, can in no wise with any convenient sense be applied: I mean of these words: "Supreme governor as well in all spiritual or ecclesiastical things or causes as temporal." Such large and ample words were in neither of the aforesaid kings' times put into the Oath. And yet they had been more tolerable in their persons (for that men be capable of spiritual government from the which a woman is expressly by nature and by Scripture excluded) than they are now. These words are such, I say, as cannot with any colorable pretext be excused.
>
> Neither is it enough to say (as the Injunctions do) that the queen's majesty intendeth not to take upon her more than King Henry her father, or King Edward her brother did, whatsoever that were, more or less; but it must also be considered what she and her successors may take upon her or them by the largeness of these words (for an Injunction cannot limit an Act of Parliament); and whether there be any either Scripture or other good doctrine ecclesiastical sufficient to satisfy the consciences that refuse . . . this oath. Which doth not only, as it did before, exclude the apostolical see, and all general councils also, as (though not in plain

---

confirmation of the royal appointee had to be made by an archbishop and two bishops or by four bishops, and in 1559 none of the bishops would play the government's game. See GH, pp. 201 ff., 206, 389, 444. "Now the pretended bishops of Protestants," wrote Stapleton elsewhere in this connection (*Fortresse*, pp. 367–68), "none being left in the realm having authority to consecrate bishops or to make priests (that being the office of only bishops), by what authority do they rule the fold of Christ's flock? . . . I speak nothing of the laws of the realm; it hath of late been sufficiently proved they are no bishops if they should be tried thereby."

words, yet in effect) in excluding the ecclesiastical authority of all foreign persons and prelates, but doth further adjoin the foresaid new addition less probable and less tolerable than was any other part of the former Oath.[16]

On May 8, 1559, Elizabeth I dissolved her first Parliament and gave her royal assent to the Act of Supremacy. This foundation stone of the Establishment repealed Mary's Act of Repeal as well as her Heresy Act and explicitly revived one of the statutes enacted by Henry's parliaments, as much of another as had not been repealed by Edward, and one statute enacted during Edward's reign. The new act went on to state that "all usurped and foreign power . . . spiritual and temporal" is forever "clearly extinguished" and that therefore "no foreign prince, prelate, state or potentate, spiritual or temporal, shall at any time after the last day of this session of Parliament use, enjoy, or exercise any manner of power, jurisdiction, superiority, pre-eminence or privilege, spiritual or ecclesiastical, within this realm." Then followed two sections with which Stapleton was, later on, to embarrass Bishop Horne of Win-

16. *Counterblast*, preface. As Hughes says (*Reformation, 3*, 72), "the Act of 1559 simply takes over the oath imposed by Henry VIII's Act of 1536," including the phrase to which Stapleton so strenuously objected. The oath of 1544 did not contain it and perhaps it was this comparison Stapleton was making. For both texts see M. A. Tierney, *Dodd's Church History of England . . . 1* (London, 1839), 417–18. Stapleton's tones of alarm are interesting if for no other reason than that they run counter to the usual explanation that "the Elizabethan legislation stood upon a different basis from that of Henry VIII, i.e. its conception of the royal supremacy. The title [Elizabeth I] chose and bequeathed to her successors to the present day sounds at first a mere modification of form without any change of meaning—'the only supreme governor of this realm as well in all spiritual or ecclesiastical things or causes as temporal.' But the explanation of the title given by Elizabeth herself . . . avoided from the first all 'caesareo-papal' interpretations." Such is the view of Arnold Oskar Meyer, *England and the Catholic Church under Queen Elizabeth* (London, 1916), pp. 22–24. But see also Powel Mills Dawley, *John Whitgift and the English Reformation* (New York, 1954), p. 57: "It is sometimes argued, and it was argued in 1559, that the distinction between 'supreme head' and 'supreme governor' made small difference in practice. On the contrary, it made small difference in theory. Elizabeth's practice was so restrained as not only to win wide acceptance on the ground of 'true obedience,' but also to endow the national Church with a surprising measure of freedom."

chester: whatever spiritual jurisdiction has ever been or lawfully may be exercised "for the visitation of the ecclesiastical state or persons," for the reformation and correction "of the same, and of all manner of errors, heresies, schisms, abuses, offenses, contempts, and enormities, shall forever, by the authority of this present Parliament, be united and annexed to the imperial crown of this realm." Furthermore, the Queen and her successors will be able through letters patent to authorize "such person or persons being natural born subjects to your highness . . . to exercise . . . all manner of jurisdictions, privileges and pre-eminences, in any wise touching or concerning any spiritual or ecclesiastical jurisdiction . . . and to visit, reform, redress, order, correct and amend all such errors, heresies, schisms, abuses, offenses, contempts and enormities whatsoever, which by any manner spiritual or ecclesiastical power . . . can or may lawfully be reformed."[17]

The sweeping powers "annexed to the imperial crown of this realm" by the act were skillfully incorporated into the oath which the act also imposed.[18] Every ecclesiastic was required to take the oath, as was anyone receiving an academic degree, and all justices, judges, mayors, "and other lay or temporal officer and minister, and every other person having your highness' fee or wages." The act distinguished between two classes of offenders, those who simply refused the oath and those who "by writing, printing, teaching, preaching, express words, deed or act . . . defend the

---

17. GH, pp. 442–49.

18. "I, A. B., do utterly testify and declare in my conscience that the queen's majesty is the only supreme governor of this realm, and of all other her highness' dominions and countries, as well in all spiritual or ecclesiastical things or causes as temporal, and that no foreign prince, person, prelate, state or potentate has or ought to have any jurisdiction, power, superiority, pre-eminence or authority ecclesiastical or spiritual within this realm; and therefore I do utterly renounce and forsake all foreign jurisdictions, power, superiorities and authorities, and do promise that from henceforth I shall bear faith and true allegiance to the queen's highness, her heirs and lawful successors, and to my power shall assist and defend all jurisdictions, pre-eminences, privileges and authorities granted or belonging to the queen's highness, her heirs and successors, or united and annexed to the imperial crown of this realm. So help me God and by the contents of this book."

authority, pre-eminence, power of jurisdiction, spiritual or ecclesiastical, of any foreign prince, prelate . . . or potentate." The
act specified that the former should lose all offices and incur a
lifelong disability to hold office; the latter, for a first offense, lost
all "their goods and chattels, as well real as personal," for a second
offense, fell under the penalties of praemunire (that is, the loss
of all property and imprisonment for life), and for a third, were
guilty of high treason.[19]

This distinction of sanction disappeared with an act passed in
1563, in which like penalties were imposed upon both groups;
for a first refusal or a first offense, loss of all property and life
imprisonment, and, for a second, death as a traitor.[20] The passage
of this harsh penal legislation brought a new crisis to all those
who had, so far, refused the tendered oath, because now, under the
new law, their continued refusal might cost them their lives. On
the other hand, the act of 1563 gave a sharp reminder to the
radical Protestant party that those who controlled the Church
of Christ in England had no intention of relaxing their hold. So,
in January 1563, as Parliament was summarily debating the new
penalties, John Feckenham, sometime Abbot of Westminster and
now prisoner in the Tower, considered with misgiving the possibility of a new commission and a new tendering of the oath,
while at Westminster, Robert Horne, sometime pastor at Frankfort and now Lord Bishop of Winchester, took his seat among
the spiritual peers and gave his hearty approval to the bill, scarcely
adverting to the reservations and qualifications he had made, once
for all, four years earlier. The duel which was about to open between these two men, the one to the right and the other to the
left of the Elizabethan center, gave occasion, immediacy, and
drama to Thomas Stapleton's literary assault on the Act of
Supremacy.

19. GH, pp. 449–55.
20. 5 Elizabeth, cap. 1. See Hughes, *Reformation, 3,* 35.

Chapter 9

THE BISHOP AND THE ABBOT

Men caught in the swirl of mighty movements are nonetheless men. They can be capable of grand achievement while remaining subject to all the ills that flesh is heir to, and if they leave an impression on the world in which they live, they do so through the vehicle of their distinct personalities. Both John Feckenham and Robert Horne had parts to play in the drama of the English Reformation. Both reflect the greatness as well as the shortcomings of the tumultuous generation they shared. But above all they remained, each of them, individuals seeking answers to imponderable questions about God and loyalty and the nature of the good life. Their confrontation, beginning in the autumn of 1563, was an instance of that permanent process in human life: men being shaped by and at the same time giving shape to the events of their time. It might stand, therefore, as a minor landmark in the history of England.

The careers of neither of them had been dull in the years prior to their association. John Feckenham, the older of the two, was born about 1507, in east Worcestershire, of well-to-do yeoman stock.[1] The family name was Homan, but young John, from the time he left his father's house and entered the novitiate of the abbey at Evesham, replaced it with the name of his native village. Bright and charming, he soon attracted a following among the younger monks, at least one of whom spoke of him almost with awe.[2] About 1536 he took up residence in Gloucester Hall, Ox-

1. For what follows see David Knowles, *The Religious Orders in England,* 3 (Cambridge, 1959), 427 ff. and the references cited there.
2. Ibid., pp. 104–05.

ford, a house of studies for Benedictines, and received in 1539 the degree of Bachelor of Divinity. He returned that uncertain summer to his monastery, prepared to assume teaching duties in the novitiate. But the times were unpropitious for monasticism, and, before the year was out, Evesham had been suppressed (November 17). Feckenham joined his brethren in the act of surrender to the crown.

Whatever his sentiments on that occasion, the ex-monk wasted no time in finding provision for himself. On the very day of Evesham's dissolution he became vicar of the parish church in Feckenham, a benefice he held, though rarely visited, for fourteen years. He added to this another living in 1544, the vicarage of Solihull in Warwickshire, and at the same time he acted as chaplain first to the Bishop of Worcester and then, by 1547, to Edmund Bonner, Bishop of London. Feckenham appears to have had little difficulty in accepting the royal supremacy, but the story was far different with regard to the continental theology. On January 16, 1547, only days before Henry VIII's death, he preached at Paul's Cross a ringing denunciation of German heresy. With Edward's accession and the assumption of power by the Protestant clique headed by Cranmer, Feckenham was clapped in the Tower, as much for his friendship with Bonner, no doubt, as for his anti-Protestant views.

Vicar Feckenham remained in that fabled prison until Mary came to the throne, except for one curious interruption. In 1551 the distinguished diplomatist and prominent Protestant gentleman Sir Philip Hoby secured his temporary release. "The very intent for the borrowing of M. Feckenham for a time out of the Tower . . . was that he should dispute, reason and have conference with certain learned men touching matters of religion then in controversy." These disputations were in due course held, the first at "my Lord Earl of Bedford's house, then lodged over the gate at the Savoy," the second at Cecil's residence "at Westminster, in the canon row," and the third at the White Friars "at the house of Sir John Cheke, Knight." And what had begun in London "did finish in Worcestershire, where M. Feckenham was born and also had a benefice. . . . By the special appointment of Sir Philip Hoby he came before M. Hooper, then taken as Bishop of Worcester." There followed "four several and solemn disputations . . . beginning in his visitation at Pershore and so finished the same in the cathedral church at Worcester." All during this parole Feckenham was "made much of and very gently used" by his Protestant opponents who, however, once the tour was ended, sent him back to the Tower.[3]

John Feckenham must have been a congenial man indeed. Even when debating principles which he would not deny at the cost of his freedom, he could be "made much of and very gently used" by his jailers. The old magic which had entranced the young monks at Evesham was evidently still at work. Nor did that geniality desert him when better days arrived for him and the shoe was placed securely (for the moment) on the other foot. In the regime of Mary the Catholic his star rose as rapidly as it had fallen with the death of her father. He was named, shortly after his release from the Tower, the Queen's confessor, and in 1554 he became Dean of St. Paul's. It was a glorious turnabout for Feckenham, busy now for the next six years with a multitude of projects. He preached the coronation sermon at Paul's Cross and began with it an impressive list of prestigious pulpit assignments. He did not, in success, cease to be his good-natured self. He befriended the Protestant Earl of Bedford and the Dudley brothers, Ambrose and Robert, later the Earls of Warwick and Leicester. At some danger to himself, he publicly advocated clemency for the Queen's sister, the Princess Elizabeth. The government sent him to the Lady Jane Grey, condemned to death, in the hopes that he might persuade her to recant her Protestantism. Though that unfortunate girl remained admirably steadfast in her religious convictions, she could turn to Feckenham on the scaffold, take his hand and say, "God will requite you, good sir, for your humanity to me."

It was a desire close to the heart of Mary Tudor to re-establish

---

3. *Counterblast,* fol. 37.

as fully as possible the Catholic life which had been so rudely interrupted by her father and brother. This ambition naturally included the setting up once again of monastic life in England, but to this work of restoration, as to so many others, the Queen found the vested interests of a generation squarely opposed. One foundation, however, she managed to restore, the Abbey of St. Peter, Westminster. On November 21, 1556, something less than forty men initiated English monasticism's brief reprise under the mitered leadership of John Feckenham. The Dean of St. Paul's gave way to the Abbot, and after seventeen years, almost to the day, Feckenham was a Benedictine once more. From what we know of his character, it seems unlikely that it was a change he sought, but we have no reason to think he undertook it reluctantly. Westminster Abbey, at the center of London's political and social life, did not oblige him to alter his busy and useful life, and, besides, it gave him a seat in the House of Lords. Furthermore (not a small matter with Feckenham), whatever sacrifices his new position entailed might have helped ease his conscience over his part in the surrender at Evesham. Cardinal Pole, the Queen's cousin and her chief adviser in religious matters, who saw Westminster revived as the first step in an important program, urged the community, made up entirely of ex-monks past forty, to live with more austerity than they had in the monasteries of their youth.

"In the event, the monastic life of the restored abbey seems to have been sober and dignified rather than austere. . . . Abbot Feckenham continued to be one of the prominent figures of the reign, speaking in parliament and Convocation, preaching at Paul's Cross and in the Abbey at the opening of parliament, disputing with heretics, assisting at the refoundation of other communities, serving on royal commissions of sewers and of exports and imports."[4] These days were, however, numbered, and when Mary died and the Abbot preached her funeral sermon, he opened with a text which struck some as succinctly stating his own situation: "And I praised the dead rather than the living; and I judged

4. Knowles, *Religious Orders*, 3, 431.

him happier than them both that is not yet born, nor hath seen the evils that are done under the sun."[5] With the new year of 1559 came the new Queen to the Abbey for the ceremonial opening of parliament. Feckenham, following the ancient ritual, greeted her in pontifical robes and offered her incense and holy water while his monks, each armed with a torch, formed a lighted gauntlet for her. "Away with those torches," Elizabeth snarled, "for we see very well." She took her seat then and listened to a married priest preach about the evils of monkery and bewail those recently executed "under pretext of heresy."

The handwriting was clear on the wall. Nevertheless, Feckenham appeared unabashed by his dim propects. He ranged himself openly on the side of the bishops in their foredoomed fight against the Acts of Supremacy and Uniformity. He spoke out strongly in the debates in the House of Lords, but the legislation passed anyway, as did the bill which dissolved the refounded monasteries. By the end of May most of his monks had prudently departed, but the Abbot stayed calmly on the scene, fulfilling the daily monastic round and puttering in his orchard during idle hours until June 29, the final day for taking the Oath of Supremacy, had come and gone. With it went the old opportunist's last chance to come to terms with the new order of things. He spent much of the next year arranging the transfer of the now defunct abbey's property, and on May 22, 1560, early in the evening, he was arrested and transported to the Tower of London. The surroundings at least were familiar, and in them he remained until October 1563 when he was released in the custody of the Bishop of Winchester.

Robert Horne, born of an old Cumberland family, was perhaps a dozen years younger than the prisoner thus committed to him.[6] Fellow of St. John's, Cambridge (1536), he had taken advanced

---

5. Eccles. 4:2–3.

6. The date for Horne's birth is about 1519. Feckenham's birthday has long been a matter of doubt and dispute. Emily Bradley (*DNB*, 6, 1146) suggests 1518, while Knowles reflects the confusion by stating it as 1505–08 in one place (p. 105 n.) and 1512–15 in another (p. 428). Stapleton, writing in 1566, refers to Feckenham as an old man.

university degrees in divinity in 1546 and 1549.[7] Like many another enthusiastic English advocate of the new continental theology, Horne had had to keep the more extreme of his Protestant views to himself as long as Henry VIII lived. But under King Edward those views did him no harm, and, with a reputation further enhanced by striking oratorical gifts, he came into much preferment. By 1550 he was Rector of All Hallows, Bread Street, and chaplain to the boy-king, and by 1551 he had been named Dean of Durham. Here he made himself highly unpopular with the chapter, whose members, traditionalists for the most part, objected to his radical theology and to the zest of his iconoclasm. On September 15, 1553, Mary's privy council summoned him to answer some unstated charge; instead of appearing, Horne fled the country with his wife Margaret ("Mistress Madge," as Stapleton delighted in calling her).

Horne was therefore in the first wave which swept a Protestant elite out of England during the early days of Queen Mary's reign. This exodus is one of the most fascinating chapters in the whole Reformation story, and "if the facts," writes its historian, "after being arranged in their chronological sequence are then impartially examined, there can be little doubt that the so-called 'flight' of 1554 was not a flight but a migration, and, as such, one of the most astute maneuvers that has ever carried a defeated political party to ultimate power." Among those who departed, one can count, with the important exception of Parker, all the clerics who later rose to significant places in the early Elizabethan Church.

> When the body of Edwardian clergy and "students," who formed a majority of the first migration, left England, they had suffered no persecution. Their party had gone out of office; and they were being called upon, in their turn, to accept changes in administrative personnel for which Edward's reign had established a precedent having less canonical justi-

7. For what follows with regard to Horne see *DNB*, 9, 1253–56; Christina Hallowell Garrett, *The Marian Exiles* (Cambridge, 1938), pp. 188–90; and M. M. Knappen, *Tudor Puritanism, A Chapter in the History of Idealism* (Chicago, 1939), pp. 118–33.

fication than Mary's. A few, certainly, had been imprisoned, but for flagrant acts of sedition, not for heresy. And with un-exampled clemency, the greater number of even these po-litical offenders were soon released. Perhaps no words more aptly describe the nature of the Protestant exodus at its in-ception than those used by Laurence Humphrey to describe the flight of his friends from Magdalen: it was a "volunta-rium in Germania exilium."[8]

The exodus did not proceed without plan. As early as December 1553, there was formed a secret "Committee of Sustainers," whose twenty-five members were all of them prominent, prosperous, Protestant, and, for the moment, at peace with Mary's regime. The board, which assumed the responsibility for the education abroad of the future clergy of the reformed Anglican communion, was dominated by the wily William Cecil and the representatives of the great Protestant clans, the Russells, the Greys, and the Parrs. It chose for its agent and treasurer a shadowy figure named Richard Chambers who, early in 1554, departed for the continent. "Father of the exiles," Heinrich Bullinger dubbed Chambers, and indeed he did play the Maecenas for the students and clerics who had scattered from Strassburg to Zurich to Geneva. Himself not a man of much education, Chambers, as he traveled from one com-munity of exiles to the next, was always accompanied by a preach-er who would have been by definition a university product and who could therefore aid Chambers in dispensing his benefactions by testing the young scholars' proficiency in the sacred sciences or languages. More often than not, Chambers' traveling companion was Robert Horne. For after spending much of the winter of 1553–54 in Strassburg, Horne and his wife had moved on to Zurich where they arrived in April at which time, presumably, the fateful contact with Chambers was made.[9]

Meantime, a situation unique among the various pockets of English Protestant exiles was developing in Frankfort. Here the

8. Garrett, p. 2.
9. Ibid., pp. 111 ff.

most carefully laid plans of the Sustainers' Committee could not prevail, because here, in microcosm, were gathered all the conflicting elements in English Protestantism which in later generations not even a civil war, a Glorious Revolution, or an Oxford Movement could put to rest. A handful of Englishmen the majority of whom were Calvinists[10] arrived at Frankfort on June 27, 1554. The tiny community—no more, at this time, than fifty members—elected two ministers, John Knox, an ardent disciple of Calvin, and Thomas Lever, a "prayer-book man," that is to say, one who favored as the source for worship the second Prayer Book of Edward VI, which, for Knox and his majority, contained far too many papal frills. Lever kept his peace until the end of October when David Whitehead, the "most heavenly professor of divinity of his time,"[11] led a party into Frankfort which swelled the non-Calvinist minority. Trouble broke out between the two now nearly equal factions during the winter, and not until the end of April 1555 could a compromise be worked out whereby a service was adopted taken partly from the Prayer Book and partly from other sources. Instrumental in bringing about this delicate agreement was one of the most distinguished of the exiles, Richard Cox, sometime almoner to King Edward VI. Cox had arrived early in March, and with him had come John Jewel and, shortly afterward, Robert Horne with his powerful and mysterious friend Chambers.

The prayer-book men now outnumbered the Calvinists, and they possessed besides, in Chambers' carefully guarded account books, the power of the purse. The position of fiery Pastor Knox was thus rendered untenable. Expelled by the community and banished from Frankfort by the nervous town magistrates, who frowned on his public denunciation of the Emperor and the Em-

---

10. The chief source for these events is William Whittingham, *A Brief Discourse of the Troubles at Frankfort,* ed. Edward Arber (London, 1908). An eyewitness part of the time, an interested party throughout, Whittingham was a dedicated Calvinist and therefore hostile to Horne and Chambers.

11. The compliment comes not unexpectedly from Anthony Wood, quoted by Garrett, p. 326.

peror's daughter-in-law, Mary of England, Knox predictably went to Geneva and waited out his exile there. By September his colleagues had joined him, and the field in Frankfort was left open to the Anglicans (if one may so designate them) with their new pastor, Whitehead.

Robert Horne had come to Frankfort at the invitation of Cox in order to assist in drawing up the compromise liturgy. He had stayed on after the departure of the Calvinists, and, in January 1556 when Whitehead resigned, he became pastor. At this point, with the way events had developed, he might well have expected a harmonious ministry. The troubles, however, had hardly begun. As one hostile observer put it, "From [the election of Horne] the . . . contentions were so sore among them, that whoso shall well weigh it with due consideration . . . shall think it to be the just judgment of our righteous God that fell upon them for supplanting a church there before them [i.e. the Calvinists] in great quietness and of much sincerity."[12]

The contentions were mostly concerned with questions of discipline and finance. The opposition to Horne had been strong from the first—indeed, so strong that he did not take office for two months after his election "till he were cleared of certain suspicions which some had bruited to the discredit of his ministry." It had not abated in the months which followed, and it reached a climax in January 1557. At supper a quarrel erupted between Horne and a prominent lay member of the community, one Thomas Ashley. It began apparently over money and then spread to the many areas in which the two men did not agree. By the end of the month, Horne had threatened to turn Ashley over to the civil magistrates, and Ashley, for his part, had appealed against his pastor to the congregation.

On January 31, 1557, at the close of a tumultuous session, the English Church in Frankfort formally deposed Robert Horne and declared itself a congregationalist polity. Horne immediately appealed to the local magistracy, which pondered the case for several

12. Whittingham, p. 96.

weeks and finally, toward the end of February, instructed the congregation to restore Horne and his associates to "their former full authority." But only days later the magistrates, weary, no doubt, of involvement in the affairs of these wild English brethren, reversed their decision and, in the name of peace, called upon the community to draw up a satisfactory constitution and to elect new officers. Throughout the month of March the English debated what form their new discipline might take, while Horne and his friends (eighteen members out of a total of sixty-two) loftily boycotted the meetings. But they appeared on March 29 to cast their votes in the election of two ministers, six elders, and four deacons, and, if a hostile source can be trusted, they attempted to stuff the ballot box. However that may have been, the election went against them and Whitehead resumed his position as pastor.

Their cause defeated, their honesty called openly into question, Horne and Chambers nevertheless lingered in Frankfort for some months, and they did not scruple to cause their erstwhile companions plenty of trouble. Then, "early in a morning" in June, they departed secretly and in haste for Strassburg, leaving behind a mutilated account book. Little is known of the rest of Horne's exile. He was at Basel in the autumn of 1558, and, just before the death of Mary, he and Chambers appeared at Geneva, "having just completed a financial visitation to the English colonies." Early in 1559 he was back in England, functioning once again as Dean of Durham, and two years later, on February 16, 1561, he was consecrated to the wealthy and prestigious See of Winchester.

Even a casual observer of Robert Horne's adventures abroad must be struck by the man's canny capacity, through good days and bad, to place himself squarely on the winning side. Whether by luck or calculation, he teamed early with Chambers, who represented the real Protestant power in England, power securely in the hands of laymen. He helped bring down Knox and his Calvinists, and, though apparently discredited by the Frankfort congregationalists, it was he and not the eminent and victorious David Whitehead who became, four short years later, a lord bishop. It does not involve an adverse judgment of his character to suggest that Horne joined Chambers because he recognized where his best opportunity for ultimate service lay. Leaving aside as irrelevant and in any case unproved the allegations about his personal honesty, Horne emerges throughout his career as a pragmatist, a realist, the likes of which neither Knox nor Stapleton could understand. Horne was prepared to accept in England as much of the Protestant theology as he could get and to trim sail whenever an ill wind blew. He knew that Elizabeth was Protestantism's only hope in the British Isles and that, without her, popery and mummery (to use his words) would continue to hold the allegiance of the people. Left to himself, Knox would have preached the gospel pure and unalloyed and would have been burned for his efforts. As events turned out, Knox scored one of the Reformation's most complete triumphs in Scotland, but those same events demonstrated that Horne had been right all along, because, without Elizabeth in England, the Scottish Kirk would have been stillborn. It comes, therefore, as no surprise that when challenged by Feckenham and Stapleton about his devotion to the lay supremacy as embodied in the settlement of 1559, Horne reacted as though his life depended upon a successful refutation. In a very real sense it did.

"It is now an whole year past," wrote the Bishop of Winchester on February 25, 1566, "since I heard of a book scattered abroad by M. Feckenham among his friends, and in April last I came by a copy thereof." Seeing the author's "proofs so slender and his manner of dealing so shameless," Horne thought at first he would not dignify it with an answer. Then realizing that the book's "chief and principal purpose . . . was to ingraft in the minds of the subjects a misliking of the queen's majesty, as though she usurped a power and authority in ecclesiastical matters whereto she hath no right," as well as to slander the realm as though it were in heresy, and to "deface" the Christian ministry, he felt compelled to reply to it.[13]

13. Quoted in *Counterblast,* fol. 10.

Feckenham, Horne went on, had written a treatise in the Tower sometime after January 12, 1563. Horne himself, however, had no inkling of this when, by the following October, the ex-Abbot of Westminster was in his custody at Waltham, an estate in Hampshire belonging to the See of Winchester. From the time of his arrival there until the end of January (1564), "there was daily conference betwixt us in matters of religion." These discussions centered around the points which Feckenham claimed prevented him from taking the oath in good conscience. After some months of debate (that is, about the end of January 1564), Feckenham appeared to Horne to be convinced and ready to conform. "Ye had nothing to object, but seemed resolved and in a manner fully satisfied." Feeling this was so, Horne, with Feckenham's own good primarily in mind, "made relation . . . to certain honorable persons of the good hope I had conceived of your conformity." But Feckenham, when he learned of this from a friend, suddenly became recalcitrant because, observed Horne, he feared what his "confederates" might do, those Catholics, that is, who had not really trusted Feckenham since the latter had broken ranks at the Westminster conference in 1559.[14] From this time, Feckenham began to use "many shifts" and "continually [to] quarrel in sophistication of words." Almost in desperation Horne demanded that he present his position in writing, which statement might then serve as a basis for debate, but this Feckenham consistently refused to do. The Bishop even wrote out an "Assertio" of Feckenham's position as he, Horne, understood it, but this, too, failed to budge his opponent from silence and evasion. Finally, "being so much pressed herewith, and perceiving that your forward quarreling with the plain words of the Statute could no longer cover your evil meaning, at length you did require that I would put in writing the words of the Oath, with the sense or interpretation added thereunto, as you, considering thereupon,

---

14. For the Westminster conference, see Birt, *Elizabethan Religious Settlement*, pp. 98–119, and especially p. 110 for Nicholas Sander's disapproval of Feckenham's conduct.

might devise the form of your propositions, whereupon afterward we might debate."

Horne, therefore, went to considerable trouble to establish that his only interpretation of the oath had been written before he knew anything at all about Feckenham's book composed in the Tower a full year before. This was extremely important to the Bishop of Winchester because, before all else, he had to disavow remarks about the supremacy he had allegedly made in response to Feckenham's scruples, remarks which, could they have been proved to be his, might have damaged him irreparably. This task he could accomplish, of course, with greater ease if he could point to the whole of Feckenham's work, from its title[15] to its conclusion, as a tissue of lies. Horne's contention was that he had not learned of the treatise's existence until February 1564 when "certain persons of worship" came to Waltham to hear something of the debate. Feckenham, after a little discussion, seemed to yield on almost every point. Later, however, when Horne had left the company for a moment, Feckenham observed to some of the visitors that though the Bishop's arguments were all valid, yet "the matter itself is grounded here," and he pointed to his heart. A little later Horne came back into the room, informed already of the admission made in his absence, and, righteously indignant, he challenged Feckenham to prove now, after such a statement, that all his arguments were not pretense and that his conscience was not at all in a very bad state, allowing him, as it apparently did, to debate these important matters while all the time his position was settled and secret. Stung by this accusation, Feckenham offered to show Horne his treatise, prepared in the Tower, which could demonstrate that his feelings about the oath did indeed reflect a delicate conscience. And so, complained Horne, the work addressed to "the L. Bishop of Winchester" had been written in

---

15. "The Resolution of such scruples of conscience, touching the Oath of Supremacy, as M. John Feckenham did deliver unto the Lord Bishop of Winchester, with his Resolutions thereunto." This text, like Horne's, was incorporated into *Counterblast,* a common practice among the controversialists and, incidentally, a roundabout way of giving publicity to one's opponent's views.

January 1563 although the worthy prelate mentioned in the title did not come to know of its existence until February 1564 and had not read it before April 1565. This, concluded Horne, will give the reader some idea of the deceit habitually practiced by John Feckenham.[16]

Stapleton, replying to this account, based himself upon private sources whose identity, unfortunately, he did not reveal. Feckenham, a prisoner in the Tower, supposed "that the Oath of Supremacy, then passed in the Parliament holden at Westminster in the fifth year of the queen's majesty's reign, should forthwith (as it was probable) be tendered him and others, gathered . . . in a schedule certain reasons why he thought he could not with safe conscience receive the said Oath." He intended to present this "schedule" to the commissioners when they approached him; instead, he eventually gave it to Horne when, nine months after its preparation (October 1563), he was transferred to Waltham by order of "the queen her highness' honorable council," the oath not yet having been tendered him. It happened thus: there were daily conferences in religion between Feckenham and Horne at Waltham, and the Bishop kept urging the Abbot to put his position in writing and "open unto him the stays of his conscience touching the Oath of the queen's highness' Supremacy, being the whole matter and cause of his trouble, with no small promises that he should sustain no harm or injury thereby; and in fine, if there came no further fruit or benefit thereof unto him, the whole matter should be safely folded up, and left in the same state where they began." With this assurance, Feckenham gave Horne the "small treatise" he had prepared in the Tower, entitled "The Answer made by M. John Feckenham, Priest and Prisoner in the Tower, to the Queen's Highness' Commissioners, touching the Oath of Supremacy." Feckenham, of course, explained to Horne the title and the occasion for writing the treatise, apparently to the latter's satisfaction. Then Horne prepared "Answers" and Feckenham "Replies" to which Horne responded with the fateful

16. *Counterblast*, fols. 10–11. The dates used in the text presume the year begins on Jan. 1.

"Resolutions," and it was a copy of this "increased work" which Feckenham, after his return to the Tower in the early autumn of 1564, sent "to the right honorable, the Lord Earl of Leicester, and . . . . to Sir William Cecil, Knight and Secretary to the queen's highness." This latter fact, said Stapleton, made clear the falseness of Horne's charge that Feckenham spread his treatise abroad in order to subvert the Queen's authority: the Abbot was "one who had as his principal and chief regard how to satisfy his own and not other men's consciences, how to save himself from slanders . . . and not to work with other men by persuasion." Furthermore, Horne's great noise about answering "this book" was ridiculous; Feckenham's little "schedule" measured but "six poor leaves"; to have answered such a vast work, Stapleton said sarcastically, makes the Bishop of Winchester "worthy for this martial prowess to be, if all other things fail, a Prelate of the Garter."[17]

Feckenham's conduct at the Westminster conference (April 1559) had drawn hostile criticism from some Catholic quarters, as Horne well knew, but Stapleton did not hesitate to defend the Abbot in this matter also. Horne could not prove, he asserted, that other Catholics after Westminster had feared for Feckenham's constancy: between him and them there had been no more than a difference of opinion about procedure. When "the right honorable Lord Keeper of the Great Seal commanded the [Catholics] in the queen her highness' name to read their [statement] first, which they refused to do . . . yet [Feckenham] for his part thought it not good to disobey the queen's highness' commands therein, and thereupon offered himself to begin the disputation, and the Lord Keeper would not permit him to do so." Many Catholics, Stapleton went on, had been slandered in connection with this conference, as if "they were not able to defend and maintain their side." Actually, the Catholics at the conference had been gagged, unable to answer the first point before the second was introduced, treated, all in all, like a landlord "that had an hundred years and more

17. Ibid., fol. 3.

quietly enjoyed his lands, suddenly . . . disturbed and dispossessed thereof, unless he could prove his possession . . . to him that had no right or interest to claim the same."[18]

But, when Feckenham protested in his little book that he could not take "book oath" to the supremacy because he did not know that the Queen was so supreme or how he might come to have such knowledge, Horne brought up a more serious and more notorious instance of his inconstancy which could not be so easily explained away. "You did know . . . and confess this supreme authority in causes ecclesiastical to be in King Henry VIII and his heirs, when your abbey of Evesham, by common consent of you and the other monks there, under the convent seal, was of your own wills, without compulsion, surrendered into his hands," and "you by his authority reformed and forsook your foolish vow and . . . superstitions of monkery, and became a secular priest. . . . This knowledge remained steadfast in you all the time of King Edward, also." Feckenham, Horne admitted, had spent some time in the Tower during Edward's reign, but not because he denied the supremacy; he had erred in "other points of religion, touching the ministration of the sacraments" in which he had ultimately conformed, and "a right honorable gentleman procured your deliverance out of the Tower."

This misstatement of Horne's about Feckenham's imprisonment during Edward's reign was a serious tactical error because it gave Stapleton the chance to blur in the reader's mind the real point Horne was trying to make. Stapleton was nothing if not a skillful debater. The Bishop of Winchester is a liar, he said in effect, because he knows very well that Feckenham had been sent to the Tower by Cranmer as a result of his views about justification and that he had not won a permanent release by conformity. Stapleton then went on to prove convincingly that Feckenham had never been a Protestant in the Edwardian sense. It must be noted, however, that Horne had never accused the ex-Abbot of holding other than papist views on justification or indeed on the

18. Ibid., fol. 13. The conference, Stapleton concluded, had been a "fruitless and a superfluous enterprise."

administration of the sacraments, for which, as he said, perhaps mistakenly, Feckenham had been imprisoned. If Stapleton's account clarified this point, it did not meet Horne's real contention, that Feckenham now piously hid behind a naïveté about the crown's supremacy that he had never shown in the days of Henry VIII. In his attempt to absolve Feckenham from his original lapse (for so it was in Stapleton's eyes), he took a line that can only be described as disastrous. Feckenham's conformity during the reigns of Henry and Edward, he suggested, had come not from "knowledge," which he declared that he did not now possess, but from an impulsive and youthful ignorance, a privation of knowledge that rendered his decision a bad one.

After this piece of sophistry, Stapleton went on to call for the testimony of the great Catholic hero, Sir Thomas More, who had admitted in his famous letter to Cromwell that his position on the divine foundation of the papacy had come only after a long time and much study. "It is less marvel, therefore," observed Stapleton, "if at the first, for lack of mature and deep consideration, many good and well-learned men otherwise, being not resolved whether this primacy were immediately instituted by God, and so thinking the less danger to relent to the king's title, especially so terrible a law enacted against deniers of the same, were, and among them also Master Feckenham, carried away with the violence of this common storm and tempest." Now, however, the divine law "is clearly known to stand against it, and although the Pope's primacy were not grounded directly upon God's word, but ordained of the Church, yet could it not be abrogated by the private consent of any one or few realms, no more than the city of London can justly abrogate an Act of Parliament." In effect, concluded Stapleton, Horne has demanded that Feckenham "once again . . . fall quite over the ears into the dirty dunghill of filthy schism and heresy."[19]

As far as Stapleton was concerned, Feckenham's seven years of imprisonment and all the consequent indignities and privations

19. Ibid., fols. 38–39.

had been as heroic as his first fall "into the dirty dunghill of schism" had been shameful. Yet one wonders if the youthful and ardent Stapleton, righteous in his own exile, might perhaps have thought that the ordeal suffered by Feckenham, Bonner, and the men like them in 1565, splendid at it was, had been merited by their original sin committed twenty-five or thirty years before.[20] Whatever he thought, the controversialist's "no quarter" instinct prevailed as he tried to explain away Feckenham's capitulation to Henry VIII with questionable theology and with the shoddy excuse that cowardice becomes less culpable if "many and well-learned men" partake of it together. Of course, it may well have been that Feckenham, judged as an individual, had not clearly understood the magnitude of the decision he had made in 1539; however, Stapleton did not know this to be so when he wrote almost thirty years later. What he did know was that the whole-sale surrender of the clergy, of whom Feckenham was one, had made possible the alienation of England "from that apostolic see from whence we received our faith."[21] Even if the theologians of the thirties had some reservations about the divine foundation of the papacy, certainly the most ill-trained of them did not really think the king could claim God's appointment to headship of the Church. The introduction of Thomas More into the discussion widely missed the mark at which the peculiar logic of controversy should aim, for the conduct of the martyr-chancellor pointed up more vividly than anything else the failure of the Henrician clergy to do its duty. "The Fortress has been betrayed," John Fisher had said, "by them that should have defended it." Stapleton knew that More had stepped into a breach deserted by clerics not unlike John Feckenham who, for all his present troubles, still had his head firmly attached to his shoulders. What the young monk of Evesham had done cheerfully enough a generation before, the former Abbot of Westminster in 1563 fiercely refused to do, but if he deserved credit for his present state of mind, and Stapleton

20. In 1539 Feckenham would have been about the same age as Stapleton in 1566.

21. *Fortresse,* p. 391.

took it for granted that he did, that in itself did not justify a shifty apology for the Abbot's earlier judgment.

Bishop Horne, however, found Feckenham's present state of mind very troublesome, particularly insofar as the report of it threw a shadow of suspicion on the Bishop's own wholehearted acceptance of the settlement of 1559. Feckenham, it will be remembered, claimed that the treatise he had composed in the Tower he had eventually shown to Horne, who in turn had attempted to "resolve" the scruples Feckenham had expressed. The original text, together with these comments and "Resolutions," had been sent by Feckenham, after his return to the Tower, to Leicester and Cecil. Horne was anxious to deny his authorship of the Resolutions, and his concern was understandable; in fact, it seems not unlikely that this anxiety had more to do with the genesis of Horne's book than his concern for the Queen's authority and for the good name of the English ministry.

Feckenham explained the Resolutions this way: expressing repeatedly his scruples about the oath during the conversations at Waltham, Horne answered him "that he did much lament that the right meaning of the Oath had not been in season open and declared unto me, when the only lack of the right understanding thereof hath been the cause of such disturbance . . . of conscience. Whereas the queen's majesty's meaning in that Oath is far otherwise than the express words are, as they lie *verbatim,* like as it doth well appear by her highness' interpretation made thereof in the Injunctions." To this Feckenham replied that he nevertheless had to swear the oath verbatim, and that even in the Injunctions the Queen still claimed the jurisdiction exercised by her father and brother—no more, indeed, but no less. "For answer his Lordship did still continue in the denial thereof, and that her highness' meaning was not to take so much of spiritual power and authority upon her as they did; with affirmation that he most assuredly knew her highness' mind therein." Well, then, asked Feckenham, what does the oath really mean? What does it include? Horne replied by writing out the true interpretation of the oath: "I, A. B., do utterly testify and declare in conscience" that the Queen is "the only supreme governor" in all her dominions in matters temporal and matters spiritual. Thus, she has jurisdiction over all persons, temporal and ecclesiastical, she has the "power" to visit "the ecclesiastical estate," to reform and correct ecclesiastical persons as well as to check all abuses and heresies. Yet, said Horne, "in no wise meaning that the kings and queens of this realm, possessors of this crown, may challenge authority or power of ministry of divine offices,[22] as to preach the word of God, to minister sacraments or rites of the Church appointed by Christ to the office of Church ministers, to excommunicate, or to bind and loose." Three of these functions belong by right to the ministry and the fourth (excommunication) to the congregation itself. It is on these grounds, the Bishop had concluded, setting down his pen, that the oath demands the renunciation of all foreign jurisdiction, whether of prince or prelate.

Horne's rejoinder to this account was a flat denial. The "resolutions" described above "be your own," he wrote to Feckenham; "either ye could not or ye were ashamed to adjoin my answer to your silly objections, and therefore ye feigned me to utter for resolutions your own peevish cavillations." He denied that he questioned in any sense the verbatim construction of the oath, and it was no less than "a malicious slander" to say that he claimed to know the Queen's mind to be other than her words expressed. Feckenham had stated in his preface that Horne "did require" him to take the oath; did not this demonstrate, the Bishop asked, certainly with more zeal than logic, that he meant the oath to be understood literally? Dozens of witnesses of the conversations at Waltham, including Feckenham's own friends, could vouch for the fact that the Bishop of Winchester never tried to mitigate or mollify in the slightest way the Queen's authority as defined by the act.[23]

22. Up to this point—that is, until he began to give examples of what he meant, to "theologize," as will be seen below—Horne quoted the Queen's Injunctions (the official explanation of what the Act of Supremacy means, called "An Admonition to Simple Men Deceived by Malicious") word for word. See GH, pp. 438 ff.

23. *Counterblast*, fols. 437–40.

Stapleton found the core of his defense of Feckenham in these conflicting accounts. Here obviously, he wrote, is a *quaestio facti* hinging upon private conversations between two individuals: did Horne write the Resolutions in response to Feckenham's inquiries about the true interpretation of the oath, or did he not? The solution of this problem Stapleton left sensibly to "the discreet consideration of the indifferent reader. Yet, so much as I know, I will say, and that is that I understand by such as have had at several times communication with M. Feckenham, and, among other things, of this conference, heard M. Feckenham say that, touching these resolutions, he hath them of M. Daniel, then secretary to M. Horne, his hand writing, ready to be shown at all times. If it be so . . . M. Daniel can and will testify the truth in case he should be required, of whose handwriting M. Feckenham saieth he hath also other things copied out."[24]

But if Horne's secretary should fail to corroborate Feckenham's story, what then? The Abbot's general position, wrote Stapleton, would not really be weakened in such an instance "for whether these resolutions be true or false the principal point is neither greatly bettered nor much hindered by them." But, even in so "unlikely" a circumstance, Feckenham would yet have the testimony of the most important witness, Horne himself. For the whole burden of the Bishop's argument, the distinction, especially, which he made between the ecclesiastical power of the Queen and that of the bishops (as will be seen below), made it highly probable that this account was exactly what Horne had been saying all along. Horne, for fear of the government, had to answer Feckenham publicly that "the right sense of the Oath is none other than it is plainly set forth," that "when I add this supremacy to be in all spiritual causes and things, I show an universal comprehension to be meant, without exception, for if ye except or take away anything it is not all." Come now, Master Horne, said Stapleton, "are not these your own words?" The Queen's authority, by Horne's own admission, is "the chiefest, principalest, and a

24. Ibid., fol. 440.

general or universal authority in all things and causes whatsoever, as to preach, to minister the sacraments, and to loose and bind. ... Is it not evident that these things are spiritual and ecclesiastical?" Nevertheless, Horne, in his theological treatise, excluded from the Queen's jurisdiction these very functions in exactly the same way Feckenham alleged he had in their private conversations. These exceptions could be safely made by virtue of the Injunctions, in which the Queen explicitly stated that she "neither does nor ever will ... challenge authority and power of the ministry of divine offices in the church." Horne's position, therefore, the government permitted; the exceptions he made to the Queen's authority on theological grounds she agreed to for political considerations, interested principally as she was in "maintaining the sovereignty and rule over all manner persons born within these her realms, dominions and countries, of what estate, either ecclesiastical or temporal, soever they be, so as no other foreign power shall or ought to have any superiority over them."[25] Why, then, Stapleton asked, should Horne call Feckenham a liar when he related that what Horne wrote publicly in 1566 he had also written privately in 1564? The difference perhaps was that though the Bishop of Winchester publicly excepted certain ministerial functions from the Queen's supremacy, which exceptions the government permitted him to make, he did not dare claim publicly to know "the queen's mind" in this matter, to suggest that one need not bother about the *verbatim* construction of the oath. The control of the church did not belong to Horne and his fellow bishops but to the Queen and her lay advisers. Horne might proclaim all he wanted that the preaching of the word or the administration of the sacraments belonged only to the bishop's office: nobody in the government intended to ascend the pulpit or invade the baptistry; but neither Horne nor anybody else could voice the logical consequent that the Queen was therefore not supreme governor in every ecclesiastical cause. This tacit contradiction was a matter of policy on both sides, and it was the skimpy veil behind

25. The expression is found in the Injunctions. See GH, pp. 438–39.

which shrank the bishops' compromise with their principles, and the politicians' cynical disregard for anything practically inexpedient.[26]

The appearance of the Resolutions, however they evolved, did not quite ring down the curtain on the Horne-Feckenham quarrel. After the Bishop had given him the Resolutions, Feckenham wrote out further objections and submitted them to Horne. After waiting some time for the rejoinders, Feckenham finally received the courteous assurance that though discussion on these matters appeared useless because of Feckenham's own firm resolution, yet he remained the honored guest of Waltham and was still, said Horne, "unto me most heartily welcome." Moreover, to Feckenham's great relief, the Bishop suspended the daily conferences, and he promised his prisoner that whatever had been written or spoken in the course of those already held would never be used against him.

The events which followed hardly lived up to the magnanimous words. First, a rumor was spread abroad by Horne's servants that Feckenham had agreed to sign certain submissive articles; then, another story fixed the date and time of his formal recantation at the parish church in Waltham. "At his open table, and in the presence of many," complained Feckenham, Horne charged him with changing his religion nine times, and, "being put in further remembrance by one M. Denny,"[27] a guest of Horne's, the Bishop added that there must indeed have been at least nineteen changes and not only nine.

Somewhat later, again at the dinner table, Horne allowed this same Denny to abuse Feckenham, to charge the former Abbot of Westminster first with incontinence, "That if I had not as many children as he he did know that I deserved to have so many;"

26. See Tierney's observations, *Church History, 1*, 243–46.

27. Henry Denny (Denie) (1540–74) was the zealous Protestant son of Sir Anthony Denny, who had received from Henry VIII some of the lands of a dissolved nunnery at Waltham. Young Henry, a cousin to Walsingham, had been abroad during Mary's reign and counted Bullinger among his friends. See Garrett, *Marian Exiles*, p. 144.

then with gluttony, "affirming that I was an epicure;" and finally with hypocrisy. Horne appeared to enjoy all this so much that Feckenham felt certain that his lordship was really responsible for it. An hour after this stormy session, Feckenham was confined to "close imprisonment" at Waltham, and, six weeks later, "much contrary to his promises before made," Horne sent him back to the Tower. "Surely, for my own part," protested Feckenham, "I was never so used, neither openly nor privately, at any man's table in my whole life."[28]

Horne's recollection of the events was of course somewhat different. As far as he could remember, Feckenham presented him with his written objections sometime between Easter Sunday and Whitsun, about the end of April 1564. Two days later, after he had read them, the Bishop berated Feckenham for the malice and stubbornness evident throughout them, and he saw to it that the religious conferences continued into the following September. It was only then that Horne found it absolutely necessary to "sequester" his prisoner because of his loose and libelous talk, especially on those occasions when the Bishop himself was absent. One Sunday in September, at the dinner table, Feckenham chided Denny (whom he knew very well, for Denny had been a guest at Waltham off and on for three months) for being a glutton. Horne, who had just returned from a tour of preaching, thought at first that this exchange would prove to be only more of the "scoffing talk" which was common between the two men; they were jolly companions, noted Horne, and Feckenham "many times" sought Denny's company "to play at the bowls, to walk in the park, and to be merry together." But when Denny, obviously angry, began to reply to Feckenham's taunt, Horne motioned him to silence and said that he marveled at the ex-monk's accusation when he, Feckenham, every day of the week, including Friday, had his three meals a day, while Denny ate but one meal three days a week and never more than two.

Then, Horne continued, after he had "in a few words calmed

28. *Counterblast,* fols. 531–32.

the storm that seemed would arise betwixt M. Denny and you," he opened the usual theological discussion, this one dealing with the distinction between mortal and venial sin. Horne's remarks on this subject infuriated Feckenham, and "ye fell into such a rage that ye not only railed against the Bishop of Salisbury [Jewel], saying he was utterly unlearned and that he would never be able to answer M. Harding's book,[29] but also openly called me in almost plain terms a heretic." When Feckenham paused for breath, Horne told him to cease his "unmannerly" talk and promised he would have more to say to him later in private. After dinner, the Bishop summoned Feckenham to the gallery adjoining the latter's room, and told him that he was tired of repeating his warnings about scurrilous and "unseemly" talk, particularly at table, which "might breed peril to yourself, blame to me, and offense to others." From that day on, Feckenham no longer sat at the Bishop's table; all his needs were seen to in his own quarters, and he was allowed conference with no one. Yet he had no other keeper than before, his own servant who had a chamber next to his. Feckenham was still free to walk in the "parks, gardens, and orchards," and thrice in the week at least, whenever Horne himself lay at Waltham, he appointed some one to walk and converse with the prisoner.

These were the true circumstances, Horne contended, which led to Feckenham's "close imprisonment" at Waltham, a not too pleasant incarceration, as the Bishop carefully pointed out. He added that he would not divulge the nature of his complaint to the government, some weeks later, which occasioned Feckenham's return to the Tower. It had nothing to do, however, with the remarks the latter had made about the Queen and the laws of the realm during the course of the debates, because Horne had promised that none of this material would be used against Feckenham, and he meant to keep his promise. If anyone is curious about the specific charge, he suggested, let him ask the lords of the Queen's council. Above all, let Feckenham himself admit that all the complaints and propaganda in his book aimed at one mark,

29. Thomas Harding (1516–72), *An Answer to M. Jewel's Challenge* (Antwerp, 1564).

the recovery of favor with the members of his own faction, who were understandably dubious about his fidelity.[30]

Stapleton reported in full these accounts of the unhappy conclusion of the association between Bishop Horne and Abbot Feckenham, but he offered little comment on them. The matter, he remarked, could not be settled with the present state of the evidence, and so he felt he "must leave this to M. Feckenham's own defense when the time shall serve." But he could not resist a final dig at Horne over the question of fasting: it would be a marvel, he thought, if Feckenham, who had never eaten three meals a day in his life,[31] should suddenly begin doing so at Waltham.

> One thing I am sure of, M. Horne, he took no part of your fleshly breakfasts and suppers that ye in good store in your house had upon Fridays and other fasting days. Which example to be shown in your house, being a man of such vocation and countenance, against the laws of the Church and the realm, how it may be allowed, I leave it to the consideration of others. For I suppose neither yourself nor Mistress Madge, with all your other fleshly company, are fallen into such weakness, feebleness and consumption, nor are of so timorous and scrupulous a conscience, that either ye need or will tarry for a licence, I will not say to be sought at Rome, but nearer at hand, at London.[32]

Who won in the Horne-Feckenham quarrel? There was much about it of which Stapleton knew nothing, and he prudently said so. Yet he saw enough, he thought, to confirm his bias, and, putting to use his gift for biting sarcasm, he wrote to Horne: "For though I say you could handle your club, your buckler and your waster well and cunningly when you were in Cambridge, whereof ye will not stick, as it is reported, now and then to talk, when

30. *Counterblast*, fols. 533–34.
31. Stapleton overstated his evidence with this remark. See *DNB*, 6, 1149.
32. *Counterblast*, fols. 534–35.

you are disposed to brag of your youthly parts there played, yet to say the truth in this combat with M. Feckenham I see no such manliness in you." Even so, the most prejudiced observer could not help seeing that Horne in some respects scored heavily against his opponent. Feckenham was consistently vague in his references to dates and places, while Horne pinpointed these matters precisely. This showed up particularly in the conflicting accounts of the final break between the two men. When describing matters of fact, Horne usually exhibited not a trace of excitement; he wrote rather like a man calm and confident that his story will be believed because it is true. The one significant exception to this, however—his furious repudiation of his alleged Resolutions—spoiled a good deal of the general effect and gave Stapleton the opportunity to make use of an entirely reasonable question: why should Feckenham be denounced as a liar for recounting as Horne's private opinion the very notions essential to the latter's public thesis as well as to the spirit of the Thirty-nine Articles?[33]

In one important sense, Horne clearly did lose the argument: Feckenham did not conform. The daily conferences, surely themselves a sign of the Bishop's and the Council's eagerness to effect a change of mind in the apparently pliant Feckenham, had been in vain, and such a result hardly tended to be of benefit to Horne, especially when the failure came into public print. One of the most interesting, and perhaps significant, discrepancies in the two accounts is the way in which each principal described his personal relations with the other. Feckenham claimed that Horne, almost until the end of their year together at Waltham, remained always the soul of amiability, gracious and courteous, and that, even after the Bishop saw the daily conferences to be useless, he nevertheless assured Feckenham that the latter was "most heartily welcome" at Waltham. Horne, on the other hand, pictured his prisoner as a contentious sophist, as a man given to buffoonery and to the pleasures of the table; more significantly, he maintained that

33. See Article XXXVII in E. J. Bicknell, *A Theological Introduction to the Thirty-Nine Articles of the Church of England*, 3d rev. ed. H. J. Carpenter (London, 1955), p. 420 and the interesting commentary, pp. 425–29.

he himself had always been the sternest of keepers, and he explicitly denied suspending the conferences. Did the acrimonious exchange at the dinner table which occasioned Feckenham's "close imprisonment" mark a sudden and distressing reversal of attitude on the part of the Bishop of Winchester or was it, as that prelate contended, merely the result of accumulated exasperation at Feckenham's continued provocative conduct and "unmannerly talk?" Horne at any rate wanted his readers to understand that he consistently had assumed a harsh line with his prisoner because Feckenham, as early as January 1564, had proved himself thoroughly unreliable and untruthful.

Stapleton, assuming as he did that Horne was lying, must have been tempted to explain the Bishop's account otherwise. Horne had not only failed to convert Feckenham, but, deceived by the Abbot's genial disposition and notorious eagerness to please, he had also assured "certain honorable persons of the good hope . . . conceived of [his] conformity." Feckenham had disappointed Horne's expectation, and, more important, the announcement of his conversion, eagerly awaited by "certain honorable persons," never came. When he was writing his account of the events a year and more afterward, Horne had to explain both his failure and his sanguine predictions. It would hardly have been prudent for him to have described his association with Feckenham in terms of long, amiable theological discussions over fowl and wine, of evening walks in the cool of Waltham's "parks, gardens and orchards." Yet if Horne's account were the true one, it is astonishing that Feckenham should have complained of ill treatment only in the last weeks of his stay with the Bishop. If the months at Waltham had been but a long series of reprimands and humiliations for Feckenham, what did it profit him to extol the Bishop's kindness and consideration? Perhaps it was only in September 1564 that the Council had begun to press Horne for results; perhaps only then was it noised abroad how well the Bishop and the Abbot got on together.

Had Stapleton suggested this explanation (and he did not), he might have found some confirmation of it in one detail of that vexing question, Horne's alleged Resolutions. The Bishop of Winchester claimed that he wrote out an interpretation of the oath after beseeching Feckenham in vain to produce his own position in writing. Only then did he discover, quite by accident, the existence of the treatise Feckenham had written in the Tower. Finally, a couple of months thereafter (April 1564), Feckenham gave him, in writing, certain "objections" which, the Bishop noted carefully, he had answered verbally. Feckenham's side of the story was that, after he had received certain assurances, he answered Horne's urgent request for a written statement by presenting him with the treatise prepared originally for the Queen's commissioners in January 1563, and, so early in the course of conferences, this document actually did serve as a basis for debate, beginning with Horne's "Answers" to the treatise and concluding with his "Resolutions" and Feckenham's consequent objections. (The Resolutions, it will be remembered, amounted to a written interpretation of the oath.) One question put considerable strain on Horne's version: if Horne had consistently urged Feckenham to write down his position (and both agreed that he had), why did the Bishop refuse to put it to the use he had suggested, when there remained, as he insisted, seven full months (February to September 1564) of daily conferences after his discovery of the treatise's existence? And why did he imply that even after the discovery was made he had not bothered to read the document? A critic more kindly disposed toward him than was Thomas Stapleton could be pardoned for suggesting that Horne, anxious as he understandably was to dissociate himself from certain unpropitious remarks attributed to him, decided to repudiate the whole context in which they were said to have been made: he could not have claimed to know the "queen's mind" as his accuser said, because he had written his interpretation of the oath independently of any of Feckenham's silly objections. This was the logic of Horne's version of the "Resolutions," and it did little to enhance his credibility.

But Stapleton spun out no theories and contented himself instead with a parting gibe which had its own significance. Would the Bishop of Winchester apply for a "licence" to eat meat on Friday? Or, to put the fundamental issue in a less jocose form, did Horne and his associates accept in conscience, as the oath required, the crown's supremacy in matters ecclesiastical? "We know and confess," he observed, "in words they say so," but "doth not all the world see that these men themselves will be supreme governors in spiritual causes, and play the popes themselves?"[34] Whatever of importance or human interest the Feckenham-Horne episode had in itself, Stapleton viewed it chiefly as a background against which to set his criticism of the lay supremacy and its embodiment in the oath. He would have been among the first to admit that the checkered career of the Abbot of Westminster was not easy to defend, that his intellectual integrity was not above suspicion, but, with the odds more heavily against him than ever before in his unluckly life, John Feckenham had held firm in the face of threats and blandishments, and for this he deserved the gratitude and the protection of the Catholic party. Feckenham had done more, albeit unconsciously. In stating his pious and respectful objections to the oath, and, above all, in revealing Horne's indiscreet remarks about the supremacy (or, it may be, in maligning him) to, of all people, Leicester and Cecil, Feckenham had forced the Bishop of Winchester to set out in detail his curious views on ecclesiastical authority, to underscore, as it were, for every literate Englishman the theoretical contradiction in the politico-religious settlement of 1559. At least Thomas Stapleton found here, in the summer of 1567, a confirmation of what he had written a year or two before: "Only the miserable clawbacks of our country, not regarding what absurdities they commit, so that their wicked heresy may take place, both against the perpetual practice of Christ's Church and against their own fellow Protestants, do place the supreme government in spiritual causes in the lay prince; I may say further, against their own consciences."[35]

34. *Fortresse,* pp. 397, 350.
35. Ibid., p. 382.

Chapter 10

THE COUNTERBLAST

However much the quarrel between Robert Horne and John
Feckenham might have reflected the personal crises of two men,
it pointed to a larger issue: could anyone, save a complete Erastian, swear the Oath of Supremacy, imposed by English law, and
still claim to be a Christian? Feckenham phrased his objection in
various ways, but ultimately it always came to the same thing.
The Act of Supremacy and its Oath "give unto the queen's majesty
all manner of jurisdictions, privileges, and preeminences in any
wise touching and concerning any spiritual or ecclesiastical jurisdiction within the realm, with a . . . flat denial of all spiritual
jurisdiction unto the bishops . . . without her highness' special
commission granted thereunto." But "the express word of God"
grants to bishops certain areas of authority, and the articles of the
Creed which deal with the Catholic Church and the Communion
of Saints involve the notion of a jurisdiction not limited to any
one community. Therefore, the Queen cannot be the supreme
governor in every ecclesiastical cause. If a man believed this line
of reasoning to be correct and nevertheless took the oath in exchange for his life, freedom, or advancement, he would commit
perjury.[1]

Robert Horne would hardly have been a man of his time had
he not characterized an opponent's position as made up of "silly
objections and peevish cavillations," as a "foul sophistication,"
and, since the opponent had once been the member of a religious
order, as "nothing else but a misshapened lump of words . . . a

1. *Counterblast*, fol. 444; also fols. 404, 417, 420.

monkish dream without rhyme or reason."[2] Verbal abuse played
its part in the sixteenth-century game of controversy, and the
Bishop of Winchester was an adept practitioner of a milder form
of the art. But he had other devices, too, the chief of which was
that most venerable of scholastic tools, the distinction. Your minor,
he said, in effect, to Feckenham, *concedo,* but your major *distinguo;*
understood properly, the Act of Supremacy involves no "flat
denial" of episcopal authority.

Theology, as it is a deductive science, demands that its agent
begin his reasoning process with some revealed principle, and
Horne of necessity had produced one. He found it in two documents, the Act of Supremacy itself, and the appendix to the
Queen's Injunctions of 1559, entitled "An Admonition to Simple
Men Deceived by Malicious." The Act of Supremacy assumed
the task of "restoring and uniting to the imperial crown of this
realm the ancient jurisdictions, authorities, superiorities, and pre-
eminences to the same of right belonging and appertaining."
Therefore, it specified that jurisdiction exercised heretofore "by
any spiritual or ecclesiastical power for the visitation of the ecclesiastical state or persons, and for reformation, order and correction of the same, and of all manner errors . . . and enormities
shall forever, by authority of this present Parliament, be united
and annexed to the imperial crown of this realm."[3] And so, in imposing the oath, the government demanded that responsible officials swear that the Queen was the "only supreme governor of
this realm . . . as well in all spiritual or ecclesiastical things or
causes as temporal," that they renounce "all foreign jurisdictions,"
and that they defend "all jurisdictions, pre-eminences, privileges
and authorities granted or belonging to the queen's highness, her
heirs and successors."[4]

The Injunctions, the second part of Horne's *locus theologicus,*
aimed at enlightening "sundry of [the Queen's] native subjects
being called to ecclesiastical ministry of the Church," who had

2. Ibid., fols. 439, 449.
3. GH, pp. 442, 447.
4. Ibid., p. 449.

been "by sinister persuasion and perverse construction induced to find some scruple in the form of an oath which by Act of the last Parliament is prescribed to be required of diverse persons for their recognition of their allegiance to her majesty." The Queen therefore assured such subjects that she "intended" by the oath to demand no more "than was acknowledged to be due to the most noble kings of famous memory, King Henry VIII . . . or King Edward VI." Furthermore, she put it down to "perverse and malicious persons" that the oath had been interpreted by some to mean "the kings and queens of this realm, possessors of this crown, may challenge authority and power of divine office in the Church. . . . For certainly her majesty neither does nor ever will challenge any other authority than that was challenged and used" by her father and her brother: "that is, under God to have the sovereignty and rule over all manner persons born within these her realms . . . either ecclesiastical or temporal."[5]

Horne took care never to exceed the literal limits set by these two authoritative pronouncements, neither in his alleged private conversations nor in his public thesis. He took care, that is, never to allow his theological argument actually to contradict the wording of the act or of the Injunctions. How successfully he combined his principle with his application of it, indeed, how true he remained to the meaning of the act, was another question. Spiritual jurisdiction, he explained, is of two kinds, cohibitive and non-cohibitive, of which the former is itself divided into two parts. The first kind of cohibitive jurisdiction is the exercise of excommunication and the "circumstances thereunto required by Christ's institution." This power belongs not to prince, bishop, or priest but only to the Church and "to those who receive commission thereunto by the Church." The second kind of cohibitive jurisdiction is that proper to the *forum causarum* or the *forum publicum et externum*. It includes the power to promulgate and to execute law, to judge in matters of controversy, "and, in surmise, to do those things that justice doth require according to the laws."

5. Ibid., pp. 438–39.

Noncohibitive jurisdiction, the Bishop continued, "is exercised and worketh in the inward and secret court of conscience: that is, the preaching of the word, ministration of the sacraments, and the absolving and retaining of sins by the word of God in the public ministry." Here is the internal forum, to which no man is summoned against his will. Here is authority exercised not by kings or magistrates but only by those "lawfully called thereunto."

For this distinction Horne cited the work of one Joannes Antonius Delphinus,[6] and, to elucidate further the second kind of cohibitive jurisdiction, the real point at issue, he quoted another scholastic, Joannes Quintinus:[7] "This cohibitive jurisdiction . . . is not properly signified by the name of the keys; for although it may be named (in some respect) a church key yet it differeth very much from the keys of the first court, that is, of the court of conscience. For the use of those keys, that are occupied in the court of conscience, belongeth only to the evangelical priests. But this jurisdiction may be lawfully exercised of those that are not ministers of the word and sacraments, and are not priests." This kind of jurisdiction, Horne pointed out, depends upon the positive law of Christian magistrates or, if these be lacking, "upon the positive rules and orders of that Church where such orders must be practiced, and not immediately upon the law of God."[8] Feckenham had been asked to swear (in 1559) that the Queen has all jurisdiction in matters ecclesiastical, although she has explicitly denied that she does or ever will "challenge authority and power of ministry of divine offices in the Church." In other words, Horne concluded, the oath requires a man to grant that the crown possesses the fullness of the second kind of cohibitive jurisdiction without troubling him over the other two kinds.

6. Giovanni Antonio Delfini (1507–61) was a conventual Franciscan, professor of logic and metaphysics at the University of Bologna, theologian at the first two sessions of the Council of Trent. See *Enciclopedia cattolica,* 4 (Citta del Vaticano), c. 1356.

7. Joannes Quintinus (1500–61), professor of law at the University of Paris, published in 1547 a commentary on Gratian. See A. Van Hove, *Prolegomena* (Mechlin, 1945), p. 561.

8. *Counterblast,* fols. 444–45.

If a Catholic author had quoted a work of Delphinus, wrote Stapleton in rebuttal, the argument would have been by Horne "with great contempt refused and rejected." Actually, this author, with whom "M. Horne thinketh so to bewitch his reader with certain magical incantations," had first made the more fundamental distinction, "as other schoolmen do," between the power of order and the power of jurisdiction. To the former belongs the power of interpreting Scripture, of confecting the sacraments, and matters of this kind. Delphinus did indeed divide jurisdiction into cohibitive and noncohibitive, but Horne deserted his author completely when he forced preaching and administration of the sacraments into the noncohibitive classification, for Delphinus restricted noncohibitive jurisdiction to sacramental confession in which alone is there in force "the secret court of conscience."[9] "Preaching and ministering of sacraments do not appertain to noncohibitive jurisdiction, as absolution doth, but to the power or key of order, which (properly to speak) is no jurisdiction at all."

Moreover, in his description of cohibitive jurisdiction, Horne had done nothing but pile up "a heap of follies and lies." Neither Delphinus nor Quintinus made the division Horne attributed to them; they did not "sever and dismember excommunication from the hearing of causes ecclesiastical . . . in public and external court." Quintinus had indeed said that those who exercise cohibitive jurisdiction need not be priests, but had it eluded Horne's notice that his author also specified that they be at least in minor orders? Why had not the Bishop explained that another of Quintinus' opinions, quoted in this connection, "that all authority to judge descendeth from the prince alone," had been lifted bodily from the author's discussion of temporal power? The restriction of the power to excommunicate "to the whole Church and congregation is a fond, foolish and frantic imagination" which Horne did not learn from any scholastic. "And as it is not far from heresy, so perchance it is not far from a praemunire. What mean you, M. Horne, by this Church?" The whole Church, taken in the

9. Stapleton cited *De potestate ecclesiastica* (Venice, 1552), Bk. II, pp. 36b, 37a.

literal sense, cannot possibly come together; and, if Horne had
in mind the general council, excommunication would be a rarity
indeed, since these great meetings convene so seldom. ("And
yet," added Stapleton, "few as they are, diverse of them have already excommunicated such heresies as ye maintain.") Even if
Horne meant simply a particular church, in its smallest and most
compact form, the thing remained impossible because every man,
woman, and child would have to be summoned and consulted,
"for they be as well parts of the Church as the wisest and eldest
in the parish." Horne had charged Feckenham with subverting
the Queen's authority. Did not his own denial of her power of excommunication amount to subversion? "Now, as I said, take ye
heed lest to your great folly [there be] annexed a dangerous
praemunire."[10]

Feckenham had objected that he could not take the oath without corrupting the Creed: "I must renounce all foreign authorities,
which for a Christian man to do is directly against these two
articles of our Creed: I do believe in the holy Catholic Church,
I do believe in the Communion of Saints."[11] Horne replied that
there was absolutely no mention of the "Catholic Church" in the
oath, and that anyway the true definition of the Church rendered

---

10. *Counterblast*, fols. 445–49. Note also the text of Article XXXIII of
the 1563 Articles (unchanged, in this instance, from the Forty-Two Articles
of 1552): "That person which by open denunciation of the Church is rightly
cut off from the unity of the Church and excommunicated, ought to be taken
of the whole multitude of the faithful as an heathen and publican, until he is
openly reconciled by penance and received into the Church by a judge that
hath authority thereunto." Stapleton objected to this exposition (which Horne
faithfully adhered to) as contrary to the oath, his point throughout. Horne
was not inconsistent with regard to the administration of the sacraments or to
preaching, and again the Articles supported him (Article XXXVII explicitly
quoted the ambiguous language of the Injunctions); the Bishop of Winchester
was allowed to specify as he and the framers of the Articles had done without
fear of government objection. But Stapleton insisted on keeping the question
on the sometimes uncomfortable ground of conscience where theory and
formulae necessarily play some part: could one agree to swear the oath, accept
the Injunctions, subscribe to the Articles, and cheer the arguments of Robert
Horne without somewhere along the line telling a lie?

11. *Counterblast*, fol. 420.

the objection meaningless.[12] But Stapleton braved the Bishop's brusque dismissal and returned to this point. "I reply: In that you exclude foreign power and authority, you exclude also the Catholic Church, which is no less foreign to you than is the Pope to whom the Church is subject. . . . What a heap of absurdities do follow thereof!"

Is the pope " 'every foreign prelate' or if he be not, why swear you against 'every foreign prelate?' Secondly, is 'every foreign prelate' the Pope? Then have we, I trow, more Popes than one." To renounce every foreign prelate applies as much, said Stapleton, to the bishops of Milan and Toledo and Reims as it does to the pope, and such an act rejects the faith not only of the pope but of all the bishops who share his faith, rejects, really, "all society, communion and fellowship of saints, that is, of faithful folk in the Church of Christ." The renunciation of every foreign prelate must include as well "the Lutheran and Sacramentary Superintendents of Geneva, of Zurich, of Basel, of Wittenberg and of all other Protestant prelates without the realm of England. . . . And so you stand post alone in matters of religion . . . as though you had a warrant from the Holy Ghost neither to fail in faith nor at any time to have princes that may fail." The oath has made an English subject not only stand by his sovereign against foreign political interference, which he would do in any case, but also give his conscientious support to the government in spiritual matters against, if need be, the decision of foreign prelates, whoever they are or under whatever auspices they teach:

12. "The Catholic Church of Christ," said Horne, "is a multitude, society and communion of saints and faithful ones that have been, shall be and are now [alive] in the earth, how and wheresoever they be divided and dispersed in time and place, the which multitude of saints have a participation in communion amongst themselves of all good things given, granted and growing from God through Christ, of spirit, faith, prayer, sacraments, remission of sins and heavenly bliss; and are united to Christ their head by faith and fastened together amongst themselves, as members of one body, with the bond of love." Commented Stapleton: "Now the definition or description of the Catholic Church, such as you bring, is much like to a shoe that serveth every foot, or to a Welshman's hose that serveth every leg." *Counterblast,* fols. 422, 431.

If all prelates and bishops of the world beside would meet together or otherwise agree in one truth, order or law ecclesiastical (which hath often been done and may always be done in General Councils) the subjects of England are bound under pain of perjury and of a praemunire to renounce all such orders, laws and concluded truths; which is shortly to say, to renounce and forswear all obedience to General Councils, that is, the whole corps of Christendom represented therein, except it should please the prince and prelates of our country to agree to the same. Which is to make our prince and our prelates either as superiors to all other princes or countries, or, at the least, as aliens and strangers from the whole body of Christendom beside, as though we had a proper Christ, a proper gospel, and looked for a proper heaven in which the other Christian nations should find no place. And what is this else but by book Oath flatly to renounce the Catholic Church and the Communion of Saints, both of which in our Creed we profess to believe.[13]

If other nations should follow the English pattern, "what end will there be of schisms and dissensions in the Church? What hope of unity can be conceived? Or how can ever unity be long maintained?" The Protestants had really scuttled the ideal of Christian unity in order, charged Stapleton, to destroy with it the concept of the general council, and particularly the effectiveness of the Council of Trent.

They which conceived and edited first this . . . part of the Oath . . . had they not (trow you, M. Horne) a direct eye to general councils, and did they not by that clause closely disburden and discharge the whole realm of obedience to general councils, namely to the general Council of Trent that then was assembled? . . . Again, if so much was not intended, how cometh it to pass in the Injunctions where the Oath is drawn (as much as may be) to a gentle exposition, this part

13. Ibid., fols. 423–26.

is not so interpreted as it might not seem to exclude the authority of general councils.[14]

In another context Horne had already made clear that his distinction of spiritual jurisdiction depended not so much upon the literal meaning of the authors cited as upon the limitations fixed by the secular state within which the Protestant conscience was permitted to function. The difficulty Horne found himself in, argued Stapleton,[15] resulted from his own inability to admit that the layman's supreme governance of the Church could be taken literally. If the rock of faith and the only source of truth were Scripture, what could a Protestant bishop possibly do with the glaringly clear biblical testimonies that churchmen did rule their flocks?[16] Take, for example, as Feckenham did, St. Paul's exhortation to the bishops of Ephesus: "Take heed to yourselves and to the whole flock of Christ in which the Holy Spirit has placed you as bishops, to rule the Church of God, which he has purchased with his blood."[17]

Horne took a scholarly approach to this serious objection, maintaining that the word which Feckenham quoted as "rule" actually in the Greek meant "feed."[18] Therefore, he said, the only kind of rule these and all bishops have been charged with is "the feeding of God's Church with the spiritual food of the gospel. So . . . the bishoply rule and government of God's Church consisteth in these three points, to feed the Church with God's word, to minister Christ's sacraments, and to bind and loose." Besides this, he added, there is another kind of rule in the Church, "which appertaineth only to kings, queens and princes, and not to the apostles, bishops and priests": This is "the supreme authority and power of the sword, to guide, care, provide, direct and aid God's

14. Ibid., fol. 429.
15. Ibid., fol. 83.
16. E.g., Heb. 13:17 and I Peter 5:2.
17. Acts 20:28.
18. The Greek verb is *poimaino,* to feed, tend; to keep flocks; to be a shepherd; metaphorically, to cherish, guide, lead, govern. The Vulgate uses the verb "regere," the Reims (1582) "rule," the King James (1611) "feed."

Church, to further, maintain and set forth true religion . . . and
to oversee . . . and correct all manner persons, with all manner
errors, superstitions, heresies . . . and enormities."[19]

"By likelihood," wrote Stapleton, "M. Horne thinketh that
there is not true rule or government but where the sword beareth
rule; wherein he thinketh as well and reasoneth as substantially
as doth M. Jewel, avouching that S. Peter was not head of the
Church, because he took up his dwelling with a poor tanner." And
then Stapleton put his finger on the spot the Lord Bishop of Winchester found most difficult to explain:

> The shepherd, M. Horne, doth not only feed his sheep and
> carefully chooseth out such ground and pasture as is most
> convenient and wholesome for them; but, besides that,
> sundereth the whole and sound from the infected and rotten,
> he greaseth and tarreth them, he bindeth, he cutteth them;
> he hath a staff with a hook to draw them in when they stray;
> he hath a staff to beat away the wolf and other ravening
> beasts. And what doth all this but resemble and express unto
> us the pastoral office of bishops and prelates? Who ought
> to tell the people what is good and bad, what is truth, what
> is falsehood, what is heresy, what is Catholic faith but these
> pastors? Where then was this lesson of late when lay men
> only, by Act of Parliament, took upon them to teach the
> whole clergy? Did not then less men than kings, queens and
> princes (who may not, you say now, claim or take upon them
> this kind of spiritual government and rule to feed the Church
> with God's word) take upon themselves to feed all the realm
> with such doctrine as it pleased the Parliament to allow, the
> Parliament, I say, of lay men only, not one bishop among
> them, you being neither by the law of God . . . neither yet
> by the law of the realm any bishops at all.[20]

Stapleton reasoned that the passage of the Act of Uniformity over
the objection of the spiritual peers and of convocation emphasized

19. Quoted in *Counterblast*, fols. 404–05.
20. Ibid., fols. 409–10.

the poverty of Horne's distinction. Certainly provisions of the act had to do with "the feeding of God's Church," strictly as episcopal function according to Horne, and yet it had been laymen only, wielding the power of the sword, who had settled the "ground and pasture":

> One thing would I fain know more of you M. Horne, if I may be so bold, and learn what you mean . . . with the "supreme authority and power of the sword" . . . with the Act of Parliament [you] take away from the clergy the power and authority to make church laws and constitutions; and you say and swear, too, that no convocation or council of bishops shall or may have force or authority to decree any constitution ecclesiastical without the prince's consent, licence and supreme authority . . . What? Did not the apostles govern the Church of Christ all the time of their abode here on earth? And when or where, I pray you, used they the power of the sword? . . . Learn now, then, M. Horne, that the Church of Christ hath a power above the sword and that . . . [it] is ruled by the spiritual keys committed to the apostles and their successors, and the transgressors of the Church's laws are punished by the sword of that spiritual jurisdiction. S. Augustine saith: "Phinees the priest slew the adulterers with the sword; which truly was signified to be done in this time with degradations and excommunications, when, in the church discipline, the visible sword should cease." Lo, M. Horne, the visible sword is no part of the church discipline now. It was among the Jews a great part of their discipline. Mark that it was no part of the Church discipline. I do not deny, as the Donatists did, that because in the apostles' time princes did not use the sword upon heretics and disobedient Christians, therefore they should not now use it. I say, with S. Augustine, this visible sword in the church discipline ceaseth. The bishop hath a far superior government and a more terrible sword to strike withal.[21]

21. Ibid., fols. 413–14.

What, then, did Stapleton think of Bishop Horne's theological distinction? "And of all madness, this is a madness, and a most open contradiction, to remove these things from the prince, as ye do, and yet to attribute to him, without exception, the supremacy 'in all things or causes ecclesiastical.' Neither M. Feckenham nor any man else may take this Oath without evident and open perjury."[22]

But Stapleton's criticism did not limit itself to Horne's deductions: it struck as well at the revealed principle itself. The distinction between cohibitive and noncohibitive jurisdiction was made possible only by a liberal interpretation of the Queen's Injunctions. Horne's explanation, said Stapleton, made but a "poor, silly and insufficient shift . . . yet it is the best ye may now find to qualify and mitigate the general words of the statute. Which indeed are so general and preemptory that they may in no wise be borne without some qualification." To fill this "notorious need," the Queen's admonition has stated "that men should not take the general clause so largely as to collect thereby that the kings or queens of this realm may challenge authority and power of ministry in the divine offices of the Church."

> Now though this be a necessary interpretation and moderation, yet this doth not take away the scruple that remaineth, staying M. Feckenham, and others, too, in taking the said Oath; for that this interpretation is not made by Act of Parliament as the statute was. Neither doth the Act or statute refer itself to any such Injunctions to be made for the qualification or restraining of anything in the Act or in any branch thereof contained, no more than it doth to M. Horne's book. Neither hath any Injunction by the law of our realm any force to restrain, weaken, mollify the rigor or generality of an Act of Parliament.[23]

The Bishop of Winchester has sworn therefore a false oath: "Swearing to all causes, the principal causes are excepted, and so

22. Ibid., fol. 411.
23. Ibid., fol. 443.

he that sweareth forsweareth." In demanding that Feckenham and, in his person, every loyal Englishman do likewise, Horne, it seemed to Stapleton, had taken a great deal upon himself:

> What if you and your fellows intend not or mean not all manner spiritual causes? Can this excuse them which swear to all from manifest perjury? How many have received the Oath which never understood word of any such limitation? If you mean indeed a limitation, M. Horne, procure then that the limitation be put into the Oath expressly, that men may swear to no more than is intended. Else if you intangle men's souls in open perjury, under a covert limitation, assure yourself that you and all other procurers hereof shall answer full dearly to God for all the souls that hereby have perished.[24]

In the final analysis, Feckenham had pressed Horne back upon the very words of the act. The Queen has "all manner jurisdictions" which "in any wise" concern "any spiritual or ecclesiastical jurisdiction . . . in any manner." She has become the single source of authority in the Church because no one except "such person or persons . . . your majesty, your heirs or successors shall think meet" assigned "by letters patent under the great seal of England" can exercise any power whatsoever. Does not this, asked Feckenham, involve "an express debar and flat denial" of episcopal jurisdiction without "her highness' special commission?"[25]

Not at all, answered Bishop Horne. "The Statute giveth, or rather restoreth, to the prince jurisdiction and authority to inquire after what sort the ecclesiastical state and persons behave themselves in their cures and charges, to reform and correct the disorders . . . rising amongst them to the hindrance of their office." Feckenham employed the expressions "all spiritual jurisdiction," "in any wise," and "all manner" as though they were meant to modify "the gift or restitution of spiritual jurisdiction made by

24. Ibid., fol. 459.
25. Ibid., fols. 449–51.

the Act unto the prince." But, said Horne, these terms have reference to "that part where the Act giveth afterward power and authority to the prince to execute the jurisdiction, now united and annexed to the crown, by meet delegates to be assigned . . . and authorized by letters patent under the great seal of England." Such universal words as "any" and "all" are "restrained and bounded within the limits of the gift"; that is—and here Horne took his courage in both hands—these terms "give rightly" to the prince universal power in matters falling under the second kind of cohibitive jurisdiction, but they do not infringe the exclusive rights of the bishops to preach and to administer the sacraments, or the right of the Church to excommunicate, because these matters lie outside the "limits of the gift."

This explanation of the limitation of the prince's power Stapleton found "a wondrous and marvelous interpretation" though he affected some concern lest the Bishop might have placed himself in a "dangerous" position: might not someone say "that you deal very ill with the words of the Act, and you express an unkindly meaning to the prince and the state?"[26] Stapleton had other questions, too. "Think you, M. Horne, that M. Feckenham hath or will allow your first and second cohibitive jurisdiction?" Does that distinction have its source "in any good divine [or] in any book of the temporal law in all England?" And even if it had, why would the prince retain the second type of cohibitive jurisdiction and not the first? Why would excommunication be severed from its proper judicial and administrative setting? Finally, when was this jurisdiction taken away from the princes so that now it must be restored to them again?

The only examples of royal commission of the kind mentioned by Horne, said Stapleton, were those issued during the reign of Edward VI. "There I find, though untruly, that all jurisdiction, as well secular as spiritual, spring from the king as supreme head of all men." By such commissions, the bishops were authorized

---

26. This was a sarcastic reference to Horne's preface, where the same question was asked of Feckenham.

not only to hear ecclesiastical cases but even to ordain[27]—both at the king's pleasure. "And three months thereafter, all bishops and archbishops were inhibited from exercising any ecclesiastical jurisdiction until the visitation appointed by the king were ended."[28] Next, citing Foxe, Stapleton recalled the case of Stephen Gardiner, who was commanded by the Protector to refrain from preaching on the controversial aspects of the Eucharist and to be content with "the expert explication of the articles prescribed unto him etc." Two years later, during his examination before the King's commissioners at Lambeth, the tenth article of the charge cited Gardiner for having disobeyed this injunction, that he "did, contrary to the said commandment and inhibition, declare diverse his judgments and opinions in the same." Gardiner's deprivation and imprisonment followed upon his disobedience in this matter. "Did not the king here take upon himself the very first cohibitive jurisdiction, as you call it? Did not he abridge Christ's commission given immediately to the bishops, and limit the exercise thereof to his own pleasure and commandment?" It must be a great comfort to know, observed Stapleton tartly, that the Queen expects no more acknowledgment of power in spiritual matters than her brother had, especially in view of her own recent restraint upon preaching. Nevertheless, "M. Horne, take heed of perjury!"[29]

For Horne had indeed dealt "very ill with the words of the Act," as Stapleton was quick to point out. The universality of expression to which Feckenham had objected in the use of words like "all" and "any" applied, said the Bishop, not to the jurisdiction given the crown but to the Queen's power of commissioning —that is, the Queen may give all her power in any case to whomsoever she pleases, but, he added, as the act specifies, this commission is restricted to "the visitation of the ecclesiastical state and persons." In other words, the government's authority, universal

---

27. Stapleton quotes a "Commissio Regia" dated Feb. 7, 1547. It is now printed in Edward Cardwell, *Documentary Annals of the Reformed Church of England,* 1 (Oxford, 1839), 1–4.

28. For an instance see ibid., pp. 24–25.

29. *Counterblast,* fols. 451–53.

as far as it goes, still is confined explicitly by the act to the second kind of cohibitive jurisdiction. This exegesis Stapleton derided as "against all order and course of writing or reason. . . . Dare you then to restrain an Act of Parliament to the only second kind of cohibitive jurisdiction, a kind of jurisdiction by yourself invented?" The clauses which Horne used thus to restrict the royal prerogative occurred in the paragraph preceding the objectionable universal expressions. Or, as Stapleton expressed it: "They go before that general gift; neither do they or can they limit that generality, going (as I have said) before it."

Stapleton further suggested that "the Reader for better trial hereof . . . consider and peruse the Act itself." Anyone who does will not find it difficult to see what he was driving at. The paragraph of the act that includes the clause "for the visitation" and so on had to do specifically with visitation; it ruled that whatever "jurisdictions" and "superiorities" had exercised that function heretofore were now "united and annexed to the imperial crown of this realm." The paragraph immediately following dealt with the Queen's power to commission fit persons to exercise her authority. First it designated how and to whom that authority might be committed, then described that authority itself, and, finally, granted that properly credited commissioners might also be appointed visitators. The second section of this paragraph, of course, was what aroused Feckenham's objections,[30] and Horne had answered them by lifting a clause from the preceding paragraph which had no connection, literary or logical, with the reprehensible phrases.[31] Had not, concluded Stapleton, Horne said "a

30. "To exercise, use, occupy and execute under your highness . . . all manner of jurisdictions, privileges and pre-eminences in any wise touching or concerning any spiritual or ecclesiastical jurisdiction. . . . And to visit, reform, redress, order, correct and amend all such errors . . . which by any manner spiritual or ecclesiastical power . . . may be lawfully reformed." GH, pp. 447–48.

31. In other words, Horne said that these sweeping powers ("any," "all") are meant to include only the Queen's rights of visitation and correction which she may delegate in their fullness: "used for the visitation of the ecclesiastical state and persons." This last phrase is found in the paragraph

great deal more against the Oath than ever M. Feckenham said?"[32]

"I marvel," Stapleton had remarked in an earlier context, "ye bearing the state of bishop have so little faith and honesty; or dwelling so nigh Winchester school, so little sight in the grammar."[33] Horne's juggling of sections within the act put the finishing touch to what his invention of cohibitive jurisdiction had begun: John Feckenham could surely be excused for objecting to the oath if Robert Horne could only swear it with the reservations he had indicated. Indeed, wrote Stapleton, "we need to wrestle no further with you, seeing you can so roundly give yourself so notable a fall."[34] The judgment Stapleton had passed on Horne elsewhere, with all its harshness and sarcasm, applied also in this instance:

> If this be your own new, fresh invention, then have you a jolly, pregnant wit, and ye have deceived as well others as the late reverend father, M. Bayne, late Bishop of Coventry and Lichfield, his expectation, sometime your reader in Cambridge that was wont to call you "quovis cornu duriorem," that is, harder than any horn. But I pray you, good Sir, is your authority invoidable? Must we needs sing "sanctus, sanctus, sanctus" to all your sayings? and say of you as Pythagoras' scholars were wont to say, "ipse dixit," and reason no further? Let poor blunt fellows be so bold upon you for once to hear from you some better authority than your own naked word for this noble exposition.

Really, however, Stapleton on this occasion was happy enough to hear only the "naked word" of the Bishop of Winchester, because it gave him an opportunity to press home two related conclusions about ecclesiastical authority within the settlement of

---

prior to the one containing the description of her powers (ibid., p. 447) and this, said Stapleton, is deception.

32. *Counterblast*, fols. 453–59.

33. Stapleton, it will be remembered, was himself an alumnus of Winchester School.

34. *Counterblast*, fol. 415.

1559. Horne, he argued, did not accept the Act of Supremacy in the government's sense because his Protestantism would not let him, and in this he was not untypical. The Queen, therefore, could find more loyalty to her person and to her dynasty among her Catholic subjects than she ever could among men who gladly perjured themselves in order to secure her favor and thus further their own designs. If Horne had been less dull or more honest, Stapleton implied, so striking a proof of Protestant deviousness as the "blast" against Feckenham might never have come to light.

> Let us now turn on the other side, and consider the fruits of M. Horne, his evangelical brethren and their obedience, that by words would seem to recognise the queen's majesty as supreme governor in all causes ecclesiastical. Who are those, then, M. Horne, I pray you, that repine at the queen's majesty's injunctions and ordinances for the decent and comely apparel, meet for such as occupy the room of the clergy? Whence came those sixteen ministers to Paris, and what ministers were they but roundcap ministers of England, fleeing the realm for disobedience? Who wrote and printed a book at Rhone against the queen's majesty's express commandment about apparel? Was it not Minister Barthelot, that published before the infamous libel against the universal Church of God? Who are they that have preached with a chain of gold about their necks instead of a tippet? Who are those that preach even in her highness' presence that the crucifix her grace hath in her chapel is the idol with the red face?[35]

These Englishmen, said Stapleton, were not exceptional though they have been somewhat more forthright than Horne and his fellow bishops. They at least could call upon the testimony of the whole Protestant world to support their statement. For example, Stapleton noted, in the preface to the *Centuria septima* it has been explicitly denied that magistrates have headship in the Church.

---

35. Ibid., fol. 22.

"These are no papists, I trow, M. Horne, but your own dear
brethren of Magdeburg, in their new story ecclesiastical, by which
they would have all the world directed; yea, in that story whereof
one parcel Illyricus and his fellows have dedicated to the queen's
majesty."[36] Luther too had repudiated the interference of the lay
power in matters of doctrine: "Non est regum aut principum
etiam veram doctrinam confirmare, sed ei subjici et servire." And
Philip Melanchthon, "the pillar and anchorhold of the Civil
Lutherans," has complained often about those rulers who exceed
proper bounds in their relationship with the Church.[37]

"Well, I suppose you will challenge him as a Lutheran. If it
must needs be so, I trust M. Calvin, your greatest apostle, shall
bear some sway with you." Horne must be aware, Stapleton presumed, of Calvin's well-known opinion about Henry VIII, contained in his commentary on the seventh chapter of the Book of
Amos: "They which in the beginning did so much extoll Henry,
King of England, and which did give him the highest authority
in the Church, they were men which lacked circumspection and
of small consideration; which things did at all times offend me
very much, for they did commit blasphemy and were blasphemers
when they did call him supreme head of the Church." When
Nowell, Elizabeth's Dean of St. Paul's, had been confronted with
this opinion of Calvin's, he had simply dismissed it as due to "false
reporters." Horne tried in his clumsy fashion to turn it back upon
Feckenham: "Ye know," the Bishop wrote darkly, "who they
were that first gave to him that title and authority." But Stapleton
did not let that inference pass: "That Calvin meaneth herein
plainly . . . the Protestants and his own dear brethren it is most
evident by his words immediately following, which are these:
'Surely, this is too much. But let it lie buried, for they offended
by inconsiderate zeal.' Tell me now, of good fellowship, M. Horne,
were they M. Feckenham's friends or yours, were they Catholics
or Protestants that Calvin here so gently excuseth?" Stapleton

36. Stapleton noted that *Centuria quarta* had been dedicated to the Queen
by "the famous liars of Magdeburg." Ibid., fol. 509.
37. Ibid.

added that Calvin had said much the same thing in his commentary on I Corinthians with regard to the Eucharistic formula. "Remembering the jolly consent of his brethren on that matter," he had suggested that the "unhappy combats" which had arisen on this score be forgotten. This is the man, said Stapleton, "whose books the Sacramentaries esteem as the second gospel. . . . This is he whose Institution[s] against Christ and the true, divine religion are in such price with you that . . . few of your Protestant fellow bishops . . . will admit any man to any cure that hath not read them, or will not promise to read them."[38]

Perhaps Horne might answer that, whatever the opinions of the continental Protestants, at least all loyal Englishmen rally round the lay supremacy. Stapleton did not think so:

> Marry, that were wonderful that if as we be sequestered and, as it were, shut up from other countries by the great ocean sea that doth environ us, so should we be shut up from the doctrine as well Catholic as also the Protestant of other countries, and that with us the Lutherans and Zwinglians should find no friends to accompany them in this as in other points. But content yourself, M. Horne, and think you, if you do not already, that either yourself or any other of your brethren like the queen's supremacy never a deal better in heart, whatsoever ye pretend and dissemble in words. Think ye that Calvin is so slenderly friended in England, his books being in so high price and estimation there? No, no, it is not to be thought. The contrary is too well known.[39]

The *Admonition* of Anthony Gilby, a leading gospeler indeed, was for Stapleton a case in point. In that work Henry VIII had been described as "a lecherous monster," a "monstrous boar," while those who supported him had been but "pigs"; together they had looted the Church of England and made it "no better

38. Ibid., fols. 506–07.
39. Ibid., fol. 22.

than the Romish Anti-christ."[40] "I trust now, M. Horne, that you will somewhat the more bear with the Catholics if they cannot well bear the service and title your companions so ill liketh."

But Stapleton had another, more serious charge. Did not Horne and his brethren, whether they pretended to accept the supremacy or not, really question Elizabeth's right to rule at all? "Who are they, I pray you, that have set forth devices of their own for the succession of the crown without the prince's knowledge?" Who has denied that any woman either by God's law or nature's may inherit a throne?[41] "No Catholic, I warrant you, but your holy brethren, so fervent in the word of the Lord." John Knox, for one, had written that royal blood had not as much to do with a king's "election" as "the ordinance which God hath established in the election of inferior judges." He would thus exclude the succession of anyone, man or woman, and "will have the kingdom go by election, that in case there be found any prince that fancieth not this new apostle, that then he may be lawfully deposed and a new brother in his room placed."[42]

The verdict of Christopher Goodman, given about the same time, differed little from that of his friend Knox. At the death of Edward VI, this "zealous brother of Calvin's school" had written five years after the event that even if Mary "had been no bastard

40. Stapleton quoted a long passage from Gilby's *Admonition* (Geneva, 1558), fol. 69.

41. But Stapleton never hesitated to say that it was worse for Elizabeth to be "supreme governor" than for her father to be "supreme head." "If teaching, preaching and disputing in matters of religion be causes and matters ecclesiastical, then there is sufficient cause why M. Feckenham may not take this oath, that a woman is supreme head [sic] in all causes spiritual and ecclesiastical. . . . Now put the case (as we saw it eight years past [i.e. in 1559]) that in a doubtful matter of doctrine and religion to be tried by Scripture and the whole number of the bishops agree upon some determinate and resolute exposition with their clergy, and would by an ecclesiastical law of convocation or council set forth the same. And how this will stand with St. Paul in this chapter [I Cor. 14:34] tell us, I pray you: presupposing (as the Statute requireth) that the prince's allowing, though she be a good woman, is necessary." *Counterblast,* fols. 419–20.

42. Ibid., fol. 24. Stapleton quoted John Knox, *Appelation and Exhortation to the Nobilitie of Scotland* (Geneva, 1558), fols. 77, 30.

as lawfully begotten as was her sister, that godly lady and meek lamb, void of all Spanish pride and strange blood," yet the first duty of all the estates had been to select the "most meetest among your brethren to have had the government over you . . . and to rule . . . carefully in the fear of God." A woman's reign "is the express sign of God's wrath, and a notable plague for the sins of the people, as was the reign of Jezebel and ungodly Athalia, special instruments of Satan and whips to his people Israel."[43]

Horne might wish to lay this sort of talk at the door of one or two extremists. "Nay, sir," replied Stapleton, "ye shall not so escape: I say this was the common consent and judgment of all your holy brethren of Geneva, as well English as other." For proof Stapleton cited the preface to Goodman's book, written by another of Bishop Horne's old acquaintances, William Whittingham. Goodman's articles and propositions, Whittingham explained, appeared first in a sermon given at Geneva, and they had the approval and admiration of "the best learned in these parties [sic]"; he enlarged the sermon and printed it "as a token of his duty and good affection toward the Church of God," and he was prepared, if it should seem good to the brethren, to translate the expanded work into other languages that "the profit thereof might be more universal." Stapleton was sifting these passages for quotation early in the summer of 1567, and who could have blamed him, then or later, if the thought crossed his mind, at once angry and wistful, of the canonry at Chichester he had given up and the fellowship at New College he had vacated. He knew, and all the world knew, that among the beneficed clergy of the Church of England were Anthony Gilby, Christopher Goodman, and William Whittingham.[44]

---

43. *Counterblast,* fol. 25, quoting Goodman, *Superior Powers,* fol. 54.

44. Beneficed they were but still suspect. When Whittingham died as Dean of Durham in 1579 (a post once held, ironically enough, by Horne), he was under investigation. Parker had considered working for the deprivation of Gilby, but the latter enjoyed the patronage of the powerful Earl of Huntingdon, who gave him the living of Ashby de la Zouche in Leicestershire, where he lived "great as a bishop" until his death in 1585. Goodman was indeed deprived of his benefice at Alford just a year after he received it, and he lived

Lo, good M. Horne, a sermon made at Geneva to all the
English brethren, not only to deprive the queen of her title
of the Supremacy in causes ecclesiastical, but even in temporal, too, and from all government, the matter being communicated to the best learned there. And then M. Calvin
and M. Beza, too, I trow, gave their verdict to this noble and
clerkly work. And so it seemeth to import the consent of all
the gehennical (I should have said Gevenical) Church. And
who are those that now rule all the roost in England but
this good brotherhood? Men no doubt well worthy, for whose
sake the Catholics should be hardly handled and to whom the
queen's majesty is (who doubteth) deeply bound, and they
worthy to be so well cherished as they are. . . . So that now
whereas the Catholics, yea, the starkest papist of all (as
these men term them) can be well content, yea, with all
their hearts, to affirm that the queen's majesty may enjoy
not only this realm but even the whole empire, and wish no
less (if it pleases God) to her highness, and find no fault but
only with that title that is not competent for her highness,
and without the which she may reign as nobly, as amply, as
honorably as ever did prince in England or elsewhere which
never affected any such title. These men who pretend to the
world to profess a wonderful sincere observation toward
God and their prince do not only spoil her of that title, but
of all her right and interest to England, France, Ireland or
elsewhere, making her incapable of all manner of civil regiment. Which, I trust, the queen's majesty, once well considering, will graciously bear with the Catholics that do not
envy her the one or the other title, but only desire that their
consciences may not be straitened for one of them. Which

---

out his days peacefully enough at Chester. These "Puritans of the disciplinarian
faction" aimed their antiroyal broadside at Mary, writes Dawley (*John Whitgift,* p. 144). "With the accession of Queen Elizabeth their tune changed."
Anyway, the point remains valid that even Goodman, for whom the Queen
(naturally enough) had a strong distaste, was given a benefice, and even after
he lost it the government left him to grow old in peace.

they upon great grounds and they verily think without impairing of her worldly estate, cannot by oath assuredly avouch; which thing they trust they may do without any just suspicion of sedition or rebellion.[45]

The danger of revolution came chiefly from those who had already proved themselves rebels. "Protestants obey until they have the power to resist. When their faction is the stronger side, as they resist both prelates and popes, so they lay at both kings and kaisers."[46]

Eloquent it may have been, but this attempt to paint Robert Horne and the radical Calvinists with the same brush gave a distorted picture. English Protestantism was not a monolith. Horne had already done battle with Whittingham and his friends at Frankfort; indeed, it is perhaps not too much to say that in that victory he had won his episcopal spurs. In the strange distinctions of Bishop Horne, Stapleton saw another version of the machinations of Goodman and Knox, and here his rigorous logic failed him. If the episcopacy preached justification by faith alone, Stapleton argued, it aimed as well at the establishment of a Calvinist theocracy. He may not have erred altogether in theory, given his first principles, but he took too little account of the readiness of practical men to modify, to compromise, to adjust. This was Stapleton's permanent and pervasive blind spot: if Robert Horne rejected the Mass and branded it idolatry, how could he sincerely hold a notion of Church government which, even if it did repudiate the pope, was at the same time "contrary to the chief master of Geneva, John Calvin, contrary to the chief masters of the Zealous Lutherans, Illyricus and his fellows, contrary to the chief master of the Civil Lutherans, Philip Melanchthon, yea, and contrary to the father of them all, Martin Luther?"

> These are no papists. They are your own dear brethren; or if they are not, defy them that we may know of what sect and company you are. What? Will you in matters of religion

45. *Counterblast*, fols. 26–27.
46. Ibid., fol. 21.

stand post alone? Will you so rent the whole coat of Christ, the unity of his dear spouse, the Church, that you alone of England will ... defend this most barbarous paradox of the prince's supreme government in all ecclesiastical causes, all, as you say, without exception? Sirs, if you list to stand alone against all and by oath hale men to your singular paradox, not only to say with you but also to swear that they think so in conscience, get you also a heaven alone, a God alone.... O, M. Horne, these absurdities be too gross and palpable ... This hath been your own device. And why? Forsooth, to erect your new religion by authority of the prince which you knew by the Church's authority could never have been erected. And so to provide for one particular case, you have made it, M. Horne, a general rule that all princes ought and must be supreme governors in all ecclesiastical causes. Which, if it be so, then why is not King Philip here and King Charles in France such supreme governors? Or if they be, with what conscience do the Geux here and the Huguenots there disobey their supreme governors, yea, and take arms against their princes' religion? ... Solve all these doubts and absurdities, M. Horne, and then require us to give ear to your book and to swear to your Oath.[47]

It was an admirably sculptured argument, but the tide of events submerged it.

What had happened before in other places happened in England. Men questioned the ancient doctrine of justification, fashioned theories of their own, and, when recognized authority called a halt, they repudiated the authority, too, to protect themselves. The Act of Supremacy had made possible the Act of Uniformity, which, in turn, grafted onto the religious practice of the English people the foreign heresy that human beings find salvation only by faith in the imputed merits of Christ. To Thomas Stapleton the Reformation meant doctrinal revolution, whether in England, Flanders, or anywhere. His view had grave limitations. It ig-

47. Ibid., fols. 509–10.

nored political and economic and geographical considerations.
It brushed aside as irrelevant generations of callous and cynical
abuse. It took for granted the bad will of every leading Protestant.
To Stapleton's credit, however, let it be said that he never forgot,
as has many a man of wider research since his time, that the Reformation was essentially a matter not of politics or economics or
psychology but of doctrine: "God of his secret and right justice
. . . hath suffered that wicked apostate, Martin Luther, first and
chiefly to upbraid the authority of our mother Church. He suffered that detestable persuasion to sink also into our hearts."[48]

And what of prophecy? "We have fallen into plenty of heresies,
from one heresy to another, from Lutheran to Sacramentary and
so forth; we stand also in danger to fall . . . from a false faith to
no faith, from heresy to paganism."[49] In England, Stapleton believed the last process was well on its way, because the reformers
had denied "that which first brought us the faith, that is, the authority of the Pope of Rome."[50]

> Woe to them that induced godly princes thereunto. For in-
> deed here hath proceeded the whole alteration of religion
> in our country. And hereof it followeth that religion in our
> country shall never be settled or of long continuance, except
> princes always of one mind and judgment do reign. Hereof
> it followeth that we shall never join in faith and doctrine
> with other Christian realms and with the whole universal
> Church, except our happe be to have a prince so affected as
> other Christian princes are. Hereof it followeth that though
> our prince be a Catholic yet this authority standing our faith
> is not authorized by God's word and the Church but by God's
> word and the prince, that is by God's word so expounded and
> preached as the prince shall command and prescribe it.
>
> Briefly, hereof it followeth that the faith of England is no
> faith at all, builded upon the authority of God and his minis-

48. *Fortresse*, p. 391.
49. Ibid., p. 41.
50. Ibid., p. 390.

ters, who have charge of our souls, but is an obedience only of a temporal law, and an opinion changeable and alterable according to the laws of the realm.

These are indeed most horrible absurdities and most direct against the unity of the Church, which above all things ought to be tendered, and without the which there is no salvation. This destroyeth the obedience of faith and setteth up only a philosophical persuasion of matters of religion. This clean defaceth all true religion and induceth in its place a civil policy. To conclude, this maketh a plain and direct way to all heresies. For if ever (which God forbid) any prince of our land should be affected to any heresy, as of Arianism or any such like, the supreme authority of the prince, remaining as the Oath granteth and King Edward practiced, should not all the bishops either be forced to preach that heresy or to lose their bishoprics, others placed in their rooms? Which to please the prince and to climb to honor would be quick enough to further the proceedings.[51]

For us, living as we do in a Western world which scholars have described as "post-Christian," these words are not without their point.

51. *Counterblast,* fol. 454.

BIBLIOGRAPHICAL NOTE

Thomas Stapleton was primarily a literary man, and therefore his place in the history of the Counter Reformation must be determined by an analysis of his own work. There is nowhere in print even a summary description of that work. No attempt, to my knowledge, has ever been made to survey his folios and thus discover the basis of the reputation he enjoyed among his contemporaries. Moreover, the books which comprise his literary testament are exceedingly difficult to obtain. His Latin *Opera,* together with translations into Latin of works originally written in English, were collected into four huge volumes and published at Paris in 1620. Of these there is but one copy to be found in the United States, while earlier editions of Stapleton's Latin works are very rare, and most of them have disappeared without a trace. The same thing is true of Stapleton's English works. Although the 1625 edition of *A Fortresse of the Faith* is relatively easy to find (because it was appended to the translation of Bede), there are only two copies available in the whole English-speaking world of the controversies with Horne and Jewel.

Also worth noting is the fact that Stapleton wrote voluminously. The collection of his Latin works approaches five million words in length, while the English would run to another million. This bulk (as much, say, as the *Œuvres* of St. Francis de Sales in the Annecy edition or the forty volumes of Newman in the standard Longmans edition), forbidding enough in itself, becomes still more awesome to the modern reader when he finds it in the sixteenth-century idiom. Stapleton's English style is charming and it often has a gorgeous Elizabethan rhythm to it, but it is complex and, for the uninitiated, sometimes difficult to unravel. As a Latin stylist, Stapleton reflected both the scholastic and humanist traditions, and the result was usually elegance and clarity, spoiled not a few times by a weakness for the contrived. Stapleton's greatest literary fault, one which makes him particularly uncongenial to the modern reader, is verbosity. This is particularly apparent in his formal theological tracts. He is content to make a point three times only if it is absolutely impossible to make it four times.

In view of these considerations, I believe the third chapter of this present study has special relevance. However, since the analysis there is pioneer work, its conclusions remain tentative and its points of emphasis may seem arbitrary.

There is no study of Stapleton's life. The biographical notices in the various great dictionaries (like the *DNB,* the *DTC,* and the more recent, but much smaller, *Oxford Dictionary of the Christian Church,* London, 1958) are either inaccurate or incomplete. The short metrical autobiographical note which Stapleton left behind (*Opera Omnia,* Vol. I) helps only in establishing general sequence, while Henry Holland's memoir (ibid.) is totally uncritical. Hints are found tucked away in various corners (e.g. in the correspondence printed in the *Douay Diaries*), but, with the present state of the evidence, little more than a skeletal outline can be constructed. One cannot help feeling that Stapleton's life story, when compared to William Allen's or, indeed, to any one of the priests who served the English mission, must have been rather dull.

The Counter Reformation itself has yet to find its historian. There are many accounts but as yet no grand synthesis. Typical of recent attempts, neither of them especially distinguished, are P. Janelle, *The Catholic Reformation* (Milwaukee, 1949) and L. Cristiani, *L'Église a l'époque du Concile de Trente* (Paris, 1948). The latter is part of the Fliche-Martin series (*Histoire de l'Église*) and carries the story up to 1563. Its companion volume, L. Willaert, *La Restauration Catholique* (Paris, 1960) continues the account, following, however, a completely topical arrangement. Both these books contain immense but undigested bibliographical lists. In J. Lortz, *Geschichte der Kirche* (Münster, 1948), one will find a brief but excellent description of what the author calls "Die Katholische Reform." No student of the period can do with-

out L. Pastor's *History of the Popes* (St. Louis, 1902–24) or
H. Jedin's *A History of the Council of Trent* (St. Louis, 1957–),
the first two volumes of which have appeared in English. For the
intellectual setting of Stapleton's controversies one should con-
sult Pontien Polman, *L'Elément historique dans la controverse
religieuse de XVIe siècle* (Gembloux, 1932).

In English history, the Counter Reformation runs roughly
parallel to the reign of Elizabeth I, and here of course the literature
is enormous. The third volume of Mgr. Philip Hughes' monu-
mental *The Reformation in England* (New York, 1954) is especially valuable for the insights it gives into both political and
theological matters. The same author's *Rome and the Counter
Reformation in England* (London, 1942) places the spotlight on
William Allen and the English mission. J. E. Neale has all students of the period in his debt for many things, including his
astute examination of the framing of the Act of Supremacy (see,
for example, *Elizabeth I and Her Parliaments, 1559–1581,* New
York, 1958). Many specialized studies, now more than a generation old, are still useful. Among them might be mentioned Henry
Birt, *The Elizabethan Religious Settlement* (London, 1907), Arnold Oskar Meyer, *England and the Catholic Church under Queen
Elizabeth* (London, 1916), and John Pollen, *The English Catholics in the Reign of Queen Elizabeth* (London, 1920). A. C. Southern, *Elizabethan Recusant Prose* (London, 1950) has given us an
extremely useful analysis of the exiles of the 1560s in their first
controversial efforts. His treatment of Stapleton is excellent. Finally, as confirmation that the intellectuals on both sides of the
Counter Reformation controversies deserve more attention than
they have received, there appeared very recently W. M. South-
gate's *John Jewel and the Problem of Doctrinal Authority* (Cambridge, 1962). Perhaps this is a happy omen for the future.

INDEX

Acceptance, doctrine of, 111–12, 113, 115, 116
Act of Repeal (of Mary), 151
Act of Supremacy (1536), 151 n.
Act of Supremacy (1559), 27, 143, 149 n., 151–53, 158, 173 n., 184–86, 195–201, 208. See also Injunctions of 1559; Oath of Supremacy; Royal supremacy; Treason Act of 1563
Act of Uniformity, 27, 158, 193–94, 208
Act of Uniformity (of Edward VI), 149 n.
Ad limina visitation, 20
Admonition to Simple Men Deceived by Malicious, An, 173 n., 185. See also Injunctions of 1559
Adrian of Utrecht (Pope Adrian VI), 2
Agazzari, Alphonsus, 48 n.
Alba (Alva), Duke of, 30
Albigenses, 130
Aldobrandini (family), 46 n.
Aldobrandini, Ippolito. See Clement VIII
Aldobrandini, Pietro, Cardinal, 47, 49
Alexander VI, Pope, 3
Allen, William, 25–26, 34–37, 40, 45–46, 47, 50, 55, 147
Anabaptists, 4, 5, 130
Anglican Church, 27, 143–49. See also Elizabethan Settlement
Antwerp, 31–33, 54 n., 123; Third Synod of, 71 n.
Aquinas, St. Thomas, 62, 80–81, 84, 95–96
Aragon, Catherine of, 148

Arius, 134
Articles of 1563, 189 n.
Ashley, Thomas, 162
Augsburg, Confession of, 98, 101, 111, 112, 132
Augustine, St., 78, 90, 95, 99, 101, 102, 105, 106, 107, 132; quoted, 102, 104, 194
Authority, nature of, 81. See also Church; Royal supremacy; Scripture, authority over interpretation of

Baius, Michael, 23, 42, 43
Bale, John, 68
Baptism, 85, 87, 91. See also Sacraments
Barlow, William, 28, 126
Barnes, Robert, 126, 148
Baronius, Caesar, 23–24
Barret, Richard, 47–48
Barthelot, Mr., 201
Bayne, M., 200
Becket, à, St. Thomas, 67–68
Bede, *Ecclesiastical History*, 55–56
Bedford, Earl of, 155, 156
Bellarmine, Robert, 23, 24, 25, 74, 75, 135
Berengarius, 130
Bernard, St., 4
Beza, Theodore, 2, 54, 72, 73, 74, 123, 128, 129, 131, 206
Biel, Gabriel, 62, 113
Boncompagni, Ugo. See Gregory XIII
Bonner, Edmund, 155, 171
Borromeo, Charles, 14, 17
Bracton, Henry de, 60
Brenz, Johann, 131